MW00463841

Psychology & Christianity

FIVE VIEWS

SECOND EDITION

EDITED BY Eric L. Johnson

WITH CONTRIBUTIONS BY David G. Myers,
Stanton L. Jones, Robert C. Roberts & P. J. Watson,
John H. Coe & Todd W. Hall, David Powlison

IVP Academic
An imprint of InterVarsity Press
Downers Grove, Illinois

InterVarsity Press
P.O. Box 1400, Downers Grove, IL 60515-1426
ivpress.com
email@ivpress.com

Second edition: ©2010 by Eric L. Johnson
First edition: ©2000 by Eric L. Johnson and Stanton L. Jones

All rights reserved. No part of this book may be reproduced in any form without written permission from
InterVarsity Press.

InterVarsity Press® is the book-publishing division of InterVarsity Christian Fellowship/USA®, a movement of
students and faculty active on campus at hundreds of universities, colleges and schools of nursing in the United States
of America, and a member movement of the International Fellowship of Evangelical Students. For information
about local and regional activities, visit intervarsity.org.

All Scripture quotations, unless otherwise indicated, are taken from the Holy Bible, New International Version®.
NIV®. Copyright ©1973, 1978, 1984 by International Bible Society. Used by permission of Zondervan Publishing
House. All rights reserved.

Design: Cindy Kiple

ISBN 978-0-8308-2848-7

Printed in the United States of America ∞

As a member of the Green Press Initiative, InterVarsity Press is committed to protecting the
environment and to the responsible use of natural resources. To learn more, visit
greenpressinitiative.org.

Library of Congress Cataloging-in-Publication Data

Psychology & Christianity: five views /edited by Eric L. Johnson;
with contributions by David G. Myers [. . . et al.].—2nd ed.
     p. cm.
   Includes bibliographical references and index.
   ISBN 978-0-8308-2848-7 (pbk.: alk. paper)
   1. Christianity—Psychology. 2. Psychology and religion. I.
Johnson, Eric L., 1956- II. Myers, David G. III. Title: Psychology and
Christianity.
   BR110.P77 2010
   261.5'15—dc22
                                                                    2010009384

| P | 25 | 24 | 23 | 22 | 21 | 20 | 19 | 18 | 17 | 16 | 15 | 14 | 13 | 12 | 11 | 10 | 9 |
| Y | 32 | 31 | 30 | 29 | 28 | 27 | 26 | 25 | 24 | 23 | 22 | 21 | 20 | 19 | 18 | 17 | 16 |

To Malcolm Jeeves, Gary Collins, John Carter,

Bruce Narramore, C. Stephen Evans, David Benner,

Jay Adams, Wayne Mack and Larry Crabb:

Forerunners.

CAPS
INTERNATIONAL

An Association for Christian Psychologists,
Therapists, Counselors and Academicians

CAPS is a vibrant Christian organization with a rich tradition. Founded in 1956 by a small group of Christian mental health professionals, chaplains and pastors, CAPS has grown to more than 2,100 members in the U.S., Canada and more than 25 other countries.

CAPS encourages in-depth consideration of therapeutic, research, theoretical and theological issues. The association is a forum for creative new ideas. In fact, their publications and conferences are the birthplace for many of the formative concepts in our field today.

CAPS members represent a variety of denominations, professional groups and theoretical orientations; yet all are united in their commitment to Christ and to professional excellence.

CAPS is a non-profit, member-supported organization. It is led by a fully functioning board of directors, and the membership has a voice in the direction of CAPS.

CAPS is more than a professional association. It is a fellowship, and in addition to national and international activities, the organization strongly encourages regional, local and area activities which provide networking and fellowship opportunities as well as professional enrichment.

To learn more about CAPS, visit www.caps.net.

CAPS BOOKS
from IVP Academic

The joint publishing venture between IVP Academic and CAPS aims to promote the understanding of the relationship between Christianity and the behavioral sciences at both the clinical/counseling and the theoretical/research levels. These books will be of particular value for students and practitioners, teachers and researchers.

For more information about CAPS Books, visit InterVarsity Press's website at www.ivpress.com/cgi-ivpress/book.pl/code=2801.

Contents

Preface to the Second Edition

It is widely acknowledged that factions in American culture have been embroiled over the past four decades in a conceptual and political battle grounded in different views of morality, values, epistemology and the role of religion in public life, a "culture war" of great importance to evangelicals (Hunter, 1991). Less well known are the similar battles waged *within* the evangelical community, one of which concerns the relation of psychology and Christianity.

What has led to this particular conflict? There are at least two factors. For one, modern psychology has become enormously influential in our culture and on the American church. And two, since its founding 130 years ago, modern psychology has been largely devoid of reference to religiousness, and often it has been downright hostile to religion, a stance that has only recently shown signs of softening. In the face of these dynamics, Christians have taken different positions regarding the extent to which they should have anything to do with modern psychology—some embracing it wholeheartedly, others rejecting it just as vigorously and many falling somewhere between. Few opportunities have arisen for Christians to dialogue publicly about these differences, about the value of psychology in general for Christians, and about the problems involved in psychological study and counseling practice for people of faith.

This book is one such opportunity, and it has been a pleasure to work on this dialogue. I wish to thank heartily the seven contributors. I have long felt a professional debt to all of them for their contributions on these matters, and I add to that a personal debt for their efforts in this project.

This second edition is distinguished from the first by the move of Stanton Jones from coeditor of the earlier edition to the representative of the integration position, with the result that I am now the sole editor of the book you now hold. Further, another view has been added to the dialogue: transformational psychology. This model had its roots in the integration tradition, but over the past twenty years, for reasons that will be explained, the various proponents of this view are advancing what amounts to a novel and distinct Christian way of thinking about psychology that must now be taken seriously.

Finally, I'd like to thank Sarah Tennant for helping with the indexes, and I want to express my appreciation for the staff at InterVarsity Press, especially Andy Le Peau and Joel Scandrett, for their guidance and support throughout the different stages of this project.

I think it would be fitting to dedicate a book such as this to some of the notable forerunners who contributed to and, in some cases, helped to establish the five positions found in this book: Malcolm Jeeves (levels of explanation); Gary Collins, John Carter and Bruce Narramore (integration); C. Stephen Evans (Christian psychology); David Benner (transformational psychology); Jay Adams and Wayne Mack (biblical counseling); and Larry Crabb (who over his career has contributed to three of the positions in this book: integration, Christian psychology and transformational psychology).

1

A Brief History of Christians in Psychology

Eric L. Johnson

FOLLOWERS OF GOD HAVE ALWAYS BEEN interested in his creation. After citing the stars in the heavens, the bestowal of rain, the growth of vegetation and the feeding of wild animals, the psalmist cries out, "How many are your works, O LORD! / In wisdom you made them all; / the earth is full of your creatures" (Ps 104:24). But of all the things in creation, of greatest interest to most of us is our own nature, for we are fascinated with the wonder of ourselves. As John Calvin wrote, a human being is a microcosm of the universe, "a rare example of God's power, goodness, and wisdom, and contains within . . . enough miracles to occupy our minds" (1559/1960, p. 54). It is not surprising then to learn that Christian thinkers over the centuries have thought deeply about psychological matters, long before modern psychology arose.

Yet Christian interest in psychology has exploded over the last fifty years. Countless books have been written by Christians that describe our personalities, our boundaries, our dysfunctional development, our relationships and their problems, how our children should be raised, and so on. However, in the midst of this explosion has been an intellectual crisis that the church has been wrestling with for even longer: over the previous 140 years, a complex and rich body of knowledge and practice has proliferated, which has understood and treated human beings in some ways that vary considerably from Christian perspectives on human life. Since this modern psychology is largely secular, there is considerable disagreement about how much the theories and findings of this type of psychology should influence, be absorbed into and even transform the way Christians think about human beings. Some Christians have embraced modern psychology's findings and theories with uncritical enthusiasm, naively trusting that its texts are a perfect reflection of human reality. Others have argued that *any* appropriation of modern psychology is "psychoheresy," since it necessarily poisons the Christians who imbibe it (Bobgan & Bobgan, 1987). This book will examine neither extreme but will consider the vast territory between them—specifically five well-thought-through views from evangelicals who offer a fairly comprehensive representation of the ways that most Christians (including nonevangelicals) understand psychology and counseling in our day.

Before summarizing the five approaches themselves, I would like to trace the historical and intellectual background for the present debate.

CHRISTIANITY AND SCIENCE

We ought to begin by noting that Christians have commonly understood that the natural order is the work of a wise Creator who continues to providentially guide it, and that it, therefore, possesses an intrinsic rationality and orderliness that can be investigated. Discovering evidence of this design brings God glory, thus its continued investigation is warranted (Hooykaas, 1972; McGrath, 2001; Stark, 2003). Indeed, it was mostly Christians in the West who founded the scientific revolution, and the main contributors to the early developments in the natural sciences— astronomy, physics, chemistry and biology—were Christians of various stripes, including Roger Bacon, Copernicus, Kepler, Galileo, Francis Bacon, Newton, Boyle, Pascal, Descartes, Ray, Linnaeus and Gassendi. Throughout the history of Christianity, science has been seen, fundamentally, as a gift of God.

CHRISTIANITY AND PSYCHOLOGY

According to most introductory textbooks in psychology, psychopathology and counseling (and even some history of psychology texts), the founding of psychology occurred in the mid- to late-1800s. As we will see, though, that was the founding of *modern* psychology. A little more investigation reveals that there was a tremendous amount of reflection, writing, counseling, psychological theorizing and even some research going on during previous centuries (Brett, 1912; Klein, 1970; Leahey, 2003; Watson & Evans, 1991). Unquestionably, the form of this older psychology was different in many respects from the empirically and statistically oriented psychology of the past hundred years. In contrast, this older psychology relied much more on the philosophical and theological reflections of Christian thinkers and ministers. Nonetheless, this was genuine psychological work and it pervades the history of Christianity (and all the major religions; see Olson, 2002; Thomas, 2001), even if most of it was characterized by less of the complexity evident in modern psychology.

The first sophisticated psychologies in the West were developed by Greek philosopher-therapists like Plato, Aristotle and Epicurus. They attempted to describe human nature, including its fundamental ills and its reparation, on the basis of personal experience and rigorous reflection in light of prior thought (Nussbaum, 1994; Watson & Evans, 1991). These thinkers explored topics like the composition and "inner" structure of human beings—memory, reason, sensation, appetite, motivation, virtues and vices, and various ideals of human maturation. The Old and New Testaments themselves contain material of great psychological import, and in the case of Paul, we might say with Brett (1912), a strongly religious "protopsychology." However, in contrast to the more rigorous writing of contemporary science, the reflections in the Bible belong to the category of "folk psychology" or "lay psychology," since they do not constitute a systematic and comprehensive exploration of human nature generated for the purpose of contributing to human knowledge (Fletcher, 1995; Thomas, 2001). Nevertheless, because Christians believe the Bible to be specially inspired by God (2 Tim 3:16), revealing matters of essential importance, Christians have usually accorded the Bible's teachings on human nature with a unique authority regarding how to think about psychological matters.

After the New Testament era, the Bible and the intellectual contributions of the Greeks both contributed to the psychological theorizing of Christians for the next fourteen hundred years. With only a limited grasp of the value of empirical study, the major teachers and writers of the early church and medieval periods were convinced that Scripture and rigorous reflection on it provided the surest route to psychological knowledge. Not surprisingly, then, the best psychological work by Christians was the result of biblical and philosophical reflection on human experience.

Though largely concerned with matters of faith and life, people like the desert fathers—Tertullian, Athanasius, Cassian, Gregory of Nyssa and Gregory the Great—wrote with often penetrating insight into the nature of the soul and soul healing. However, Augustine, with his massive intellect, is widely recognized as the first great Christian "psychologist" (see Watson & Evans, 1991). Steeped in the Scriptures and the thought of the earlier church fathers, Augustine's understanding of human beings was also flavored by the philosophical tradition inspired by Plato. Nevertheless, his work on love, sin, grace, memory, mental illumination, wisdom, volition and the experience of time provides a wealth of psychological insight and suggestions for further investigations.

Strongly influenced by Augustine but much more systematic (and, therefore, more directly helpful for developing psychological theory) was Thomas Aquinas (Watson & Evans, 1991). This meticulous thinker devoted his life to relating the Christian faith to the thought of another brilliant but mostly nonreligious philosopher, Aristotle. Aquinas unified the best of the Augustinian and Aristotelian traditions and produced an influential body of psychological thought, covering the appetites, the will, habits, the virtues and vices, the emotions, memory, and the intellect.

It is worth underlining that the two greatest intellectual lights of the church's first fifteen hundred years, Augustine and Aquinas, drew heavily in their theological and psychological work on the philosophical traditions of the two greatest (non-Christian) Greek philosophers—Plato and Aristotle respectively. And the distinct approaches of Augustine and Aquinas contributed to genuine differences in thought and orientation, though these differences have sometimes been exaggerated (MacIntyre, 1990). In a very real sense, the works of both represent an "integration" of Christian and non-Christian psychology, though Aquinas was engaged in such integration more self-consciously than Augustine, who was more explicitly working out the differences between Christian and pagan thought (between the "City of God" and the "City of Humanity").

Many Christians in the Middle Ages in addition to Aquinas wrote on psychological and soul-care topics, including Bernard of Clairvaux, Symeon the New Theologian, Gregory Palamas, Anselm, Bonaventure, Duns Scotus, Walter Hilton, Julian of Norwich, William of Ockham and

Thomas á Kempis. The more philosophically inclined writers typically focused on concerns like the structure of the soul and knowledge, whereas the more spiritually inclined focused on the love and experience of God and spiritual development. The latter was the special focus of the monasteries and the priests, and the healing of souls was understood to be central to the mission of the church—long before modern psychotherapy came on the scene (McNeill, 1951; Oden, 1989).

The Renaissance, Reformation and Counter-Reformation released a new psychological curiosity in the church. For example, Reformers like Luther and Calvin reflected deeply on sin, grace, knowledge, faith and the nature of the Christian life, and Catholics like Teresa of Ávila, John of the Cross and Ignatius of Loyola described spiritual development with unparalleled clarity. However, similar to much of the work of earlier Christians, the main focus of this quasi-psychological writing was more pastoral than scientific: the cure and upbuilding of the Christian soul. It was, according to Charry (1997), *aretegenic*, directed toward the shaping of one's moral and spiritual character and the enhancement of the believer's relationship with God, and in some cases, it addressed what would be considered "therapeutic" concerns today (such as the resolution of severe "melancholy").

In the Reformation traditions this pastoral psychology reached its zenith in the Puritan, Pietist and evangelical movements. Writers like Richard Baxter, John Owen, George Herbert, William Law, John Gerhardt, John Wesley, Jonathan Edwards and John Newton developed sophisticated and nuanced understandings of psychospiritual problems—like sin, melancholy, assurance and spiritual desertions—and how to promote spiritual healing and development in Christ.

In addition, Christian philosophers after the Middle Ages continued to reason carefully about human nature in works of great psychological significance, including such luminaries as René Descartes, Giovanni Vico, John Locke, Bishop George Berkeley, Thomas Reid, Bishop Joseph Butler, Gottfried Leibniz and Blaise Pascal—some of these are recognized as figures who influenced the later founding of modern psychology.

Possibly the most significant Christian psychology author since the Middle Ages was Søren Kierkegaard, who used the word *psychology* to describe some of his works, and who wrote some profound psychological works. Over the course of a decade, he brilliantly described (in sometimes deliberately unsettling ways) the nature of personhood, sin, anxiety and despair, the unconscious (before Freud was even born!), subjectivity, and human and spiritual development from a deeply Christian perspective. Kierkegaard is, as well, the only Christian thinker who can be considered a father to a major, modern approach to psychological theory and therapy—existential psychology (though he would have vigorously rejected its secular agenda).

So if we define psychology broadly as a rigorous inquiry into human nature and how to treat its problems and advance its well-being, Christians have been thinking and practicing psychology for centuries. Believing that God had revealed the most important truths about human beings in the Bible, they learned there that God created the world and that human beings were specially created in his image. But they also learned that something was terribly wrong with human beings—they were sinners and needed to be rescued from their plight, for which they bore responsibility. Because humans were created in God's image, they were endowed with reason, so they could apprehend truth in the Bible and in the created order. In the Bible, they found God's norms for human beings and his design for the flourishing of human life through the salvation obtained through faith in Christ on the basis of his life, death and resurrection. Using this worldview, Christians were able to contribute novel and significant psychological insights in such areas as the nature of human reason, sensation, memory, attention, the appetites, the emotions, volition, the unconscious and the experience of time. In addition, Christians developed hypotheses about moral, spiritual and character development; the role of God and grace in human and spiritual development; the nature and impact of sin; techniques for overcoming sin and brokenness (the spiritual disciplines, as well as herbal remedies and common-sense helps); the psychology of religion; the relation of free will and determinism; biological and social origins of psychopathology; body-soul relations; and even some of the bases for scientific research. Thus, Christians had a broad and rich tradition of understanding human beings and treating their problems long before modern psychology came on the scene.

LATE MODERNISM AND THE "NEW PSYCHOLOGY"

Modernism is generally considered to be a worldview or framework of

Western thought that arose in the 1600s, advanced considerably in the 1800s and became dominant in the West during the twentieth century. To some extent, it was a reaction to the religious conflicts that had dominated Christian Europe since the Reformation, reaching a sad denouement in the Thirty Years' War (1618-1648). Modernism's main assumptions include the following:

1. Special revelation and tradition can no longer be regarded as ultimate authorities, because appeals to such sources obviously can not resolve the serious religious-intellectual (and societal) conflicts confronting Europe.

2. Human knowledge must be based on a more sure foundation, and that foundation is presumed to be located in human reason especially but also in human consciousness and experience—basically all aspects of the individual self.

3. The goal of human knowledge is universal understanding, obtained by objective means that all interested parties can use, thus privileging no one perspective and granting a fundamental epistemological equality to all.

4. The natural sciences are held up as the model for human understanding, since they demonstrate the power of human reason and observation (experience) to yield universal knowledge. The natural sciences are characterized by the combination of careful empirical investigation with the application of mathematics (one of reason's most powerful tools), which can yield formulas that correspond to causal relations in the world, as demonstrated magisterially in Isaac Newton's *Principia Mathematica*.

Modernism can be broken down roughly into two periods. The philosophers Descartes, Locke and later Kant (among others) were primary contributors to *early* modernism, which was distinguished by philosophical explorations based on the above assumptions, as well as on continuing adherence to some measure of religious faith, usually Christian (Hume would be the main exception).

However, by the middle of the 1800s, *late* modernism was developing as a result of four new, largely interrelated, intellectual trends. The most significant for our purposes was the widespread secularization that began to appear in the West during this period. As with any complex and controver-

sial concept, understandings of secularism differ. According to theistic philosopher Charles Taylor (2007), there are three facets: (1) the exclusion of
religious discourse from the public square, including government and science; (2) the reduction in religious belief and practice; and (3) the increased
viability of other worldview options. Smith (2003) argues that secularization
has been nothing short of a revolution, promoted by an avid, growing intellectual elite, who perceived current Christian attitudes and beliefs as
regressive (i.e., characterized by censorship, moral repression, and anti-
evolution and anti-intellectualist sentiments). It was also fostered by many
cultural and psychological factors, like the theory of evolution, positivism,
common-sense realism, a new economic power-class, changing academic
standards, and anti-Catholicism and division among Protestant leaders.

As a result of such dynamics, explicitly religious speech, values and
norms were gradually evacuated from public discourse and relegated to
religious institutions and the private sphere. This process is by no means
complete, and is still being contested, particularly in the southeastern
United States. However, by most accounts, the revolution has been over for
many decades (with a few "faith-based" qualifications) in the centers of
intellectual and therapeutic power in the West—that is, in its educational,
government, medical, social welfare, mental health and media institutions
(Marsden, 1994; Smith, 2003; Taylor, 2007).

Evidence that the revolution is over abounds. For over a century, the
majority of the West's most influential authors, thinkers, scientists and
celebrities have not been religious, and of those who have been, their religion has generally not been public. On the contrary, many of the shapers
of Western culture over the past hundred years have publicly disparaged
traditional religious perspectives (e.g., Marx, Nietzsche, Freud, H. G.
Wells, John Dewey, Bertrand Russell, Jean-Paul Sartre, Michel Foucault,
Richard Rorty, Daniel Dennett and Richard Dawkins). Perhaps the most
telling example of this revolution is the shift of European and American
institutions of higher learning, which have so markedly moved from their
Judeo-Christian origins to secular sensibilities. Institution by institution,
colleges and universities have shed their original commitments to glorifying Christ and proclaiming the Christian gospel to embrace a secularized
definition of mission and identity (Marsden, 1994; Smith, 2003).

Doubtless, some secondary benefits have accrued in Western culture

that we take for granted today, which occurred as a result o
loosening of religious cultural restrictions. For example, secularism helped
put an end to the violent religious conflicts among Christians that characterized the 1600s (but which are still found in Muslim regions of the world);
it made possible a common educational system; it allowed people of different faith communities (Christian, Jewish, agnostic) to socialize, work together, learn from each other, and focus in their common cultural pursuits
on those beliefs that most people hold in common, rather than on those
that divide; and most important for the church, it helps Christians distinguish merely cultural Christianity from the genuine article. Indeed, some
argue that such benefits are internal to Christianity itself (Stark, 2003).

Secularization by itself, however, could not have had the influence it did,
had it not been joined in the minds of many to another very significant cultural development: the application of natural science methods to the study
of human beings and the treatment of their problems. Careful observation,
the use of mathematics and often the experimental manipulation of variables
had proven successful in previous centuries in astronomy, physics, chemistry
and biology. In the late 1800s and early 1900s these methods began to be
applied to the study of society, human consciousness and behavior, econom-
ics and business, and education—and with notable results. The glue that
brought and has kept secularism and natural science methods together is the
philosophy of science and knowledge known as *positivism.*

In three successive waves, Auguste Comte (1798-1857), Ernst Mach
(1838-1916), and the logical positivists, Carnap, Schlick, Ayers, etc. (in the
first half of the twentieth century), composed increasingly sophisticated
versions of the view that "positive" knowledge was only that which could
be verified by empirical research. As a result, the methods of natural science were believed to provide the only legitimate means for obtaining
knowledge. According to such criteria, ethical and metaphysical claims
(regarding the nature of human beings and God) are not knowledge; they
are just opinions that have no place in science. The "new psychology" in
America was based on this model of science (e.g., James, 1890; Thorndike,
1905; Watson, 1913; for discussion see Danziger, 1979; Klein, 1970; Leahey, 2003; Toulmin & Leary, 1992), and it was taken to its logical extreme
in behaviorism, which dominated modern psychology from 1930 to 1960,
when most research psychologists concentrated on animal research and

carefully controlled studies of environmental stimuli and the behavior they illicited. Human consciousness and thought were largely ignored.

In time, positivism was thoroughly discredited by philosophers of science (Kuhn, 1962; Suppe, 1977). In the 1960s, as part of a "cognitive revolution," modern psychology began a partial correction and pulled away from the radical positivism of behaviorism and returned to the study of mental phenomena. However, it has never repudiated the overall framework of positivism, so it still works broadly within what could be a called a neopositivist paradigm.[1]

Late modernism was also shaped pervasively by the theory of evolution. Darwin's *Origin of the Species*, published in 1859, was immediately welcomed by the growing numbers of secular intellectuals who needed a naturalistic "origin story"—a modernist metanarrative—that was based on empirical research rather than revelation and that was believed to allow humans to explain their existence without reference to a Creator. Evolutionary theory's seeming optimism about the inevitable improvability of humankind was easily joined to the sense of progress fostered by the scientific and industrial revolutions. With regard to psychology, evolution legitimated the study of animals that have features in common with humans in their nervous systems and learning capacities. This led to the subdiscipline of comparative psychology, and it eventually contributed many notable findings in neuropsychology, childhood development and learning.[2]

Finally, whereas confidence in human reason was unparalleled in the first two centuries of the modern era, reaching a climax in the Enlighten-

---

[1]There are signs, however, that the positivist foundation is beginning to crack. The positive psychology movement, the work of leaders like Bandura (2001) and others (Baer, Kaufman & Baumeister, 2008; Martin, Sugarman & Thompson, 2003) on human and moral agency, and a renewed openness to spirituality and religion demonstrate a growing willingness within to question some of positivism's basic assumptions.

[2]Given Christianity's high view of human beings as images of God, it is unlikely that Christians would have invested so heavily in this kind of research on their own, without the impetus of another worldview. Yet comparative psychology research has yielded important and fascinating findings. In retrospect, it must be said that there is nothing in Christianity per se that is inconsistent with the study of animal psychology to enable us to understand ourselves better. Humans are undeniably a kind of animal, and God is certainly entitled to use the same basic neurological template for other animals, as he used in the design of humans. Good Christians disagree about the compatability of evolution with Christianity, yet most Christians recognize that some evolution occurs throughout the biological world. At the same time, most Christians also admit that *naturalistic* evolution—a mindless process shaped merely by natural selection and genetic mutation, without *any* involvement by God—is antithetical to the Christian faith.

ment (the late 1700s), such exuberance was checked in the Romantic movement, which led to a more substantial critique that came to typify late modernism. As a result of the questions put to reason by Marx, Nietzsche and Freud (as well as Kierkegaard), it became a truism that reason itself can be deceived, so its deliverances could not be unquestioningly trusted. They had to be critiqued—but by what or whom? Late modernism really had nowhere else to turn except to reason. So, while the limits of reason were at least being acknowledged, late modernism had nothing to offer in its place. This realization eventually contributed to the relativism of postmodernism, which came later in the twentieth century.

Throughout the 1800s, late modernism grew in cultural influence, at the same time that the new psychology was being established. Beginning in the early- to mid-1800s, European studies on the nervous system and sensory experience demonstrated that aspects of human subjectivity could be objectively studied and measured. The discovery that lawful relationships exist between stimuli in the world and our experience of them proved that natural science methods could be usefully applied to the internal world of human beings. Wilhelm Wundt, a professor of physiological psychology at the University of Leipzig, is considered the father of modern psychology. In 1879 he was the first to set up an explicit psychology laboratory for the purpose of studying immediate human experience—a move that is commonly accepted as modern psychology's birth. In 1881 he established a journal to publish the results of its research, and he founded the first graduate program with this orientation. Most simply, Wundt was the first to demarcate psychology as a distinct, empirical discipline, staffed by its own specialists (Danziger, 1979). Wundt's influence was enormous, and similar laboratories and programs soon sprung up throughout Europe and the United States. As the impetus to turn psychology into a natural science grew across the West, biblical study and philosophical reflection were systematically excluded as sources of knowledge about human nature, in favor of the empirical investigation of the structures and processes of the senses, mind, memory and behavior (Toulmin & Leary, 1992). So different in method from what went before, this seemed to many to be the founding of an entirely new discipline.

The establishment of this experimental discipline in America occurred

nonetheless
Alluring

relatively quickly with William James as its American forerunner. He became a physiology professor at Harvard in 1872 and taught "Relations Between Psychology and Physiology" in 1875. G. Stanley Hall was America's first professor of psychology, appointed at Johns Hopkins in 1884. G. T. Ladd (1887) surveyed the available research on the nervous system and sensory experience in *Elements of Physiological Psychology*. In 1889, *The American Journal of Psychology* was begun by Hall, which was the first journal in English dedicated to this new approach to psychology. Soon after, James (1890) completed his classic, masterfully written overview of the state of the field, *Principles of Psychology*. The American Psychological Association was founded in 1892, and by 1900, psychology departments had been founded at a number of major universities. Modern psychology was well on its way to laying claim to having "the monopoly of psychological truth" (Danziger, 1979, p. 28).

Along with the growth of positivist research on human beings, others were attempting to address psychological problems according to the same assumptions. In marked contrast to the historical care of souls that Christians and Jews had been doing for centuries, psychotherapy and counseling began to be done without reference to God or supernatural intervention, and training programs were created with academic standards comparable to those in the sciences. The development of clinical psychology and advances in psychiatry helped to fill the void left by religious communities that were, by and large, abandoning their historic calling to care for and cure the soul.

Freudian psychoanalysis, in particular, offered a somewhat disturbing but nonetheless profound model for treating mental problems, and it was quickly embraced by some American psychologists, psychiatrists and, even more, by the culture at large, because of its apparent sophistication, alleged empirical basis and alluring examination of the mysterious unconscious. Though increasingly criticized in coming decades, psychoanalysis was seen at the time as generally consistent with the new psychology, because it shared most of its assumptions.

The new psychology promised to offer a better basis for understanding human life and the improvement of humankind—without religion—so it is no surprise that many of its early leaders were raised in the Christian or Jewish faiths and came later to reject, at least, orthodox versions of these faiths (a process termed *deconversion;* Barbour, 1994).[3] The only place in modern psychology that religion was permitted was as an object of study, in the psychology of religion. Living in a culture still largely religious, some secular psychologists sought to study religion as if it were a merely natural phenomenon, supposedly without assuming any stance toward the phenomenon itself. As a result, many studies of religious behavior and phenomena were published around the turn of the century, the most influential being *The Varieties of Religious Experience* by William James (1903). But this was at best a last gasp of religiousness among modern psychologists; the tide was clearly turning against belief in the metaphysical and supernatural. As a result, as the first generation of American psychologists died out, few of the next generation were drawn to study religious experience, and the field virtually dried up for well over a half century.

Modern psychology quickly proved its value by amassing a substantial body of research and theory within a few decades, regarding topics that had never been so carefully examined: human sensation and perception, brain-mind relations, memory, emotions, unconscious motives, behavioral conditioning, intelligence, personality, and mental problems—and by providing a secular way to treat such problems. American universities embraced the new psychology. As a result, within a couple of generations, it became the only officially sanctioned version of psychology in universities in the West, providing an alternative framework to theism for understanding human beings, and this new psychology promised a truly scientific cure for humanity's problems, in which all open-minded, modern Americans could hope.[4]

Today, over 140 years after the founding of modern psychology, the application of natural-science methods to the study of human beings has increased our understanding of human beings enormously.[5] And given our

---

[3]This trajectory can be documented in the lives of G. Stanley Hall, John Dewey, William James, Joseph Jastrow, James Rowland Angell, James Mark Baldwin, J. B. Watson, William McDougall, B. F. Skinner, Carl Rogers and Abraham Maslow, as well as Europeans like Freud, Jung and Piaget.

[4]As John B. Watson both inticed and prophesied, "I am trying to dangle a stimulus in front of you, a verbal stimulus which, if acted upon, will gradually change this universe. For the universe will change if you bring up your children . . . in behavioristic freedom. . . . Will not these children in turn, with their better ways of living and thinking, replace us as society and in turn bring up their children in a still more scientific way, until the world finally becomes a place fit for human habitation" (Watson, 1930, p. 304).

[5]At the same time, critics have rightly recognized the limitations of using methods derived from

faith in the Creator of human beings, Christians should in principle rejoice over all knowledge about humans derived from any legitimate source. Yet, as we saw above, the church also has its own long, rich tradition of psychological theorizing and practice, a tradition that existed long before the birth of modern psychology. This has led to the oft-cited observation that "psychology has a long past but a short history" (e.g., Danziger, 1979). Much of that "long past," of course, belongs to Christianity; whereas the "short history" belongs to late modernism. The challenge for the church has been that modern psychology has always consisted of more than just objective descriptions of the facts; it is both a contributor to and a beneficiary of the secular revolution that has taken over the intellectual leadership of the West (Johnson, 2007; Smith, 2003). The collision of these two traditions has created the intellectual crisis that is at the heart of this book.

THE CHURCH'S INTELLECTUAL CRISIS ABOUT PSYCHOLOGY

For over thirty years, the renowned contemporary philosopher of ethics Alasdair MacIntyre (1984, 1989, 1990) has engaged in a massive exposition of the conflicts that have arisen in the modern era among Western philosophies of ethics. In the process of his discussions, he has reflected deeply about what happens when intellectual traditions collide. MacIntyre says that "traditions, when vital, embody continuities of conflict" (1984, p. 222). They consist of the ongoing disagreements that occur among the members of their "community"—thoughtful adherents spread across the

---

the study of the natural world (physics, chemistry, biology) to study human beings, given that humans possess unique psychological features not found in the natural world (e.g., the experience of self-awareness, freedom, morality, values, religiosity) (Martin, Sugarman & Thompson, 2003; Van Leeuwen, 1982, 1985; Varela & Shear, 1999). Though some unique features of human life have been observed and measured (e.g., in the positive psychology movement), critics have argued that natural-science methods inevitably lead to a truncated body of psychological research, since they cannot "detect" that which is most distinctive about human beings (reality from the "inside"). As a result, alternative methods have been advocated to augment natural-science research (e.g., phenomenological study, participant observation, discourse analysis, narrative psychology), methods that attempt to take into account the subjective perspective and self-understanding of the person(s) being studied. Though these methods are becoming more widely used (e.g., feminist and postmodern researchers are particularly open to them), mainstream psychologists continue to favor natural-science approaches. Christians, of course, have a stake in such issues since we assume that adult humans are persons: self-aware, responsible, relatively free and moral beings, and therefore, not mere mechanisms or computing organisms (Van Leeuwen, 1982, 1985).

generations of its life. He defines a living tradition as a "historically extended, socially embodied argument, an argument precisely in part about the goods which constitute that tradition" (1984, p. 222). The "goods" in dispute include a tradition's beliefs, standards and practices.

The *beliefs* that may distinguish one tradition from another include worldview beliefs, as well as the nature of human beings and how to understand them (e.g., beliefs about human origins, their metaphysical composition, humanity's optimal or mature state and how to facilitate its development, psychopathology and how to address it, as well as beliefs about the legitimate sources of knowledge). A tradition's *standards* refer to criteria that are used to evaluate soundness in belief and practice, maturity, and wisdom. Finally, a tradition's distinctive *practices* (for our purposes) have to do with the means of obtaining valid and useful information regarding human beings (e.g., biblical, theological, spiritual, philosophical, empirical, scientific, experiential, moral), as well as the promotion of proper human development and the remediation of psychopathology.

There are many different kinds of traditions: craft, artistic, intellectual and religious, just to name a few, and each can be composed of various subtraditions as well. Living traditions are characterized by conflict, because its members are constantly raising questions about its goods. Dead traditions either have no living adherents or those they have simply recite the sayings of its past, without questions. In his exposition, MacIntyre slyly implies that a *living* intellectual tradition possesses searching, inquisitive minds who lead it into better, more comprehensive understanding by way of working through disputes. Given such an assumption, one of the most stimulating events in a tradition's history can be its encounters with other traditions, traditions which have strengths that reveal the weaknesses in the earlier tradition. Discerning adherents can then take advantage of this critical interaction and make use of the strengths of the "new" rival tradition to enrich their own. At the same time—and here is where things get challenging and controversial—such explorations (practices, themselves needing critical evaluation) run the danger of diluting the tradition's distinctiveness. Too much borrowing from an alien tradition can lead to the disintegration of one's own tradition and sometimes even to its disappearance. Consequently, the value of such encounters has to be gauged by whether it leads to an outcome essential for a tradition's well-being: its renewal and reinvigoration by a fresh, contemporary reinvestment and rearticulation of its own resources.

Encounters between traditions are complicated by the fact that members of the traditions are differentially trained. Some may be schooled only in the goods of their own tradition, whereas others may be trained primarily in the rival tradition. MacIntyre considers the persons best equipped to contribute to the debate between two rival traditions to be those trained in the discourse of both. Such individuals "are inhabitants of boundary situations, generally incurring the suspicion and misunderstanding of members of both of the contending parties" (1990, p. 114), since those well educated in only one tradition can only interpret the work of the other in terms of their own tradition's discourse and its goods—the beliefs, standards and practices they already understand and know to be authoritative—making communication (and even trust) difficult between those who are differentially trained. Indeed, those who use only "one language" simply lack enough background knowledge to be able to really understand the potentials and pitfalls of the debate.

MacIntyre's analysis also addresses what constitutes a *crisis* for a tradition. This occurs when tradition A encounters rival tradition B that has such compelling beliefs, standards and practices that those of tradition A are called into serious question. MacIntyre (1989, 1990) says that tradition A resolves such a crisis by the construction of a narrative of the encounter, which includes the following elements: the basic rationality and legitimacy of tradition A; an acknowledgment of its weaknesses revealed by its rival and how it has adequately addressed them and revised itself accordingly; and the exposure of the (more) significant weaknesses that remain unresolved in tradition B, resulting in an account that shows the compelling superiority of the revised tradition A to its rival.

MacIntyre repeatedly makes the point that the biggest obstacle to traditions engaging in mutual, beneficial interaction is the fact that each tradition's beliefs, standards and practices are the means by which an adherent evaluates another tradition, so the very means for determining rational superiority and weakness are themselves part of the debate. Therefore, traditions sometimes discount and ignore each other, and typically only engage in dialogue when they are forced to, either of social necessity or perhaps because of moral and intellectual integrity.

amass a stunning dazzling array of systems + techniques

Our focus in this book, of course, is on two traditions interested in the nature of human beings and how to promote their well-being—two historically extended and socially embodied communities of inquiry and therapy—the Christian and the (late) modern. As noted above, Christianity has its own substantial psychological and soul-care tradition, beginning in the Bible and continuing for the next two millenia, with many permutations over the generations, and consisting of many psychological and soul-care subtraditions (Catholic, Orthodox and Protestant). The new psychology also constitutes a tradition, though of course it is much younger. However, its shorter history is more than compensated for by its vast output and the broad range of topics that it has addressed (and it too is made up of subtraditions—known as psychoanalytic, behavioral, cognitive and so on).

Furthermore, this book concerns the intellectual (and soul-care) crisis that the Christian community was thrown into since modern psychology rose to preeminence—a very serious crisis indeed. Think about it. Which of the two communities exercise the most influence in our culture at large (in its universities, scholarly media, and mental health and therapy institutions), and which has the greater influence on the other? To state the obvious, it has been largely one-directional: the Christian community has had very little explicit, constructive influence on the contemporary psychological scene, and what influence it has had was accomplished by playing according to the rules of late modernism and not by being explicitly Christian. By contrast, the modern psychological community has had an enormous influence on the Christian community, within the latter's counseling centers and colleges and universities, some of its books, and even within its churches.

Why did this crisis occur? As suggested above, modern psychology has amassed a stunning set of empirical findings regarding human beings and developed many psychological theories of great complexity, using novel empirical methods to discover aspects of human nature never before known, and so never discussed in the Christian tradition. Furthermore, this "new tradition" has developed a dazzling array of systems and techniques for improving human psychological well-being, far outstripping in scientific complexity the work of the Christian tradition. Today we live in a science-oriented culture, and modern psychology has been more scientific than any of its predecessors and worldview alternatives. In addition, modern psychology has simply made what the majority of (mostly modernist) intellectuals today consider to be a compelling case: that its version of human beings is simply better than those that went before it—more accurate, more comprehensive and less distorted. All of this has contributed to a crisis in the church.

Is Christianity a living or dead tradition of psychology and therapy? There is evidence, some of it included in this book, that it is very much alive! However, it seems that it took quite a while for Christians to recognize the intellectual crisis that was occurring. We turn next to consider some of the early attempts by Christians to respond to the crisis.

RESPONSES OF CHRISTIANS TO THE "NEW PSYCHOLOGY"

A few Christians actually contributed to the founding of modern psychology. Decades prior, there were some phrenologists who were Christians (Vande Kemp, 1998).[6] Franz Brentano was a devout, if controversial Christian (a former Catholic priest), whose "Act psychology" made a significant impact on European psychology of the day (Watson & Evans, 1991), and who was shaped significantly by his training in Catholic (and Aristotelian) thought. The pious scholar-president of Princeton, James McCosh, published works on cognition and emotion that, though still heavily influenced by philosophy, took seriously the role of physiology in the mind (see Maier, 2005).[7]

However, among the leaders of the new psychology in America, those who maintained a Protestant religious faith tended to be of a more liberal

---

[6]Originating in the 1800s, phrenology was a simplistic "faculty neuropsychology" that nonetheless contributed to modern neuropsychology. Containing both truth and error, it traced the supposedly corresponding regions of the personality, brain and cranium.

[7]Spilka (1987) has suggested that the openness of McCosh to the latest physiological research may have been fostered by his acceptance of Common Sense Realism (an influential epistemology endorsed by many of the preeminent evangelical scholars and administrators of the 1800s; Marsden, 1994; Noll, 1994). This philosophy, originated by the eighteenth-century Christian philosopher Thomas Reid, justified confidence in human abilities to know truths regarding the natural order. These abilities, it was believed, were universally bestowed by the Creator on all persons; hence its proponents saw science as an ally to theology by providing evidence of God's design (Spilka, 1987). So this philosophy encouraged Christians to trust the contemporary research and theorizing of scientists, whether Christian or not, without, at the same time, questioning the underlying modernist assumptions that were implicitly guiding the work (Marsden, 1994).

theological orientation than McCosh. A wayward seminarian in his youth, G. Stanley Hall became one of the most significant early figures in modern psychology in America, establishing the first formal psychology laboratory in the United States, starting the first English-language journal devoted exclusively to psychology, founding the American Psychological Association and becoming its first president (Watson & Evans, 1991). The theologian-turned-psychologist G. T. Ladd (1887) wrote what was for twenty years the most important work in English on physiological psychology, and he also became the second president of the American Psychological Association (before William James!). Late in their careers, both Ladd (1915, 1918) and Hall (1917) examined religion in light of modern psychology and liberal theology.

Over the next few decades, other liberal Protestants (most notably Boisen [1936]) began to explore the value of modern depth psychologies for the church. At the same time they also sought to challenge the pervasive naturalism out of which modern psychology originated, eventually forming a significant movement (e.g., Clinebell, 1966; Hiltner, 1943; Oates, 1962), and contributed to Clinical Pastoral Education (CPE), which has trained thousands of mainline ministers and chaplains in pastoral care from the mid-twentieth century to the present. Generally speaking, however, liberal Protestants largely accommodated themselves to the modernism they sought to influence—modern psychologists were far more influential in their works than Scripture. The relation of faith and psychology was largely one-directional, resulting in a reshaping of the faith by the incorporation of modern values (greater individualism, softened personal morality and reason/science as more authoritative than biblical revelation; see Holifield, 1983; Johnson, 2007, chap. 2; Oden, 1984).[8]

This overall orientation has continued to the present with a more postmodern flavor, though with increased sophistication (Browning, 1991; Capps, 1990; Howe, 1995). Although some have been willing to critique

---

[8]Notably, the founding members of the editorial board of the journal that originated out of this movement, *Pastoral Psychology*, included Rollo May and Carl R. Rogers, along with Hiltner and Oates. May's theological views may have fit well there (he was even a personal friend of Paul Tillich's). However, the inclusion of Rogers on the board, given his lifelong rejection of orthodox Christianity, demonstrates the kind of "openness" and accommodation to contemporary trends in culture for which liberal theology was well known throughout the twentieth century. (The editors are listed in Vande Kemp, 1984.)

mainstream psychology (e.g., Browning & Cooper, 2004), they still demonstrate a greater openness to contemporary values and thought, as well as a greater skepticism toward the Bible, than seems compatible with classical Christianity.

Catholics were also involved in the new psychology. The Reverend Edward Pace began teaching psychology courses at the Catholic University of America in 1891, after having studied with Wundt. Pace was also a founding member of the APA (Misiak & Staudt, 1954; Gillespie, 2001). Later Catholics may have been the first identifiable Christians who sought to provide texts that *supplemented* the literature of empirically based psychology with religiously grounded discussions on the person or soul (though more cautious Catholic voices also protested the new psychology, Misiak & Staudt, 1954, pp. 4-7). This "supplemental" activism was likely due, in part, to the Thomistic revival that began in the last decades of the nineteenth century and continued throughout the first half of the twentieth (Gillespie, 2001). The fact that Thomas Aquinas's corpus is psychologically rich, explicitly open to empirical research (à la Aristotle) yet requires the use of philosophy (or reason) to deal with human nature in all its fullness may have influenced Catholics to augment modern psychology literature with additional philosophical considerations, including topics like the will and soul-body relations.[9]

In contrast to Catholics and liberal Protestants, there is not much evidence that conservative Protestants thought much about psychology in the early twentieth century. Just as psychology was gradually becoming a part of the core curriculum in the social sciences at the major colleges and universities, an examination of course catalogues of Christian liberal arts colleges from the 1920s and 1930s (e.g., Wheaton and Calvin) shows that they also began offering courses in modern psychology around that time.

---

[9]The Catholic historians of psychology Misiak and Staudt (1954) defend this approach, agreeing with modern disciplinary divisions and seeing psychology, philosophy and theology as methodologically distinct, though forming a hierarchy of knowledge. On that basis they argue against a specifically Catholic (and by implication, Christian) psychology: "When psychologists confine themselves to the study of human behavior, as it can be experimentally studied, they are merely restricting their field of inquiry; they are not necessarily denying the existence of the soul" (p. 13). However, they also state that Catholics "will always endeavor to integrate psychology, philosophy and theology" (p. 14), but since the three disciplines all seek the truth from different vantage points (theology through revelation, philosophy through reason, and psychology through observation), there will be no genuine contradiction between them.

A few Christians criticized the new psychology for its materialism and agnosticism (e.g., Wickham, 1928), and a few isolated works can be found that take modern psychology seriously but argue for a Christian perspective (e.g., Murray, 1938; Norlie, 1924). However, conservatives were generally moving away from intellectual engagement with the wider culture, which they saw as spiritually blind. This was the heyday of fundamentalism, and fundamentalists, by and large, were not interested in cultural issues, higher learning and scholarship (Noll, 1994; Smith, 2003). In addition, they tended to be practice-oriented if not anti-intellectual, more interested in soul-winning and missions than in claiming culture for Christ (Noll, 1994). They were, for the most part, separationists, desiring to avoid contamination by the world (including the world of ungodly thinking; e.g., at the universities). For many fundamentalists, learning the Bible was seen as the primary goal of higher education (rather than learning about things like psychology). As a result, during this time they began forming their own postsecondary educational institutions: Bible colleges.

Another factor that may help explain the lack of interest in psychology and counseling is that, contrary to their Puritan and pietist heritage, conservative Christians at that time did not pay attention to inner matters of the soul and its well-being. In spite of some evidence to the contrary (e.g., in some of the movement's hymns), the bulk of fundamentalist literature focused on doctrinal beliefs (like end-times prophecy), moral issues and evangelism. The state of one's soul—apart from whether one was born again—was largely neglected. As a result, for decades the most sophisticated pastoral care literature was written by more liberal Christians.

It really wasn't until after World War II that conservative Protestants began to move out of their cultural ghettos and think more seriously about how their faith bears on the sciences and arts. A group of fundamentalists began to articulate a more activist role in culture and higher learning, calling themselves evangelicals (Carpenter, 1997). It was only in the 1950s that we find evangelicals beginning to engage psychology in any concerted way.

EARLY EVANGELICAL ACTIVITY IN PSYCHOLOGY

Hardly a revolutionary thinker, Hildreth Cross, head of the psychology department at Taylor University, published in 1952 *An Introduction to Psychology: An Evangelical Approach,* which presented psychology positively but screened through the Word of God" (preface). Though simplistic by most standards, it nonetheless combined information from modern psychology with Christian interpretation and evaluation. Critical of evolution, it included many citations from the Bible and an affirmation of supernatural reality in human life, while somewhat superficially presenting some of the main topics covered in any introduction to psychology of the day. The book concluded with a study of the "dynamic Christian personality," in which the influence of redemption on the human personality is described with explicit dependence on Scripture and theology.

A group of conservative Christians, practicing psychologists mostly from a Reformed theological persuasion, got together in 1954 and 1955 for conferences that explored the relation of psychology, psychiatry and religion. In 1956 they formed the Christian Association for Psychological Studies (CAPS <www.caps.net>), continuing to hold conferences that explore how a person's faith relates to the findings of modern psychology, with a special emphasis on counseling. CAPS still has annual conferences, though their identity has broadened substantially beyond its roots in the Reformed community.

Clyde Narramore was a practicing psychologist and began a radio program in 1954 called "Psychology for Living" that eventually played on over two hundred Christian stations nationally. He later published an influential book (1960) outlining a Christian approach to therapy that incorporated a high view of Scripture along with a Christianized form of the person-centered counseling of Carl Rogers. Even more explicit than Narramore in his appreciation for a model of therapy that originated outside Christianity, Tweedie (1961) wrote a book critiquing but still largely supporting the view of persons and therapy found in the work of Viktor Frankl. In different ways these authors argued that modern psychotherapy can contribute to the psychological well-being of evangelical Christians.

During the 1960s the works of Paul Tournier (1965)—a physician-psychotherapist from Switzerland who was schooled in the Freudian and Jungian traditions and had converted to Christianity in midlife—were being translated into English, and the writings of this wise, seasoned Christian therapist proved to be eye-opening to many evangelicals hungry for literature that offered a depth psychology from a Christian perspective.

Eventually, a number of evangelicals began to sense the need for advanced training in a psychology that was shaped by a Christian worldview. Fuller Theological Seminary was the first evangelical school to begin a doctoral program in clinical psychology (1964), and Rosemead School of Psychology followed within a few years (1968), founded by Clyde Narramore and Bruce Narramore, his nephew. Shortly after its inception, Rosemead initiated the *Journal of Psychology and Theology* (1973), providing the first academic forum for evangelicals in psychology. CAPS began publishing the *CAPS Bulletin* in 1975 (which was retitled the *Journal of Psychology and Christianity* in 1982). In some ways the 1970s were a turning point for evangelicals in psychology. Increasingly, books were being written by evangelicals that dealt with psychological topics or counseling, applying insights and techniques derived from modern psychology to such topics as child rearing, marriage, self-esteem, and personal and spiritual growth (e.g., Collins, 1969; Dobson, 1970; Narramore, 1978). Yet this was also the decade in which serious concerns began to be raised about the perceived dangers of accommodating the Christian tradition to that of modern psychology—and thus initiating the intellectual crisis that gave rise to the five positions in this book.

The biblical counseling view. Jay Adams, professor of practical theology at Westminster Theological Seminary, instigated the crisis with the publication of his widely read *Competent to Counsel* (1970), in which he severely criticized modern psychiatry and psychotherapy, arguing that they were pervasively secular. He argued that they were, alternately, deterministic in their understanding of psychopathology and human-centered in their therapy, and in both ways, fundamentally opposed to Christianity. Adams urged Christians to repudiate the dominant Freudian and humanistic methods of counseling. In his own model, "nouthetic counseling" (from the Greek *noutheteo,* "to admonish"), he taught that genuine Christian counseling regards the Bible to be sufficient for the spiritual needs of God's people. Consequently, he advocated that Christians should focus their attention in counseling primarily on repentance from sin (since sin causes most problems that modern psychology tries to address) and Christ as God's solution to our problems. He also believed that pastors should be the primary counselors in the Christian community. Adams founded the Christian Counseling and Educational Foundation (CCEF) in 1968, and the *Journal of Pastoral Practice* in 1977, to help the church meet counseling needs biblically (Powlison, 2010).

Through his numerous books (e.g., 1973, 1979; now over seventy) and their forceful, prophetic style, Adams mobilized many Christians to counsel in strict accordance with Scripture and reject any reliance on modern psychology, and he and others became increasingly critical of the writing and practice of Christian counselors, who they believed were synthesizing Christianity with secular thought (see Bobgan and Bobgan, 1987; MacArthur and Mack, 2005). With help from his colleague at CCEF, John Bettler, Adams and others founded the National Association of Nouthetic Counselors (www.nanc.org) in 1976. In addition to Westminster Theological Seminary, other seminaries began offering counseling programs that centered on the use of the Bible in counseling theory and practice (e.g., The Master's College and Seminary in 1990). Eventually the movement made more clear its central focus by changing the name of the approach from "nouthetic" to simply "biblical" counseling (indicated by the name change in 1993 from *Journal of Pastoral Practice* to *Journal of Biblical Counseling*, as well as by books like MacArthur & Mack, 2005). The movement is by no means monolithic, and over time differences of method and substance have become more obvious, as some have questioned parts of Adams's teachings (Powlison, 1988; Schwab, 2003; Welch, 2002) and critically appropriated some of the research of modern psychology (Welch, 1998, 2005). Adams left CCEF in the mid-1990s in protest, and since then, CCEF has become the leader of this reorientation of the original vision (Lane & Tripp, 2006; Powlison, 2003, 2005; Welch, 2005). In addition, new groups have arisen that, in different ways, are similarly moving beyond Adams's nouthetic model, while still preserving the core concerns of the movement, including the International Association of Biblical Counselors (www.iabc.net) and the Association of Biblical Counselors (www.christiancounseling.com). These changes in turn led Adams and others to start the *Journal of Modern Ministry* in 2005 and the Institute for Nouthetic Studies (www.nouthetic.org).

Many Christians, however, did not find the biblical counseling critique persuasive and pushed back. For example, counselors and therapists who worked with people outside the church, people with little or no religious faith and with problems that are not addressed in the Scriptures, did not find it relevant. Moreover, those educated and trained at secular graduate programs believed that modern psychology had more value than biblical counselors were suggesting, especially psychology teachers and researchers who had studied modern psychology in depth. As a result, the biblical counseling movement was labeled "antipsychology" by some (e.g., Beck & Banks, 1992). In addition, there was a growing realization that some conservative churches were misusing the Bible and doing damage to people in their authoritarian subcultures (something also acknowledged by those in biblical counseling). Such abuses led some Christians to be skeptical of Bible-based counseling and more supportive of counseling that concentrated on psychological dynamics, rather than solely on the spiritual realm. In the context of this foment in the 1970s, two evangelical approaches more favorable to modern psychology began to be more clearly formulated.

The levels-of-explanation view. The "levels-of-explanation" (LOE) approach assumes a sharp distinction between the disciplines (or "levels") of psychology and theology (Jeeves, 1976, 1997; Myers, 1978). Influenced by the physicist Richard Bube (1971), proponents of this approach maintain that all levels of reality are important (the physical, chemical, biological, psychological, social and theological), that each dimension or level of reality is accessible to study by the unique methods appropriate to it that have been developed by the corresponding discipline, and that the boundaries of each discipline, therefore, should not be blurred. To confuse these levels results in a misunderstanding of reality by blending together concepts that are, in fact, very different and do not really cohere (e.g., sin and brain dysfunction). Furthermore, the understanding of each level is assumed to offer a distinct perspective that is essentially independent of the understandings of other levels. Hence, this approach has also been called perspectivalism (Evans, 1977). Theology and psychology, in particular, use different methods of investigation, have different objects of study and answer different questions. Confusing them would distort both (though this model's proponents encourage interdisciplinary dialogue, "after hours" so to speak, in order to get the fullest picture of human nature possible). There is comparatively little interest in the effects of secular modernism on psychology, for its proponents believe strongly that science properly conducted is the best way to eliminate such bias. To bring theological matters into the science of psychology would only undermine the objectivity and integrity of the scientific method.

Significantly, most of the advocates of the LOE approach have been academics and researchers, Christians teaching at Christian and non-Christian colleges and universities. Some of them (like Brown and Jeeves, 2009; Jeeves, 1976, 1997) have done research in neuropsychology, where it is hard to conceive of a distinctly Christian approach that would make any difference. On the contrary, there has been concern in this group that true science will be impeded by the intrusion of faith beliefs from *any* quarter that cannot be empirically established. Science can only proceed on the basis of an objective study of reality that is accessible to direct observation and that can be replicated by any interested investigators.

It should also be pointed out that it is not necessary to endorse this approach *formally* in order to assume it *implicitly* in one's work (e.g., in teaching, writing or counseling). A number of Christians have contributed significantly to the field of contemporary psychology in just that way; for example, in the psychology of religion (Hood, Hill & Spilka, 2009), spirituality (Plante, 2009), forgiveness research and therapy (Worthington, 2005), the role of values in psychotherapy (Worthington, Kurusu, McCullough & Sandage, 1996), and positive psychology (Emmons & McCullough, 2004). Such work subscribes to the rules of modern psychological discourse, yet shows how the Christian tradition can influence modern psychology *indirectly, from within.*

The integration view. Integration is an approach also formulated in the 1970s, that is more open to modern psychology than biblical counseling, but is generally more sympathetic to its critique than the levels-of-explanation approach. Concerned about the naturalism and secular humanism that has shaped modern psychology and counseling literature, the proponents of this view (often counselors and therapists) recognize that the Christian faith has something important to contribute to contemporary psychology and counseling. However, they also respect the scientific merit of psychology as it is today and, therefore, have concluded that the Christian faith and contemporary psychology ought to be related somehow. The majority affirm "interdisciplinary integration," the integration of the discipline of psychology with the discipline of Christian theology (e.g., Beck & Demarest, 2005; Carter & Narramore, 1979; Collins, 1977; Shults & Sandage, 2006).

These integrationists believe both disciplines address, in different ways, the nature of human beings, how they develop, what has gone wrong with them and how they can overcome what has gone wrong. However, there is a range of responses to this overlap. Narramore (1973) argued that integration aims "to combine the special revelation of God's Word with the general revelation studied by the psychological sciences and professions" (p. 17).

Collins (1973) more radically sought to place psychology on a different foundation, one that is "consistent with and built upon the Bible," in order to develop a "biblically based psychology" (p. 26). Both legitimize the composition of a distinct "integration" literature (in contrast to the LOE view), where the two disciplines are more or less blended together, either throughout the text (Collins, 1980; Crabb, 1977; McMinn & Campbell, 2007; McMinn, 2008; Narramore, 1984) or in summary sections or chapters (see Shults & Sandage, 2006; Beck & Demarest, 2005).

Jones & Butman (1991) offer another approach to integration, in which one integrates Christian worldview beliefs with the science and practice of psychology, not theological beliefs (since they belong to another discipline; pp. 19-20). This sounds superficially similar to LOE, but it involves an unusually thorough, critical reinterpretation of modern psychology literature in terms of a Christian worldview, derived from Scripture. Over the past decade, new exemplary integration work has appeared, suggesting that this approach has been experiencing something of a renewal (Beck & Demarest, 2005; McMinn, 2008; McMinn & Campbell, 2007; Shults & Sandage, 2006; Yarhouse & Sells, 2008).

Integration has had a big impact on the evangelical community. Integration books written for Christian laypeople—covering many kinds of psychological topics, including marriage, recovery, self-concept and family-of-origin issues—have sold well. Christian radio programs by integrationists like Dobson, Minirth and Meier, and Cloud and Townsend have been popular. Integration-based counseling and treatment centers are found throughout the United States, in some cases run as a ministry of local churches. Integration is the orientation officially promoted at the major Christian-counseling graduate programs (for example, the doctoral programs at Wheaton College, George Fox College, Seattle Pacific University, Azusa Pacific University and Regent University, in addition to Fuller and Rosemead). The CAPS organization recently celebrated its fiftieth anniversary and compiled a definitive collection of integration articles for the occasion (Stevenson, Eck & Hill, 2007), and has appealed especially to masters- and doctoral-level counseling professionals and academics. In the 1990s, Gary Collins and Tim Clinton formed the American Association of Christian Counselors (www.aacc.net) to reach broader groups (laypeople and ministers, as well as counseling professionals) with a slightly more conservative theological stance than CAPS, and it has exploded to become perhaps the largest Christian organization in the world (see Clinton & Ohlschlager, 2002).[10]

The Christian psychology view. Related to the waning of the influence of logical positivism, Christian philosophy has experienced a significant comeback in recent decades through the work of thinkers like Alvin Plantinga (1984, 2000), Nicholas Wolterstorff, William Alston and now many others. Demonstrating a marked independence of thought from mainstream philosophical currents, Christian philosophers have developed distinctly Christian positions on many common philosophical topics and explored many other topics of interest only to theists.

One of these philosophers, C. Stephen Evans (1989, 1990), was inspired, in part, by the Christian philosopher/psychologist Søren Kierkegaard and has argued that what has happened recently in the field of philosophy could just as legitimately happen in the field of psychology, and he challenged Christians in psychology to develop their own theories, research and practice that flow from Christian beliefs about human beings—while continuing to participate actively in the broader field. Another Christian philosopher, Nancey Murphy (2005), has advocated the development of a psychology research program shaped by a Radical Reformation perspective.[11] From a different vantage point, theologians Ellen Charry (1997), Ray Anderson (1990; Speidell, 2007) and Andrew Purves (2004) have examined Christian theological resources regarding the care of souls and shown how they provide an alternative paradigm to secular models of therapy.

A few actual psychologists have been moving in the same directions. Van Leeuwen (1982, 1985) and Vitz (1987, 1994) anticipated this orientation with their Christian reconceptualizations of aspects or figures of psy-

---

[10]Collins is no longer associated with AACC.
[11]Dueck and Reimer (2009) have developed a similar orientation to psychotherapy, with a stronger postmodern tone.

chology, and Vitz has continued to pursue that agenda (1999, 2009; with Felch, 2006). Johnson (2007) attempted a similar reconceptualization of the field of counseling. P. J. Watson has pursued a Christian psychology research program for over twenty-five years (see my introduction of him below). The Society for Christian Psychology (www.Christianpsych.org) was established in 2004 to help advance this agenda, and it publishes the journal *Edification*, as a division of AACC. In addition, IGNIS, the Institute for Christian Psychology in Kitzingen, Germany, has been developing a Christian psychology for over twenty-five years. Meanwhile, the faculty at the Institute for the Psychological Sciences are working on a distinctly Catholic psychotherapy (Brugger, 2009).

Some Christian counseling authors have been working, at least implicitly, within a Christian psychology orientation. Larry Crabb (1987, 2002) has moved away from the integration approach of his early books, and has been pursuing a more theological and ecclesiological course in his writing on psychological and spiritual growth. Similarly, Crabb's former colleague Dan Allender (2000) has written a number of books, frequently with Old Testament theologian Tremper Longman III (e.g., 1994), which explore psychological topics with an unusually strong theological underpinning. Others whose writing exemplify this orientation—given the extent to which Christian considerations and resources set the agenda of their psychology and counseling, rather than modern psychology—include Neil Anderson (1990), Diane Langberg (1997), Leanne Payne (1995) and Sandra Wilson (2001).

The transformational psychology view. Over the years, a significant number of integrationists have questioned whether the primary focus of integration should be on intellectual matters or on personal, ethical, experiential and spiritual matters. They have argued that *how* Christians live out their Christianity in the field of psychology and counseling is at least as important as seeking to understand human beings Christianly (see, for example, Dueck, 1995; Farnsworth, 1985; Shults & Sandage, 2006; Sorenson, 1996a, 1996b).

In the previous edition of this book (2000), Stanton Jones and I argued that these types of concerns did not warrant a separate approach (pp. 244-46). However, since that was written, I have changed my mind—as not only have these ethical-relational concerns been increasingly well articulated (see, e.g., Coe, 1999; Shults & Sandage, 2006) but they have been linked to the recent interest among evangelicals in spiritual formation and spiritual direction (Foster, 1978; Willard, 1998).

David Benner (1988) was the first evangelical psychotherapist to advocate looking to the history of Christian spirituality to provide a model of soul care that places Christian concerns central to the counselor's agenda, and he has continued to develop this orientation (1999, 2003). Since then, many others have moved in similar directions, including Gary Moon (1996, 2004; and with Benner, 2004) Larry Crabb (2005, 2007), Siang-Yang Tan (2003), and Tan and Douglas Gregg (1997), Terry Wardle (2003), and Sandra Wilson (1998). Two periodicals have also been developed that promote this approach: *Conversations* (edited by Benner, Crabb and Moon) and the *Journal of Spiritual Formation and Soul Care* (from Biola University's Institute for Spiritual Formation).

So this book provides an opportunity to understand the intellectual crisis facing the church in the area surrounding psychology and counseling, and it does this by exploring five major positions evangelicals have taken regarding the relationship of psychology and the Christian faith. There are, of course, other ways of understanding that relationship, and some nonevangelical Christians sometimes use other terms for similar positions. Furthermore, there are many who do not neatly fit into just one of these approaches, and some have shifted over the years (like Larry Crabb). Nevertheless, these five views seem to represent the most distinctive, most clearly articulated evangelical approaches to psychology and counseling to date.

INTRODUCTION OF THE AUTHORS

David G. Myers, psychology professor at Hope College, is the representative of the levels-of-explanation approach. His contributions to contemporary psychology have been considerable, particularly his introductory (2010, 9th ed.) and social psychology textbooks (2008, 9th ed.) and a number of popular condensations of psychology research. Of special importance for this book are his reflections on the relation of faith and psychology (1978, 1991, 1996; and with Malcolm Jeeves, 1987).

Stanton L. Jones was recruited to be the representative of the integration position. After establishing the Psy.D. program at Wheaton College, he became Wheaton's provost in 1996. He has long been a leading second-generation integrationist (1986; with Richard Butman, 1991), and he has sought to engage mainstream psychology from that vantage point (1994, 2000). He has also made a mark in the ecclesial and psychological debates regarding homosexuality (with Mark Yarhouse, 2000, 2007).

Robert C. Roberts, distinguished professor of ethics at Baylor University, is one of the authors representing the Christian psychology approach. A noted philosopher who has written or edited ten books and over ninety articles on the virtues, emotions, epistemology and Søren Kierkegaard (2003, in preparation), he has also written or edited a number of books and articles that specifically advance the project of Christian psychology (1987, 1993, 2001, 2007; with Mark Talbot, 1997).

He is joined by *P. J. Watson,* University of Chattanooga Foundation Professor of Psychology and the chair of the psychology department at the University of Tennessee-Chattanooga. Watson is the editor of the *Journal of Psychology* and has published over 150 studies on a wide array of psychological topics. He has also conducted empirical studies of aspects of Christian psychology (with Morris & Hood, 1988a, 1988b; with Morris, Loy, Hamrick & Grizzle, 2007) and the antireligious bias present in some contemporary psychology (Watson, Morris & Hood, 1987; Watson, Milliron, Morris & Hood, 1995). He is also the editor of *Edification.*

A proponent of the newest position, transformational psychology, is *John H. Coe.* Since 1988 Coe has been associate professor of theology and philosophy at Rosemead Graduate School of Psychology at Biola University. He is also the director of the Institute of Spiritual Formation and is associate professor of spiritual theology and philosophy at Talbot Theological Seminary, also at Biola. He has written two articles (1999, 2000) and given many presentations that anticipate this approach. With Todd W. Hall (2010), he has recently completed a book that more fully develops this model.

Todd W. Hall is associate professor of psychology, also at Rosemead School of Psychology, and he has served as the editor of the *Journal of Psychology and Theology* for ten years. Hall is also the director of the Institute for Research on Psychology and Spirituality. He has published numerous articles in the field (e.g., with Edwards, 2002; and with Noffke, 2008) and edited an important work with Mark McMinn (2003).

Finally, the biblical counseling approach has **David Powlison** as its representative. In addition to counseling at the Christian Counseling & Educational Foundation and teaching at Westminister Theological Seminary for three decades, Powlison has been the editor of the *Journal of Biblical Counseling* (JBC) since 1992. He has written many seminal biblical counseling articles and chapters (1988, 1995, 2000), the most important of which have been collected in two books so far (2003, 2005), as well as the definitive history and analysis of the first thirty years of the biblical counseling movement (2010).

FOR THE STUDENT: ISSUES THAT DISTINGUISH CHRISTIAN APPROACHES TO PSYCHOLOGY

There are at least five issues that distinguish the approaches toward psychology and counseling represented in this book, so here are some guidelines for students regarding what to focus on while they read.

1. Perhaps the main issue distinguishing the five views concerns the possible *sources* of psychological knowledge: empirical research, Scripture and theology, philosophy, personal experience, and history.

2. Another difference is the degree to which the contributors are *more critical* in their interpretation of contemporary psychology or *more trusting*.

3. Still another issue is whether the goal of Christians in psychology should be to pursue a *distinctive understanding* of human nature, to which only Christians would subscribe, or a *universal understanding* that all psychologists, regardless of their worldview, can recognize and affirm.

4. The authors differ in how much they consider their primary allegiance in psychology and counseling to be the *church* or *the broader community of scholars and practitioners* in one's culture.

5. Finally, some of the representatives appear to understand the primary task of psychology to be the *acquisition of knowledge* about human beings, whereas others seem to think it should be the *renovation* of human beings and the cultivation of godliness, moral character and love.

The reader might try to identify the positions that each view assumes regarding these five significant issues.

Now consider yourself invited into a conversation among some of the significant Christians in the fields of psychology and counseling today.

REFERENCES
Adams, J. E. (1970). *Competent to counsel.* Phillipsburg, NJ: Presbyterian & Reformed.

———. (1973). *Christian counselor's manual.* Phillipsburg, NJ: Presbyterian & Reformed.

———. (1979). *More than redemption.* Grand Rapids, MI: Baker.

Allender, D. B. (2000). *The healing path.* Colorado Springs: Waterbrook.

Allender, D. B., & Longman, T., III. (1990). *Bold love.* Colorado Springs: NavPress.

———. (1994). *The cry of the soul: How our emotions reveal our deepest questions about God.* Colorado Springs: NavPress.

Anderson, N. T. (1990). *The bondage breaker.* Eugene, OR: Harvest House.

Anderson, R. S. (1990). *Christians who counsel: The vocation of wholistic therapy.* Grand Rapids, MI: Zondervan.

Baer, J., Kaufman, J. C., & Baumeister, R. F. (2008). *Are we free? Psychology and free will.* New York: Oxford University Press.

Bandura, A. (2001). Social cognitive theory: An agentic perspective. *Annual Review, 52,* 1-26.

Barbour, J. D. (1994). *Versions of deconversion: Autobiography and the loss of faith.* Charlottesville: University Press of Virginia.

Beck, J. R., & Banks, J. W. (1992). Christian anti-psychology: Hints of an historical analogue. *Journal of Psychology and Theology, 20,* 3-10.

Beck, J. R., & Demarest, B. (2005). *The human person in theology and psychology: A biblical anthropology for the twenty-first century.* Grand Rapids, MI: Kregel.

Benner, D. G. (1988). *Psychotherapy and the spiritual quest.* Grand Rapids, MI: Baker.

———. (1999). *Care of souls: Revisioning Christian nurture and counsel.* Grand Rapids, MI: Baker.

———. (2003). *Surrender to love: Discovering the heart of Christian spirituality.* Downers Grove, IL: InterVarsity Press.

Bobgan, M., & Bobgan, B. (1987). *Psychoheresy: The psychological seduction of Christianity.* Santa Barbara, CA: Eastgate.

Boisen, A. T. (1936). *The exploration of the inner world.* Chicago: Willett, Clark.

Brett, G. S. (1912). *A history of psychology: Ancient and patristic.* London: George Allen.

Brown, W. S., & Jeeves, M. (2009). *Neuroscience, psychology, and religion: Illusions, delusion, and realities about human nature.* West Conshohocken, PA: Templeton Press.

Browning, D. S. (1991). *A fundamental practical theology.* Minneapolis: Fortress.

Browning, D. S., & Cooper, T. D. (2004). *Religious thought and the modern psychotherapies* (2nd ed.). Minneapolis: Fortress.

Brugger, E. C. (Ed.). (2009). Special issue: Catholic psychology. *Edification: The Journal of the Society for Christian Psychology, 3*(1).

Bube, R. (1971). *The human quest.* Waco, TX: Word.

Calvin, J. (1960). *Institutes of the Christian religion* (Vol. 1). (F. L. Battles, Trans.). Philadelphia: Westminster Press.

Capps, D. (1990). *Reframing: A new method in pastoral care.* Minneapolis: Fortress.

Carpenter, J. (1997). *Revive us again: The reawakening of American fundamentalism.* New York: Oxford University Press.

Carter, J. D., & Narramore, B. (1979). *The integration of psychology and theology: An introduction.* Grand Rapids, MI: Zondervan.

Charry, E. T. (1997). *By the renewing of your minds: The pastoral function of Christian doctrine.* New York: Oxford University Press.

Clinebell, H. J., Jr. (1966). *Basic types of pastoral counseling.* Nashville: Abingdon.

Clinton, T., & Ohlschlager, G. (Eds.). (2002). *Competent Christian counseling.* Colorado Springs: Waterbrook.

Coe, J. H. (1999). Beyond relationality: Musings towards a pneumadynamic approach to personality and psychopathology. *Journal of Psychology and Christianity, 18,* 109-28.

———. (2000). Musing on the *Dark Night of the Soul:* Insights from St. John of the Cross on a developmental spirituality. *Journal of Psychology and Theology, 28*(4), 293-307.

Coe, J. H., & Hall, T. W. (2010). *Psychology in the Spirit: Contours of a transformational psychology.* Downers Grove, IL: IVP Academic.

Collins, G. R. (1969). *Search for reality: Psychology and the Christian.* Wheaton: Key.

———. (1973). Psychology on a new foundation: A proposal for the future. *Journal of Psychology and Theology, 1,* 19-27.

———. (1977). *The rebuilding of psychology: An integration of psychology and Christianity.* Wheaton, IL: Tyndale House.

———. (1980). *Christian counseling: A comprehensive guide.* Waco, TX: Word.

Crabb, L. J., Jr. (1977). *Effective biblical counseling.* Grand Rapids, MI: Zondervan.

———. (1987). *Inside out.* Colorado Springs: NavPress.

———. (2002). *The pressure's off.* Colorado Springs: Waterbrook.

———. (2005). *The papa prayer: The prayer you've never prayed.* Nashville: Thomas Nelson.

———. (2007). *Becoming a true spiritual community: A profound vision of what the church can be.* Nashville: Thomas Nelson.

Cross, H. (1952). *An introduction to psychology: An evangelical approach.* Grand Rapids, MI: Zondervan.

Danziger, K. (1979). The positivist repudiation of Wundt. *Journal of the History of the Behavioral Sciences, 15,* 205-30.

Dobson, J. (1970). *Dare to discipline.* Wheaton, IL: Tyndale House.

Dueck, A. (1995). *Between Jerusalem and Athens: Ethical perspectives on culture, religion, and psychotherapy.* Grand Rapids, MI: Baker.

Dueck, A., & Reimer, K. (2009). *A peaceable psychology: Christian therapy in a world of many cultures.* Grand Rapids, MI: Brazos Press.

Emmons, R. A., & McCullough, M. E. (2004). *The psychology of gratitude.* New York: Oxford University Press.

Evans, C. S. (1977). *Preserving the person: A look at the human sciences.* Downers Grove, IL: InterVarsity Press.

———. (1989). *Wisdom and humanness in psychology: Prospects for a Christian approach.* Grand Rapids, MI: Zondervan.

———. (1990). *Søren Kierkegaard's Christian psychology.* Grand Rapids, MI: Zondervan.

Farnsworth, K. E. (1985). *Whole-hearted integration: Harmonizing psychology and Christianity through word and deed.* Grand Rapids, MI: Baker.

Fletcher, G. J. O. (1995). *The scientific credibility of folk psychology.* Hillsdale, NJ: Lawrence Erlbaum.

Foster, R. J. (1978). *Celebration of discipline.* San Francisco: Harper.

Gillespie, C. K., S.J. (2001). *Psychology and American Catholicism: From confession to therapy?* New York: Crossroad.

Hall, G. S. (1917). *Jesus, the Christ, in the light of psychology.* New York: Doubleday.

Hall, T. W., & Edwards, K. J. (2002). The spiritual assessment inventory: A theistic model and measure for assessing spiritual development. *Journal for the Scientific Study of Religion, 41*(2), 341-57.

Hall, T. W., & McMinn, M. R. (Eds.). (2003). *Spiritual formation, counseling, and psychotherapy.* New York: Nova Science.

Hiltner, S. (1943). *Religion and health.* New York: Macmillan.

Holifield, E. B. (1983). *A history of pastoral care in America: From salvation to self-realization.* Nashville: Abingdon.

Hood, R. W., Jr., Hill, P. C., & Spilka, B. (2009). *The psychology of religion: An empirical approach* (4th ed.). New York: Guilford.

Hooykaas, R. (1972). *Religion and the rise of modern science.* Grand Rapids, MI: Eerdmans.

Howe, L. T. (1995). *The image of God: A theology for pastoral care and counseling.* Nashville: Abingdon.

Hunter, J. D. (1991). *Culture wars: The struggle to define America.* New York: Basic Books.

James, W. (1890). *Principles of psychology.* New York: Henry Holt.

———. (1903). *The varieties of religious experience.* New York: Longmans, Green.

Jeeves, M. (1976). *Psychology and Christianity: The view both ways.* Downers Grove, IL: InterVarsity Press.

———. (1997). *Human nature at the millennium: Reflections on the integration of psychology and Christianity.* Grand Rapids, MI: Baker.

Johnson, E. L. (2007). *Foundations for soul care: A Christian psychology proposal.* Downers Grove, IL: IVP Academic.

Jones, S. L. (Ed.). (1986). *Psychology and the Christian faith: An introductory reader.* Grand Rapids, MI: Baker.

———. (1994). A constructive relationship for religion with the science and profession of psychology: Perhaps the boldest model yet. *American Psychologist, 49*(3), 184-99.

———. (2000). Religion and psychology: Theories and methods. In A. Kazdin (Ed.), *Encyclopedia of psychology* (Vol. 7, pp. 38-42). Washington, DC: American Psychological Association.

Jones, S. L., & Butman, R. (1991). *Modern psychotherapies: A comprehensive Christian appraisal.* Downers Grove, IL: InterVarsity Press.

Jones, S. L., & Yarhouse, M. (2000). *Homosexuality: The use of scientific research in the church's moral debate.* Downers Grove, IL: InterVarsity Press.

———. (2007). *Ex-gays? A longitudinal study of religiously mediated change in sexual orientation.* Downers Grove, IL: IVP Academic.

Klein, D. B. (1970). *A history of scientific psychology: Its origins and philosophical backgrounds.* New York: Basic Books.

Kuhn, T. S. (1962). *The structure of scientific revolutions.* Chicago: University of Chicago Press.

Ladd, G. T. (1887). *Elements of physiological psychology.* New York: Charles Scribner's Sons.

———. (1915). *What may I hope? An inquiry into the sources and reasonableness of the hopes of humanity, especially the social and religious.* New York and London: Longmans, Green.

———. (1918). *The secret of personality: The problem of man's personal life as viewed in the light of an hypothesis of man's religious faith.* New York and London: Longmans, Green.

Lane, T. S., & Tripp, P. D. (2006). *Relationships: A mess worth making.* Greensboro, NC: New Growth Press.

Langberg, D. M. (1997). *Counseling survivors of sexual abuse.* Wheaton, IL: Tyndale House.

Leahey, T. H. (2003). *A history of psychology: Main currents in psychological thought* (6th ed.). Upper Saddle River, NJ: Prentice Hall.

MacArthur, J., & Mack, W. A. (Eds.). (2005). *Counseling: How to counsel biblically.* Nashville: Thomas Nelson.

MacIntyre, A. (1984). *After virtue* (2nd ed.). South Bend, IN: University of Notre Dame Press.

———. (1989). Epistemological crises, narrative, and philosophy of science. In S. Hauerwas & L. G. Jones (Eds.), *Why narrative? Readings in narrative theology* (pp. 138-57). Grand Rapids, MI: Eerdmans. (Original work published 1977)

———. (1990). *Three rival versions of moral enquiry: Encyclopaedia, genealogy, and tradition.* South Bend, IN: University of Notre Dame Press.

Maier, B. (2005). *The separation of psychology and theology at Princeton, 1868-1903: The intellectual achievement of James McCosh and James Mark Baldwin.* Lewiston, NY: Edwin Mellen Press.

Martin, J., Sugarman, J., & Thompson, J. (2003). *Psychology and the question of agency.* Albany: State University of New York Press.

Marsden, G. (1994). *The soul of the American university.* Oxford: Oxford University Press.

McGrath, A. E. (2001). *A scientific theology: Vol. 1. Nature.* Grand Rapids, MI: Eerdmans.

McMinn, M. R. (2008). *Sin and grace in Christian counseling: An integrative paradigm.* Downers Grove, IL: IVP Academic.

McMinn, M. R., & Campbell, C. D. (2007). *Integrative psychotherapy: Toward a comprehensive Christian appraisal.* Downers Grove, IL: IVP Academic.

McNeill, J. T. (1951). *A history of the cure of souls.* New York: Harper & Row.

Misiak, H., & Staudt, V. G. (1954). *Catholics in psychology: A historical survey.* New York: McGraw-Hill.

Moon, G. W. (1996). *Homework for Eden: Confessions about the journey of a soul.* LifeSprings Resources.

———. (2004). *Falling for God: Saying yes to his extravagant proposal.* Colorado Springs: WaterBrook.

Moon, G. W., & Benner, D. G. (2004). *Spiritual direction and the care of souls: A guide to Christian approaches and practices.* Downers Grove, IL: InterVarsity Press.

Murphy, N. (2005). Constructing a radical-reformation research program in psychology. In A. Dueck & C. Lee (Eds.), *Why psychology needs theology: A radical reformation perspective* (pp. 53-78). Grand Rapids, MI: Eerdmans.

Murray, J. A. C. (1938). *An introduction to a Christian psycho-therapy.* Edinburgh: T & T Clark.

Myers, D. G. (1978). *The human puzzle: Psychological research and Christian belief.* New York: Harper & Row.

———. (1991). Steering between extremes: On being a Christian scholar within psychology. *Christian Scholar's Review, 20,* 376-83.

———. (1996). On professing psychological science and Christian faith. *Journal of Psychology and Christianity, 15,* 143-49.

———. (2008). *Social psychology* (9th ed.). New York: McGraw-Hill.

———. (2010). *Psychology* (9th ed.). New York: Worth.

Myers, D. G., & Jeeves, M. (1987). *Psychology through the eyes of faith.* San Francisco: Harper & Row.

Narramore, B. (1973). Perspectives on the integration of psychology and theology. *Journal of Psychology and Theology, 1,* 3-17.

———. (1978). *You're someone special.* Grand Rapids, MI: Zondervan.

———. (1984). *No condemnation: Rethinking guilt motivation in counseling, preaching, & parenting.* Grand Rapids, MI: Zondervan.

Narramore, C. M. (1960). *The psychology of counseling: Professional techniques for pastors, teachers, youth leaders, and all who are engaged in the incomparable art of counseling.* Grand Rapids, MI: Zondervan.

Noffke, J., & Hall, T. W. (2008). Attachment theory and God image. In G. Moriarity & L. Hoffman (Eds.), *Handbook of God image*. Florence, KY: Routledge.

Noll, M. (1994). *The scandal of the evangelical mind*. Grand Rapids, MI: Eerdmans.

Norlie, O. M. (1924). *An elementary Christian psychology*. Minneapolis: Augsburg.

Nussbaum, M. C. (1994). *The therapy of desire: Theory and practice in Hellenistic ethics*. Princeton, NJ: Princeton University Press.

Oates, W. (1962). *Protestant pastoral counseling*. Philadelphia: Westminster Press.

Oden, T. C. (1984). *Care of souls in the classic tradition*. Theology and pastoral care series (D. S. Browning, Ed.). Philadelphia: Fortress.

————. (1989). *Pastoral counsel*. Classical Pastoral Care (Vol. 3). New York: Crossroad.

Olson, R. P. (2002). *Religious theories of personality and psychotherapy: East meets west*. New York: Haworth.

Payne, L. (1995). *The healing presence: Curing the soul through union with Christ*. Grand Rapids, MI: Baker.

Plante, T. G. (2009). *Spiritual practices in psychotherapy*. Washington, DC: American Psychological Association.

Plantinga, A. (1984). Advice to Christian philosophers. *Faith and Philosophy, 1*, 253-71.

————. (2000). *Warranted Christian belief*. New York: Oxford University Press.

Powlison, D. (1988). Crucial issues in contemporary biblical counseling. *The Journal of Pastoral Practice, 9*, 3-10.

————. (1995). Idols of the heart and "Vanity Fair." *Journal of Biblical Counseling, 13*, 35-50.

————. (2000). Affirmations & denials: A proposed definition of biblical counseling. *Journal of Biblical Counseling, 19*(1), 18-25.

————. (2003). *Seeing with new eyes: Counseling and the human condition through the lens of Scripture*. Phillipsburg, NJ: P & R.

————. (2005). *Speaking truth in love*. Phillipsburg, NJ: P & R.

————. (2010). *The biblical counseling movement: History and context*. Greensboro, NC: New Growth Press.

Purves, A. (2004). *Reconstructing pastoral theology: A christological foundation*. Louisville, KY: Westminster John Knox.

Roberts, R. C. (1987). Psychotherapeutic virtues and the grammar of faith. *Journal of Psychology and Theology, 15*, 191-204.

————. (1993). *Taking the word to heart*. Grand Rapids, MI: Eerdmans.

————. (2001). Outline of Pauline psychotherapy. In M. R. McMinn & T. R. Phillips (Eds.), *Care for the soul* (pp. 134-63). Downers Grove, IL: InterVarsity Press.

————. (2003). *Emotions: An essay in aid of moral psychology*. Cambridge: Cambridge University Press.

————. (2007). *Spiritual emotions: A psychology of Christian virtues*. Grand Rapids, MI: Eerdmans.

————. (in preparation). *Emotions and virtues: An essay in moral psychology*.

Roberts, R. C., & Talbot, M. R. (Eds.). (1997). *Limning the psyche: Explorations in Christian psychology*. Grand Rapids, MI: Eerdmans.

Schwab, G. M. (2003). Critique of 'habituation' as a biblical model of change. *Journal of Biblical Counseling, 21*(2), 67-83.

Shults, F. L., & Sandage, S. J. (2006). *Transforming spirituality: Integrating theology and psychology*. Grand Rapids, MI: Baker.

Smith, C. (2003). Introduction: Rethinking the secularization of American public life. In C. Smith (Ed.), *The secular revolution: Power, interests, and conflict in the secularization of American public life* (pp. 1-96). Berkeley, CA: University of California Press.

Sorenson, R. L. (1996a). Where are the nine? *Journal of Psychology and Theology, 24*, 179-96.

————. (1996b). The tenth leper. *Journal of Psychology and Theology, 24,* 197-211.

Speidell, T. H. (Ed.). (2007). Special issue: The work of Ray S. Anderson. *Edification: The Journal of the Society for Christian Psychology, 1*(2).

Spilka, B. (1987). Religion and science in early American psychology. *Journal of Psychology and Theology, 15,* 3-9.

Stark, R. (2003). *For the glory of God: How monotheism led to reformations, science, witch-hunts, and the end of slavery.* Princeton, NJ: Princeton University Press.

Stevenson, D. H., Eck, B. E., & Hill, P. C. (Eds.). (2007). *Psychology and Christianity integration: Seminal works that shaped the movement.* Batavia, IL: Christian Association for Psychological Studies.

Suppe, F. (Ed.). (1977). *The structure of scientific theories* (2nd ed.). Urbana: University of Illinois Press.

Tan, S.-Y. (2003). *Rest: Experiencing God's peace in a restless world.* Vancouver, BC: Regent College Publishing.

Tan, S.-Y., & Gregg, D. H. (1997). *Disciplines of the Holy Spirit.* Grand Rapids, MI: Zondervan.

Taylor, C. (2007). *A secular age.* Cambridge, MA: Harvard University Press.

Thomas, R. M. (2001). *Folk psychologies across cultures.* Thousand Oaks, CA: Sage.

Thorndike, E. (1905). *The elements of psychology.* New York: A. G. Seiler.

Toulmin, S., & Leary, D. E. (1992). The cult of empiricism in psychology, and beyond. In S. Koch & D. E. Leary (Eds.), *A century of psychology as science* (pp. 594-617). New York: McGraw-Hill.

Tournier, P. (1965). *The healing of persons.* New York: Harper & Row.

Tweedie, D. F., Jr. (1961). *Logotherapy and the Christian faith: An evaluation of Frankl's existential approach to psychotherapy from a Christian viewpoint.* Grand Rapids, MI: Baker.

Vande Kemp, H. (1984). *Psychology and theology in western thought: 1672-1965: A historical and annotated bibliography.* Millwood, NY: Kraus.

————. (1998). Christian psychologies for the twenty-first century: Lessons from history. *Journal of Psychology and Christianity, 17,* 197-204.

Van Leeuwen, M. S. (1982). *Sorcerer's apprentice: A Christian looks at the changing face of psychology.* Downer's Grove, IL: InterVarsity Press.

————. (1985). *The person in psychology.* Grand Rapids, MI: Eerdmans.

Varela, F. J., & Shear, J. (Eds.). (1999). *The view from within: First-person approaches to the study of consciousness.* Thorverton, UK: Imprint Academic.

Vitz, P. C. (1987). *Sigmund Freud's Christian unconscious.* New York: Guilford.

————. (1994). *Psychology as religion: The cult of self-worship.* Grand Rapids, MI: Eerdmans. (Original work published 1977)

————. (1999). *Faith of the fatherless: The psychology of atheism.* Dallas: Spence.

————. (2009). Reconceiving personality theory from a Catholic Christian perspective. *Edification: The Journal of the Society for Christian Psychology, 3*(1), 42-50.

Vitz, P. C., & Felch, S. M. (2006). *The self: Beyond the postmodern crisis.* Wilmington, DE: ISI Books.

Wardle, T. (2003). *The transforming path: A Christ-centered approach to spiritual formation.* Abilene, TX: Leafwood.

Watson, J. B. (1913). Psychology as the behaviorist views it. *Psychological Review, 20,* 158-77.

————. (1930). *Behaviorism.* New York: W. W. Norton.

Watson, P. J., Milliron, J. T., Morris, R. J., & Hood, R. W., Jr. (1995). Religion and the self as text: Toward a Christian translation of self-actualization. *Journal of Psychology and Theology, 23,* 180-89.

Watson, P. J., Morris, R. J., & Hood, R. W., Jr. (1987). Antireligious humanistic values, guilt, and self esteem. *Journal for the Scientific Study of Religion, 26*, 535-46.

———. (1988a). Sin and self-functioning, Part 1: Grace, guilt, and self-consciousness. *Journal of Psychology and Theology, 16*, 254-69.

———. (1988b). Sin and self-functioning, Part 2: Grace, guilt, and psychological adjustment. *Journal of Psychology and Theology, 16*, 270-81.

Watson, P. J., Morris, R. J., Loy, T., Hamrick, M. B., & Grizzle, S. (2007). Beliefs about sin: Adaptive implications in relationships with religious orientation, self-esteem, and measures of the narcissistic, depressed and anxious self. *Edification: Journal of the Society for Christian Psychology, 1*, 57-67.

Watson, R. I., & Evans, R. B. (1991). *The great psychologists: A history of psychological thought.* New York: HarperCollins.

Welch, E. (1998). *Blame it on the brain?* Phillipsburg, NJ: P & R.

———. (2002). How theology shapes ministry: Jay Adam's view of the flesh as an alternative. *Journal of Biblical Counseling, 20*(3), 16-25.

———. (2005). *Depression: A stubborn darkness.* Greensboro, NC: New Growth Press.

Wickham, H. (1928). *The misbehaviorists.* New York: Dial Press.

Willard, D. (1998). *The divine conspiracy.* San Francisco: HarperSanFrancisco.

Wilson, S. D. (1998). *Into Abba's arms.* Wheaton, IL: Tyndale House.

———. (2001). *Hurt people hurt people.* Grand Rapids, MI: Discovery House.

Worthington, E. L., Jr. (2005). *Handbook of forgiveness.* New York: Brunner-Routledge.

Worthington, E. L., Jr., Kurusu, T., McCullough, M. E., & Sandage, S. J. (1996). Empirical research on religion and psychotherapeutic processes and outcomes: A ten-year review and research prospectus. *Psychological Bulletin, 119*, 448-87.

Yarhouse, M. A., & Sells, J. N. (2008). *Family therapies: A comprehensive Christian appraisal.* Downers Grove, IL: IVP Academic.

2

A Levels-of-Explanation View

David G. Myers

As CONTRIBUTORS TO THIS VOLUME, we share a common Christian faith and an engagement with some form of psychology. But our assignment here is to explore our differences, which involve differing understandings of psychology.[1] I write as an active Christian, one who begins each day by engaging the Word and the world, via Bible reading, prayer and the *New York Times*. I also represent psychology as it exists in most universities and colleges; as it is tested by the Advanced Placement, CLEP and GRE psychology exams; and as it is portrayed in essentially every introductory psychology text, including my own.

The definitions of this mainstream psychology have varied over time. For William James (*The Principles of Psychology*, 1890) psychology was *the science of mental life*. By the mid-twentieth century it had become *the science of behavior*. Today we synthesize this history by defining psychology as *the science of behavior and mental processes*. Over time, these varied definitions have agreed: psychology is a *science*. Scientific inquiry begins with a *curiosity* and a *humility* that motivates us to test competing ideas, including our own.

So, those of us in psychological science are sometimes asked, how do you reconcile your commitment to psychological science with your commitment to the Christian faith? (1) How do they fit together? (2) Are they mutually supportive? (3) Are there points of tension?

My answers, in brief, are: (1) They fit together nicely. A humble faith in God and awareness of human fallibility motivates rigorous, open-minded sci-

---

[1]Parts of this chapter are adapted from Myers (1991, 1994, 1995, 1996, 2000a, 2000b, 2007) and Myers and Jeeves (2002).

ence. (2) Psychological science supports much biblical and theological wisdom. Whether viewed through the lens of ancient biblical wisdom or modern psychological science, the story of human nature is much the same. (3) The discoveries of psychological science do challenge some traditional Christian understandings. An ever-reforming faith will always be open to learning from both the book of God's Word and the book of God's works.

SCIENCE AND FAITH

Many secularists and Christians alike see science and faith as enemies. On one side, the "new atheist" Sam Harris (2006, p. 47) writes that religion is "both false and dangerous." His kindred spirit, scientist Richard Dawkins (1997, p. 26), agrees that faith is not only wrong—a mental "virus"—but also "one of the world's great evils." The universe has "no design, no purpose, no evil and good, nothing but blind pitiless indifference," notes Dawkins (1995). Harris and Dawkins extend the historic replacement of supernatural with natural explanations. When our ancestors came to see bolts of lightning as acts of nature, they ceased seeing them as acts of God. When the new atheists see humans as products of evolutionary history, they often cease viewing them as special creatures of God. Science and religion, it may seem, sit on opposite ends of an explanatory teeter-totter.

Actually, say historians of science, many of the founders of modern science were people whose religious convictions made them humble before nature and skeptical of human authority (Hooykaas, 1972; Merton, 1938/1970). The Christian convictions of Blaise Pascal, Francis Bacon, Isaac Newton and even Galileo led them to distrust human intuition, and to explore God's creation and submit their ideas to testing. Whether searching for truth in special revelation (the book of God's Word) or natural revelation (the book of God's works), they viewed themselves in God's service.

If, as once supposed, nature is sacred (for example, if nature is alive with river goddesses and sun gods), then we ought not tamper with it. But if, as the scientific pioneers assumed, it is an intelligible creation—a work to be enjoyed and managed—then let us seek its truths by observing and experimenting. And let us do so freely, knowing that our ultimate allegiance is not to human doctrine but to God alone. Let us humbly test our ideas. If nature does not conform to our presumptions, so much the worse for our presumptions. Disciplined, rigorous inquiry—checking our theories against reality—is part of what it means to love God with our minds.[2] "Test everything; hold fast to what is good," Saint Paul advised the Thessalonians (1 Thess 5:21).

These attitudes of humility before the created world and skepticism of human ideas also underlie psychological science. The Christian psychologist-neuroscientist Donald MacKay encouraged us "to 'tell it like it is,' knowing that the Author is at our elbow, a silent judge of the accuracy with which we claim to describe the world He has created" (1984). If God is the ultimate author of whatever truth psychological science glimpses, then I can accept that truth, however surprising or unsettling. Openness to scientific inquiry becomes not just my right but my religious duty.

Levels of explanation. "Reality is a multi-layered unity," wrote the British physicist-priest John Polkinghorne (1986). "I can perceive another person as an aggregation of atoms, an open biochemical system in interaction with the environment, a specimen of *homo sapiens,* an object of beauty, someone whose needs deserve my respect and compassion, a brother for whom Christ died. All are true and all mysteriously coinhere in that one person."

In *Psychology Through the Eyes of Faith* (2002), Malcolm Jeeves and I illustrate the different levels of analysis (or "levels of explanation") appropriate to a multilayered reality. Each academic discipline provides a perspective from which we can study nature and our place in it. These range from the scientific fields that study the most elementary building blocks of nature up to philosophy and theology, which address some of life's global questions.

Which perspective is pertinent depends on what you want to talk about. Take romantic love, for example. A physiologist might describe love as a state of arousal. A social psychologist would examine how various characteristics and conditions—good looks, similarity of the partners, sheer repeated exposure to one another—enhance the emotion of love. A poet would express the sublime experience that love can sometimes be. A theologian might describe love as the God-given goal of human relationships. Since love can often be described simultaneously at various levels, we need not assume that one level is causing the other—by supposing, for example, that a brain state is causing the emotion of love or that the emotion is causing the brain state. The emotional and physiological views are simply two complementary perspectives.

---

[2]"You shall love the Lord your God with all your heart, and with all your soul, and with all your mind" (Mt 22:37). Scripture quotations in this chapter, unless otherwise noted, are from the New Revised Standard Version of the Bible.

The multilayered ways of looking at a phenomenon like romantic love often correlate, enabling us to build bridges between different perspectives. A religious explanation of the incest taboo (in terms of divine will or a moral absolute) fits nicely with a biological explanation (in terms of the genetic penalty that offspring pay for inbreeding) and a sociological explanation (in terms of preserving the marital and family units). To say that religious and scientific levels of explanation often complement one another does not preclude conflict. It just means that different types of analysis can fit coherently together. In God's world, all truth is one.

Recognizing the complementary relationship of various explanatory levels (figure 1) liberates us from useless argument over whether we should view human nature scientifically or subjectively: it's not an either-or matter. "Try as it might," explained sociologist Andrew Greeley (1976), "psychology cannot explain the purpose of human existence, the meaning of human life, the ultimate destiny of the human person." Psychology is one important perspective from which we can view and understand ourselves, but it is not the only one.

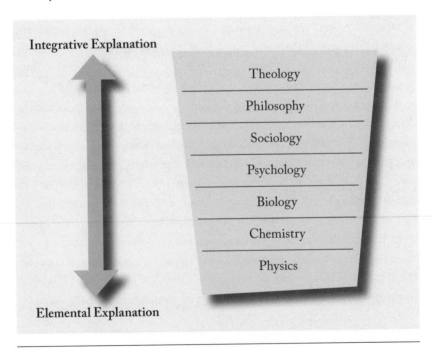

Figure 1.

PARTIAL HIERARCHY OF DISCIPLINES

The disciplines range from basic sciences that study nature's building blocks up to integrative disciplines that study complex systems. A successful explanation of human functioning at one level need not contradict explanations at other levels.

Psychological science and hidden values. Postmodernists and fundamentalists often resist psychological science. They say that psychology is so ideologically loaded that we should not swallow it uncritically. Being wary of hidden presuppositions and values, they would prefer we squeeze psychology into the contours of their ideology. For example, postmodernists have said that scientific concepts are socially constructed fictions. Intelligence, they have said, is a concept we humans created and defined. Because personal values guide theory and research, truth becomes personal and subjective. In the quest for truth, we follow our biases, our cultural bent. So, they say, we must be wary of psychology's biases and values (a message you will read elsewhere in this book).

Psychological scientists agree that many important questions lie beyond the reach of science, and they agree that personal beliefs often shape perceptions. But they also believe that there is a real world out there and that we advance truth by checking our hunches against it. Madame Curie did not just construct the concept of radium, she discovered radium. It really exists. In the social sciences, pure objectivity, like pure righteousness, may be unattainable, but should we not pursue it as an ideal? Better to humble ourselves before reliable evidence than to cling to our presumptions.

The list of popular beliefs that have crashed against a wall of observations is long and growing. No longer do many of us believe that sleepwalkers are acting out their dreams, that hypnosis uncovers long-buried memories, that our two cerebral hemispheres are functionally equivalent, that newborns are dumb to the world, that traumatic experiences tend to be massively repressed but recoverable much later, or that electroconvulsive therapy is a barbaric and ineffective treatment for profound depression.

Still, psychology's critics score points. Although psychological science helps us answer some important questions, it cannot answer all questions. "Bear in mind psychology's limits," I remind students:

Don't expect it to answer the ultimate questions, such as those posed by Russian novelist Leo Tolstoy (1904): "Why should I live? Why should I do anything? Is there in life any purpose which the inevitable death that awaits me does not undo and destroy?" Instead, expect that psychology will help you understand why people think, feel, and act as they do. Then you should find the study of psychology fascinating and useful. (Myers, 2010, pp. 12-13)

Moreover, values indeed guide our research and reporting. Ironically, it is experiments—on "confirmation bias," "belief perseverance," "mental set" and the "overconfidence phenomenon"—that most convincingly demonstrate the critics' point: *belief guides perception*. When first viewing the "canals" on Mars through telescopes, some astronomers and writers perceived them as the product of intelligent life. They were, but the intelligence was on the viewing end of the telescope. To believe is to see.

Our values also leak through our choice of topics, our examples and emphases, and our labeling of phenomena. Consider our terminology. Should we call sexually restrained people "erotophobic" or "sexually conservative"? Should we label those who say nice things about themselves on personality tests as "high self-esteem" or "defensive"? Should we congratulate socially responsive people for their "social sensitivity" or disparage them for their tractable "conformity"? (Reflecting our culture's individualistic values, American psychology values the independent self rather than the interdependent self valued in many Asian and Third World cultures.) Without discarding scientific rigor, we can rightly expose psychology's implied values.

So, neither psychological science nor our reporting of it is dispassionate. Our preconceived ideas and values guide our theory development, our interpretations, our topics of choice and our language. In questing for truth we follow our hunches, our biases, our voices within. Perusing our results we are, at times, like the many voters who, while observing presidential debates, perceive their own predebate views confirmed. As C. S. Lewis noted, "What we learn from experience depends on the kind of philosophy we bring to experience" (1947, p. 11). Similarly, we teachers and authors cannot leave our values at home. In deciding *what* to report and *how* to report it, our own sympathies subtly steer us.

Being mindful of hidden values within psychological science should motivate us to clean the cloudy spectacles through which we view the world. Knowing that no one is immune to error and bias, we can be wary of absolutizing human interpretations of either natural or biblical data. We can steer between the two extremes of being naive about a value-laden psychology that pretends to be value-neutral, and being tempted to an unrestrained subjectivism that dismisses evidence as nothing but collected biases. In the ever-reforming spirit of humility, we can also put testable ideas to the test. If we think capital punishment does or does not deter crime more than other available punishments, we can utter our personal opinions. Or we can ask whether states with a death penalty have lower homicide rates, whether their rates have dropped after instituting the death penalty, and whether they have risen when abandoning the penalty. In checking our personal predictions against reality, we emulate the empiricism of Moses: "If a prophet speaks in the name of the LORD and what he says does not come true, then it is not the LORD's message" (Deut 18:22 TEV).

Psychological science and spiritual awe. So far I have suggested that people of faith, being sensitive to hidden values, can embrace psychological science as one way to explore the human creature. There is another reason why people of faith can welcome rather than fear the advance of psychological science. At the core of the religious impulse is a sense of awe and wonder—that bewildered sense that, as J. B. S. Haldane (1928/1971) said, "the universe is not only queerer than we suppose, but queerer than we can suppose." Such awe comes more genuinely from science than pseudoscience.

Consider how we perceive the world. What is truly extraordinary is not extrasensory perception, claims for which inevitably dissolve on investigation.[3] What is extraordinary is rather our very ordinary moment-to-moment sensory experiences of organizing formless neural impulses into colorful sights and meaningful sounds.

Think about it. As you look at someone, particles of light energy are being absorbed by your eyes' receptor cells, converted into neural signals that activate neighboring cells, which, down the line, transmit a million electrochemical messages per moment up to your brain. There, separate parts of your brain process information about color, form, motion and

---

[3]The repeated scientific debunking of claims of paranormal, supernatural human abilities (including telepathy, clairvoyance, precognition, past-life regression, and out-of-body, frequent-flyer programs) provides our first example of the congeniality of psychological science and biblical faith. The scientific refutation of New Age ideas about humans as extensions of God supports biblical presumptions about our human limits as finite creatures of God.

depth, and then—in some still-mysterious way—combine this information to form a consciously perceived image that is instantly compared with previously stored images and recognized as, say, your grandmother. The whole process is as complex as taking a house apart, splinter by splinter, transporting it to a different location, and then, through the efforts of millions of specialized workers, putting it back together. Voilà! The material brain gives rise to consciousness. That all of this happens instantly, effortlessly and continuously is better than cool; it is truly amazing and bewildering. In explaining such phenomena I empathize with Job: "I have uttered what I did not understand, things too wonderful for me" (Job 42:3).

RELATING CHRISTIAN FAITH AND PSYCHOLOGICAL RESEARCH

Faith connects to psychological science not only by motivating scientific inquiry and sensitizing us to implicit values, but as table 1 indicates, in other ways as well. We can, for example, make religion a dependent variable by studying the psychology of religion. (Why do some people, but not others, take the leap of faith?) We can make religion an independent variable by asking whether it predicts attitudes and behaviors. (Are people of faith noticeably more or less prejudiced? generous? happy?) And we can ask how insights into human nature that are gleaned from psychological research correspond to biblical and theological understandings. As when boring a tunnel from two directions, the excitement comes in discovering how close the two approaches are to connecting.

In times past, scholars connecting faith and psychology drew on the old personality theories, as when suggesting that Freud's ideas of aggressive, narcissistic motivations complemented Calvin's idea of original sin. A newer approach relates ancient religious understandings to big ideas from psychological research. In any academic field, the results of tens of thousands of studies, the conclusions of thousands of investigators, the insights of hundreds of theorists, can usually be boiled down to a few overriding ideas. Biology offers us principles such as natural selection and adaptation. Sociology builds on concepts such as social structure, cultural relativity and societal organization. Music exploits our ideas of rhythm, melody and harmony.

In my specialty of social psychology, what are the really big ideas? And how well do these big ideas about human nature connect with Judeo-

Table 1. Seven Ways to Relate Faith and Psychology (adapted from Myers, 1995)

Strategies for Relating Faith and Psychology	Personal Examples
1. *Faith motivates science.* Believing that "in everything we deal with God" (Calvin), and aiming to worship God with our minds, we can rigorously search God's world, seeking to discern its truths, while recognizing the limits of science.	1. Experiments on "group polarization" (exploring how group discussion changes and strengthens attitudes) 2. Reviewing studies of subjective well-being (who is happy?)
2. *Faith mandates skeptical scrutiny.* In the ever-reforming spirit of humility, we put testable claims to the test.	1. Scrutinizing claims of the efficacy of intercessory prayer and faith healing 2. Reporting tests of New Age claims of reincarnation, channeling, fortune-telling, aura readings, telepathy, clairvoyance, astrology (and their implications of human godlike powers)
3. *Expressing faith-rooted values.* Like everyone, we infuse certain assumptions and values into our teaching, writing, research and practice.	Writings for Christian and secular audiences
4. *Giving psychology to the church.* We can also apply psychology's insights to the church's life. For some, this means merging Christian and psychological insights pertinent to counseling and clinical practice.	Applying social influence and memory principles to the creation of memorable, persuasive sermons and effective evangelism
5. *Relating psychological and religious descriptions of human nature.* We can map human nature from two directions, asking how well psychological and biblical understandings correlate.	Relating psychological research (in biological, developmental, cognitive and social psychology) to Christian belief
6. *Studying determinants of religious experience.* The psychology of religion can explore influences on spirituality, religious commitment, charismatic behavior, etc. Who believes—and why?	Exploring parallels between (a) research on the interplay between attitudes and behavior, and (b) biblical-theological thinking about the interplay between faith and action
7. *Studying religion's effects.* Is faith a *predictor* of people's attitudes? emotions? behavior?	Summarizing links between faith and joy (religious commitment and self-reported life satisfaction and happiness)

Christian understandings? I discern four pairs of complementary truths. As Pascal reminded us three hundred years ago, no single truth is ever sufficient, because the world is not simple. Any truth separated from its complementary truth is a half-truth.

Rationality and irrationality. How "noble in reason" and "infinite in faculties" is the human intellect, rhapsodized Shakespeare's Hamlet. In some ways, indeed, our cognitive capacities are awesome. The three-pound tissue in our skulls contains circuitry more complex than all the telephone networks on the planet, enabling us to process information automatically or with great effort, to remember vast quantities of information, and to make snap judgments using intuitive rules called heuristics. As intuitive scientists, we explain our worlds efficiently and with enough accuracy for our daily needs.

Yes, Jewish and Christian theologians have long said, we are awesome. We are made in the divine image and given stewardship of the earth and its creatures. We are the summit of the Creator's work, God's own children.

Yet our explanations are vulnerable to error, insist social psychologists. In ways we are often unaware, our explanations and social judgments are vulnerable to error. When observing others, we are sometimes too prone to be biased by our preconceptions. We "see" illusory relationships and causes. We treat people in ways that trigger them to fulfill our expectations. We are swayed more by vivid anecdotes than by statistical reality. We attribute others' behavior to their dispositions (e.g., presuming that someone who acts strangely must *be* strange). Failing to recognize such errors in our thinking, we are prone to overconfidence.

Such conclusions have a familiar ring to theologians, who remind us that we are finite creatures of the one who declares "I am God, and there is none like me" and that "as the heavens are higher than the earth, / so are my ways higher than your ways / and my thoughts than your thoughts" (Is 46:9; 55:9 RSV). As God's children we have dignity but not deity. Thus we must be skeptical of those who claim for themselves godlike powers of omniscience (reading others' minds, foretelling the future), omnipresence (viewing happenings in remote locations) and omnipotence (creating or altering physical reality with mental power). We should be wary even of those who idolize their religion, presuming their doctrinal fine points to be absolute truth. Always, we see reality through a dim mirror.

Self-serving bias and self-esteem. Our self-understanding is a fragile container of truth. Heeding the ancient admonition to "know thyself," we analyze our behavior, but not impartially. A self-serving bias appears in our differing explanations for our successes and failures, for our good deeds and bad. On any socially desirable dimension, we commonly view ourselves as relatively superior—as more ethical, socially skilled and tolerant than our average peer. Moreover, we justify our past behaviors. We have an inflated confidence in the accuracy of our beliefs. We misremember our own pasts in self-enhancing ways. And we overestimate how virtuously we would behave in situations that draw less-than-virtuous behavior out of most people. Researcher Anthony Greenwald (1980, 1984) spoke for dozens of researchers: "People experience life through a self-centered filter."

That conclusion echoes a very old religious idea—that self-righteous pride is the fundamental sin, the original sin, the deadliest of the seven deadly sins. Thus the psalmist could declare that "no one can see his own errors" (Ps 19:12) and the Pharisee could thank God "that I am not like other men" (Lk 18:11) (and you and I can thank God that we are not like the Pharisee). Pride goes before a fall. It corrodes our relations with one another, leading to conflicts between partners in marriage, management and labor, and nations at war. Each side views its motives alone as pure, its actions beyond reproach. But so does its opposition, continuing the conflict.

Yet self-esteem pays dividends. Self-affirmation is often adaptive. It helps maintain our confidence and minimize depression. To doubt our efficacy and to blame ourselves for our failures is a recipe for failure, loneliness or dejection. People made to feel secure and valued exhibit less prejudice and contempt for others.

Again there is a religious parallel. To sense divine grace—the Christian parallel to psychology's "unconditional positive regard"—is to be liberated from both self-protective pride and self-condemnation. To feel profoundly affirmed, just as I am, lessens my need to define my self-worth in terms of achievements, prestige, or material and physical well-being. It is rather like insecure Pinocchio saying to his maker, Geppetto, "Papa, I am not sure who I am. But if I'm all right with you, then I guess I'm all right with me."

Attitudes and behavior. Studies during the 1960s shocked social psychologists with revelations that our attitudes sometimes lie dormant, overwhelmed by other influences. But follow-up research was reassuring. When relevant and brought to mind, our attitudes influence our behavior. Thus our political attitudes influence our behavior in the voting booth. Our smoking attitudes influence our susceptibility to peer pressures to smoke. Change the way people think and, whether we call such persuasion "education" or "propaganda," the impact may be considerable.

Social psychologists have repeatedly shown that the reverse is also true: We are as likely to act ourselves into a way of thinking as to think ourselves into action. We are as likely to believe in what we have stood up for as to stand up for what we believe. Especially when we feel responsible for how we have acted, our attitudes follow our behavior. This self-persuasion enables all sorts of people—political campaigners, lovers, even terrorists—to believe more strongly in that which they have witnessed or suffered.

This realization—that inner attitude and outer behavior, like chicken and egg, generate one another—parallels a Judeo-Christian idea: inner faith and outer action likewise feed one another. Thus, *faith is a source of action*. Elijah is overwhelmed by the holy as he huddles in a cave. Paul is converted on the Damascus road. Ezekiel, Isaiah and Jeremiah undergo inner transformations. In each case, a new spiritual consciousness produces a new pattern of behavior.

But *faith is also a consequence of action*. Throughout the Old and New Testaments, faith is nurtured by obedient action. The Hebrew word for *know* is usually an action verb, something one does. To know love, one must not only know about love, one must act lovingly. Philosophers and theologians note how faith grows as people act on what little faith they have. Rather than insist that people believe before they pray, Talmudic scholars would encourage rabbis to pray, trusting that belief would follow. "The proof of Christianity really consists in 'following,'" declared Søren Kierkegaard (1851/1944). To attain faith, said Pascal, "follow the way by which [the committed] began; by acting as if they believed, taking the holy water, having masses said, etc. Even this will naturally make you believe" (1670/1965). C. S. Lewis (1960) concurred:

> Believe in God and you will have to face hours when it seems obvious that this material world is the only reality; disbelieve in Him and you must face hours when this material world seems to shout at you that it is not all. No conviction, religious or irreligious, will, of itself, end once and for all [these

doubts] in the soul. Only the practice of Faith resulting in the habit of Faith will gradually do that. (1960)

Persons and situations. My final two-sided truth is that people and situations influence each other. We see this, first, in the evidence that social situations powerfully affect our behavior. As vividly shown in studies of conformity, role-playing, persuasion and group influence, we are the creatures of our social worlds.

The most dramatic findings come from experiments that put well-intentioned people in evil situations to see whether good or evil prevailed. To a dismaying extent, evil pressures overwhelmed good intentions, inducing people to conform to falsehoods or capitulate to cruelty. Faced with a powerful situation, nice people often do not behave so nicely. Depending on the social context, most of us are capable of acting kindly or brutally, independently or submissively, wisely or foolishly. In one irony-laden experiment, most seminary students en route to recording an extemporaneous talk on the Good Samaritan parable failed to stop and give aid to a slumped, groaning person—if they had been pressed to hurry beforehand (Darley & Batson, 1973). External social forces shape our social behavior.

The social psychological concept of powers greater than the individual parallels the religious idea of transcendent good and evil powers (the latter symbolized in the creation story as a seductive serpent). Evil involves not only individual rotten apples here and there. It is also a product of "principalities and powers"—corrosive forces that can ruin a barrel of apples. And because evil is collective as well as personal, responding to it takes a communal religious life.

Although powerful situations may override people's individual dispositions, social psychologists do not view humans as passive tumbleweeds, blown this way and that by the social winds. Facing the same situation, different people may react differently, depending on their personality and culture. Feeling coerced by blatant pressure, they will sometimes react in ways that restore their sense of freedom. In a numerical minority, they will sometimes oppose and sway the majority. When they believe in themselves (maintaining an "internal locus of control"), they sometimes work wonders. Moreover, people choose their situations—their college environments, their jobs, their locales. And their social expectations are sometimes self-fulfilling, as when they expect someone to be warm or hostile and the person becomes so. In such ways, we are the creators of our social worlds.

To most religious traditions, that rings true. We are morally responsible, accountable for how we use whatever freedom we have. What we decide matters. The stream of causation from past to future runs through our choices.

Faced with these pairs of complementary ideas, framed either psychologically or theologically, we are like someone stranded in a deep well with two ropes dangling down. If we grab either one alone we sink deeper into the well. Only when we hold both ropes can we climb out, because at the top, beyond where we can see, they come together around a pulley. Grabbing only the rope of rationality or irrationality, of self-serving pride or self-esteem, of attitudes-affect-behavior or behavior-affects-attitudes, of personal or situational causation, plunges us to the bottom of the well. So we grab both ropes, perhaps without fully grasping how they come together. In doing so, we may be comforted that in both science and religion, accepting complementary principles is sometimes more honest than an oversimplified theory that ignores half the evidence. For the scissors of truth, we need both blades.

PSYCHOLOGICAL SCIENCE SUPPORTS FAMILY VALUES

Christians are predisposed not only to certain understandings of human nature but also to values such as love, joy, peace and other "fruits of the Spirit." As followers of the one who bade children to come to him, Christians also care about the well-being of children and the social ecology that nurtures them (intact families, responsible media, healthy faith communities). Social-science research findings generally affirm those values. To see how, consider some facts of contemporary life.

In many ways, these are the best of times. Thanks partly to the doubling of married women's employment, the average real income in the United States (even after the recent decline) is nearly triple that in 1960. As you would therefore expect, our money buys more things. We have espresso coffee, iPods, laptops and smart phones. We eat out two-and-a-half times as often, enjoy a longer life expectancy, and support equal opportunities for women and ethnic minorities.

Had you fallen asleep in 1960 and awakened in the twenty-first century, would you—overwhelmed by all these good tidings—also feel pleased at the cultural shift? Here are some other facts that would greet you (Myers, 2000b). Since 1960 in the United States:

- Child abuse and neglect reports have increased.

- Cohabitation, which predicts increased risk of divorce, has increased more than tenfold.

- The 5 percent of babies born to unmarried parents has increased to nearly 40 percent.

- The number of children who do not live with two parents has grown to three in ten.

- Child, adolescent and adult obesity rates have soared.

Concerned Christian family advocates believe that the ideal ecology for rearing children is two adults committed to each other and to their children. Are they right? Does family structure indeed affect children's well-being? Or is it simply a proxy for another factor such as poverty, race or parental education?

Sociologists and psychologists have generated a mountain of data hoping to answer that question. One strategy has been to compare children of different family structures while statistically extracting the influence of other entangled factors. Such data come from Nicholas Zill's summary of a 1981 child health survey of 15,416 randomly sampled children, conducted by the National Center for Health Statistics, and from a 1988 repeat survey of 17,110 more children. Zill and his colleagues (Dawson, 1991; Peterson & Zill, 1986; Zill, 1988; Zill et al., 1993) recognized that intact and broken families differ in many ways: race, children's ages, parental education, family size and income (poverty, we know, can be socially corrosive). To see if those were the only factors at work, he statistically adjusted scores to extract such influences. Even so, children of intact families were less likely to display antisocial and "acting out" behavior. Those living with both parents were half as likely as those living without fathers to have been suspended or expelled from school or to have had misbehavior reported by the school. In the 1988 national survey, children in intact families were half as vulnerable to school problems and were a third less likely to repeat a grade, regardless of their age or race.

The other strategy has been to follow children's lives through time, noting their well-being before and after parental divorce. A monumental but rarely discussed study by Andrew Cherlin and others (1991, 1995, 1998; Chase-Lansdale et al., 1995) began when researchers interviewed 17,414 women—the mothers of 98 percent of all British children born during the first full week of March 1958. British parents and teachers rated the behavior of nearly 12,000 of these children as seven-year-olds and again four years later, knowing that by then some would have experienced their parents' divorce. At the second rating, boys whose parents had divorced during the four years had about 25 percent more behavior problems than those whose families remained intact.

But were these children's postdivorce problems influenced by the marriage breaking up, or were they the result of the marital problems that preceded the divorce? "Staying in an unhappy marriage is psychologically damaging," asserted Pepper Schwartz (1995), "and staying only for the children's sake is ultimately not in your interest or anyone else's." So rather than stay together for the sake of the children, should unhappy couples divorce for the sake of the children?

When the children had reached age twenty-three, the intrepid researchers traced and interviewed 12,537 of the original sample, enabling them to compare those who, at age seven, were living with two biological parents with those living with one biological parent, and to compare those whose parents had divorced with those whose parents had not divorced by age sixteen. Controlling for predivorce family problems did not weaken the divorce effect. Moreover, among children of divorce, 45 percent had cohabited—a rate more than double the approximately 19 percent among children of intact marriages. "Parental divorce seems to have stimulated a pattern of behavior characterized by early homeleaving due to conflict with parents and stepparents and early sexual activity outside marriage—leading, in this cohort, to a greater likelihood of premarital birth and cohabitation," said the researchers. Yet another follow-up, with 11,759 of the participants at age thirty-three, confirmed the emotional aftermath of the chain of events that often began with parental divorce. The bottom line from this important study is that by launching children into "negative life trajectories through adolescence into adulthood," divorce predicts increased social problems.

For victims of abuse, infidelity, alcoholism or financial irresponsibility, divorce is sometimes the lesser of two evils. (We are all earthen vessels.

We all at some time find ourselves broken, if not in our love life, then in our parenting, our friendships or our vocations.) Moreover, most children of nonmarried or divorced parents thrive. Nevertheless, the results of these national studies are confirmed by dozens of others that reveal the toxicity of family disruption for many children. Why this is so is a complicated story, apparently having less to do with parenting differences than with the poverty, broken attachments, dislocations and altered peer relationships associated with family fracturing and parental absence. If normal variations in well-meaning parenting matter less than most people suppose, family collapse and its associated social ecology matters more than many suppose. (So too do the post-1960 increases in materialism, individualism, and media modeling of impulsive sexuality and violence. But those stories are for another bedtime.)

FAITH AND WELL-BEING

These findings are the tip of an iceberg of data that support the social and family values linked with religious faith. So does an active faith, therefore, enhance social and psychological well-being? Or is religion, as Freud (1928/1964) surmised, corrosive to happiness by creating an "obsessional neurosis" that entails guilt, repressed sexuality and suppressed emotions (p. 71)? Another one of the new atheists, Christopher Hitchens (2007), argues that religion is "violent, irrational, intolerant, allied to racism and tribalism and bigotry, invested in ignorance and hostile to free inquiry, contemptuous of women and coercive toward children" (p. 56). Accumulating evidence reveals that some forms of religious experience do correlate with prejudice and guilt.

However, as I document in *A Friendly Letter to Skeptics and Atheists: Musings on Why God Is Good and Faith Isn't Evil* (2008), the data also reveal that, in general, an active faith correlates with social and personal health and well-being. First, actively religious North Americans are much less likely than irreligious people to become delinquent, to abuse drugs and alcohol, to divorce, and to commit suicide (Batson, Schoenrade & Ventis, 1993; Colasanto & Shriver, 1989). Thanks in part to their lesser rates of smoking and drinking, religiously active people even tend to be physically healthier and to live longer (Koenig, 1997; Matthews & Larson, 1997).

Second, other studies have probed the correlation between faith and coping with crises (Myers, 1992). Compared to religiously inactive widows, recently widowed women who worship regularly report more joy in their lives. Among mothers of developmentally challenged children, those with a deep religious faith are less vulnerable to depression. People of faith also tend to retain or recover greater happiness after suffering divorce, unemployment, serious illness or a disability. In later life, according to one meta-analysis, the two best predictors of life satisfaction have been health and religiousness.

Third, in surveys in various nations, religiously active people also report somewhat higher levels of happiness (Inglehart, 1990). Consider a Gallup (1984) U.S. survey. Those responding with highest scores on a spiritual commitment scale (by agreeing, for example, that "my religious faith is the most important influence in my life") were twice as likely as those lowest in spiritual commitment to declare themselves very happy. National Opinion Research Center surveys reveal higher levels of "very happy" people

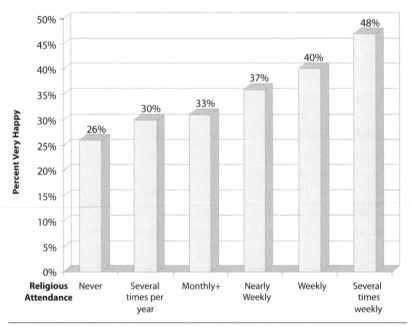

Figure 2. Religious attendance and happiness (data from 42,845 participants in the General Social Surveys, National Opinion Research Center, 1972 to 2008)

among those who feel "close to God." Self-rated spirituality and happiness may both be socially desirable responses, however. Would the happiness correlation extend to a behavioral measure of religiosity? As figure 2 indicates, it does. The evidence similarly indicates that strong religiosity predicts heightened generosity with time and money (Myers, 2008).

What explains these links between faith and personal and social well-being? Is it the close, supportive relationships—the "fellowship of kindred spirits," the "bearing of one another's burdens," "the ties of love that bind"—provided by faith communities? Is it the sense of meaning and purpose that many people derive from their faith? Is it a worldview that offers answers to life's deepest questions and an optimistic appraisal of life's events? Is it the hope that faith affords when facing "the terror resulting from our awareness of vulnerability and death" (Solomon, Greenberg & Pyszczynski, 1991)? Such are among the proposed explanations.

WHEN PSYCHOLOGICAL SCIENCE CHALLENGES FAITH

We have seen how psychological research affirms faith-rooted assumptions about human nature, faith-rooted values and faith-related well-being. Although psychological science is largely congenial to faith, it does sometimes motivate us to rethink certain cherished ideas and to revisit Scripture. As ecological findings drove biblical scholars to reread the biblical mandates concerning our environmental stewardship, so recent psychological findings have stimulated new questions among people of faith. One example below comes from research on illusory thinking, another from new information about sexual orientation. Such findings have prompted some of us to rethink our presumptions about both prayer and sexual orientation—and to look more closely at what the Bible does and does not say. Mindful that we are fallible creatures, the scientific challenge to some of our assumptions should neither startle nor threaten us. As we worship God with our minds and with humility of spirit, we should expect our "ever-reforming" faith to change and grow.

Example 1: Testing prayer. We pray, asking in faith. Sick, we pray for healing. Fearful, we pray for safety. Hopeful, we pray for success. Suffering drought, we pray for rain. Sharing our prayer experiences, we may recall times when God has answered our petitions and our intercessions for others.

And then along comes psychological experiments showing that we humans often perceive relationships where none exist (especially where we expect to see them), perceive causal connections among events that are only coincidentally correlated, and believe that we are controlling events that are actually beyond our control.

These experiments have been extended to studies of gambling behavior, stock-market predictions, clinical assessments of personality, superstitious behavior and intuitions about ESP. The unchallenged verdict: we easily misperceive our behavior as correlated with subsequent events, and thus we easily delude ourselves into thinking that we can predict or control uncontrollable events. Thus gamblers often act as if they can control mere chance events. They may feel more confident when allowed to spin the wheel or throw the die (throwing softly when hoping for a low number and hard for a high number). The gambling industry thrives on such illusory thinking.

Reading this research has provoked some of us to wonder whether illusory thinking similarly contaminates people's beliefs regarding the power of their petitionary prayers. If indeed we are predisposed to find order in random events, to interpret outcomes guided by our preconceptions, to search for and recall instances that confirm our beliefs, and to be more persuaded by vivid anecdotes than by statistical reality, then might we not misunderstand the efficacy of petitionary prayer? Is prayer not a made-to-order arena for the operation of illusory thinking principles?

If that sounds heretical, it may be reassuring to remember that warnings about false prayer come from believers as well as from skeptics. There was no stronger skeptic of false piety than Jesus. If it is heretical to think too little of the power of our prayers, is it not more heretical to think of God as a sort of celestial Santa Claus who grants our wishes if we are good?

Well then, say some researchers from both the skeptic and believer camps, why not settle the issue empirically? Why not put prayer to the test? Recognizing the mixed results and design problems in earlier prayer experiments, a massive Harvard Medical School-related prayer experiment was undertaken. One large group of coronary-bypass patients was prayed for, one not. These patients participated voluntarily, but without knowing whether they were being prayed for or not. To assess a possible placebo effect, a third group was being prayed for and knew it. From a scientific perspective, the study seemed flawless. It exploited the clinical trial methodology used in evaluating the healing powers of a new drug.

What result would you predict from this effort to put prayer to the test? Knowing of this experiment from its beginning, I published (in some articles at <davidmyers.org>) my prediction of *no* prayer effect. As I report in my introductory psychology texts, we now have impressive evidence of links between faith and health (more good news from psychology for people of faith). Nevertheless, as a person of faith, I had three reasons for predicting that intercessory prayer would not exhibit significant healing powers for the experiment's cardiac-care patients.

First, *the prayer concept being tested was more akin to magic than to a biblical understanding of prayer to an omniscient and sovereign God.* In the biblical view, God underlies the whole creation. God is not some little spiritual factor that occasionally deflects nature's course, but God is the ground of all being. God works, not in the gaps of what we do not yet understand, but in and through nature, including the healing ministries that led people of faith to spread medicine and hospitals worldwide. Thus, while our Lord's model prayer welcomes our acknowledging our dependence on God for our basic necessities ("our daily bread"), it does not view God as a celestial vending machine, whose levers we pull with our prayers. Indeed, would the all-wise, all-knowing, all-loving God of the Bible be uninformed or uncaring apart from our prayers? Doesn't presuming that we creatures can pull God's strings violate biblical admonitions to humbly recognize our place as finite creatures of the infinite God? No wonder we are counseled to offer prayers of adoration, praise, confession, thanksgiving, dedication and meditation, as well as to ask for what will (spiritually if not materially) be given. Prayer, J. I. Packer (1961) has written, "is not an attempt to force God's hand, but a humble acknowledgment of helplessness and dependence" (p. 11).

Second, even for those who believe that God intervenes in response to our prayers, there were practical reasons for expecting null effects:

The noise factor. Given that 92 percent of Americans express belief in God (Banks, 2008), all patients undergoing cardiac bypass surgery will already be receiving prayer—by spouses, children, siblings, friends, colleagues, and congregants or fellow believers, if not by themselves. Do these fervent prayers constitute a mere "noise factor" above which the signal of additional prayers may rouse God? Does God follow a dose-response curve (i.e., more prayers yield more response)? Does God count votes? Are the pleading, earnest prayers of patients and those who love them not sufficiently persuasive (as if God needs to be informed or persuaded of our needs)? Are the distant prayers of strangers participating in an experiment also needed?

The doubt factor. To be sure, some Christians believe that prayers, uttered in believing faith, are potent. But how many people of faith also believe that prayers called forth by a doubting (open-minded, testing) scientist will be similarly effective?

God is not mocked. During the British prayer-test controversy of 1872 (over a hypothetical proposal for a similar experiment), Christians recalled that in response to one of his temptations, Jesus declared that we ought not put God to the test. Reflecting on a proposal to test prayers for randomly selected preterm babies, Keith Stewart Thompson (1996) questioned "whether all such experiments come close to blasphemy. If the health outcomes of the prayed-for subjects turn out to be significantly better than for the others, the experimenter will have set up a situation in which God has, as it were, been made to show his (or her) hand." C. S. Lewis (1947) observed, regarding any effort to prove prayer, that the "impossibility of empirical proof is a spiritual necessity" lest a person begin to "feel like a magician" (p. 215). Indeed, if this experiment were to show that numbers of pray-ers matter—that distant strangers' prayers boost recovery chances—might rich people not want, in hopes of gaining God's attention, to pay indulgences to others who will pray for them?

Third, *the evidence of history suggests that the prayers of finite humans do not manipulate an infinite God.* If they could and did, how many droughts, floods, hurricanes and plagues would have been averted? How many stillborn infants or children with disabilities would have been born healthy? And consider the Bible's own evidence: How should the unanswered prayers of Job, Paul and even Jesus (in petitioning that the cup might pass) inform our theology of prayer? If the rain falls on my picnic, does it mean I pray with too little faith or that the rain falls both on those who believe and those who do not? Should we pray to God as manipulative adolescents—or as dependent preschoolers, whose loving parents, already knowing their children's needs, welcome the intimacy?

As we awaited the much-anticipated results of this mother-of-all prayer experiments, data from other prayer experiments surfaced. As I report in *A Friendly Letter to Skeptics and Atheists,*

- A 1997 experiment on "Intercessory Prayer in the Treatment of Alcohol Abuse and Dependence" found no measurable effect of intercessory prayer.

- A 1998 experiment with arthritis patients found no significant effect from distant prayer.

- A 1999 study of 990 coronary-care patients—who were unaware of the study—reported about 10 percent fewer complications for the half who received prayers "for a speedy recovery with no complications." But there was no difference in specific major complications such as cardiac arrest, hypertension and pneumonia. The median hospital stay was the same 4.0 days for both groups.

- A 2001 Mayo Clinic study of 799 coronary-care patients offered a simple result: "As delivered in this study, intercessory prayer had no significant effect on medical outcomes."

- A 2005 Duke University study of 848 coronary patients found no significant difference in clinical outcomes between those prayed for and those not.

Climaxing this string of negative results came the final blow: intercessory prayer in the Harvard prayer experiment had no positive effect on recovery from bypass surgery (Benson et al., 2006).

Henri Nouwen once suggested that clearing the decks of some of the false gods of popular religion may prepare our hearts for the God of the Bible. The Bible does not promise that we will escape misfortune, sickness and death. Rather, it offers a perspective from which to view misfortune, a promise that God is with us in our suffering, and a hope that suffering and even death will ultimately be redeemed. In the Christian understanding, God is not a genie whom we call forth with our prayers but the creator and sustainer of all that is. When the Pharisees asked Jesus for a way to validate the kingdom of God, he answered, "The kingdom of God is not coming with things that can be observed; . . . for, in fact, the kingdom of God is among you" (Lk 17:20-21).

The Lord's Prayer, the model prayer for Christians that I pray daily, affirms God's nature and our human dependence even for daily bread. We can approach God as a child might approach a benevolent parent who knows the child's needs but also cherishes the relationship. Through prayer, people of faith voice their praise and gratitude, confess their wrongs, utter their hearts' concerns and desires, open themselves to the Spirit, and seek the grace to live as God's people.

Example 2: The question of sexual orientation. I see myself as a family-values guy. In my psychology textbooks, I document the corrosive effects of pornography, teen sexual activity and family decline. I have been on the advisory board of the marriage-promoting National Marriage Project, whose cohabitation report concludes that trial marriages undermine marriage. And I have authored *The American Paradox: Spiritual Hunger in an Age of Plenty* (2000b) to document the post-1960s social recession and its roots in radical individualism, the sexual revolution, and the decline of marriage and the two-parent family.

Hearing me speak on such things, a friend remarked, "You've become more conservative." No, I said, I've always been pretty conservative on these family concerns, because the data are so persuasive.

New data have, however, dragged me, along with other Christian thinkers such as William Stacy Johnson (2006) and Jack Rogers (2006), to revise my understanding of sexual orientation. Here are some of the observations that challenged my former assumptions (for documentation, see Myers & Scanzoni, 2006):

There is no known parental or psychological influence on sexual orientation. Factors once believed crucial actually seem not to matter. Sexual orientation appears not to be influenced by child abuse, social example, overprotective mothering, distant fathering or having gay parents. We may yet discover some parental or psychological influence. But, for now, if some new parents were to seek my advice on how to influence the sexual orientation of their newborn, I could only say, after a half century of research, that we are clueless. We simply do not know what, if anything, parents can do to influence sexual orientation.

Unlike sexual behavior and other moral behaviors, sexual orientation appears unaffected by an active faith. Earlier I noted that, compared with people who attend church rarely, those who attend regularly are less likely to be juvenile delinquents, abuse drugs and alcohol, and divorce. In a recent National Opinion Research Center survey, they were also one-third as likely to have cohabited before marriage, and they reported having had many fewer sexual partners. Yet, for the males, they were no less likely to have had a homosexual relationship (Smith, 1996). This unpublicized finding is worth pondering. If male sexual orientation is a spiritually influenced lifestyle choice, then should same-sex relationships not—like those other disapproved tendencies—be less common among people of faith?

Today's greater tolerance seems not to have amplified homosexuality. Homosexuals are a small minority, roughly two or three percent of the population, and their numbers appear not to have grown with the emergence of a gay rights movement or with the passage of gay rights laws. Contrary to the concern that gay role models would entice more people into homosexuality, surveys suggest no increase in the homosexual minority. In 1988, when the National Opinion Research Center first asked American males about their sexual partners (with procedures that assured anonymity), 97 percent of those sexually active reported having exclusively female partners during the previous year. In 2004, the result was still 97 percent.

Biological factors are looking more and more important. This scientific story is still being written and the light is still dim, so we had all best be tentative. Nevertheless, we have learned, first, that biological siblings of gay people, especially their identical twins, are somewhat more likely than people without close gay relatives to themselves be gay. Evidence points to both prenatal influences and to brain differences in a region known to influence sexual behavior. (A similar brain difference has been observed in male sheep that display same-sex attraction.) These and other biological factors help explain a dozen you-never-would-have-guessed discoveries of gay-straight differences in traits ranging from fingerprint patterns to skill at mentally rotating geometric figures. The emerging conclusion: sexual orientation (most clearly so for males) is a natural disposition, not a voluntary moral choice. (I document these and other findings in my text *Psychology*, 9th edition. For a book-length exploration of the biology of sexual orientation, see Wilson & Rahman, 2005.)

Efforts to change a person's sexual orientation usually (some say, virtually always) fail. People who have experimented with homosexual behavior (as many heterosexual people do) can turn away from it. Homosexuals, like heterosexuals, can become celibate. Or they can marry against their desires (with risk of future divorce) and have children. But research on efforts to help people do a 180-degree reversal of their sexual orientation—their feelings and fantasies—reveals that, though many have tried, hoping upon hope to escape their culture's contempt, few have succeeded. "Can therapy change sexual orientation?" asks an American Psychological Association statement (www.apa.org). "No. [It] is not changeable." There are anecdotes of ex-gays, but these are offset by anecdotes of ex-ex-gays—often the same people, a few years later.

The Bible has little, if anything, to say about an enduring sexual orientation (a modern concept) or about loving, long-term, same-sex partnerships. Out of 31,103 verses in the Protestant Bible, only seven frequently quoted verses (none of which are the words of Jesus) speak directly of same-sex behavior—and mostly in the context of idolatry, temple prostitution, adultery, child exploitation or violence. Some biblical scholars and theologians, such as Robert Gagnon (2002) in *The Bible and Homosexual Practice: Texts and Hermeneutics,* have assembled a biblical case against same-sex sexual relationships. Others, such as William Stacy Johnson (2006), in *A Time to Embrace: Same-Gender Relationships in Religion, Law, and Politics*, offer a biblical case that supports same-sex partnerships. Their differences, and those among the authors in this volume, involve not biblical commitment but interpretation.[4]

To suggest that sexual orientation may be disposed rather than chosen leaves moral issues open. Shall we regard homosexuality as, like left-handedness, a natural part of human diversity, or as a lamentable aberration such as dyslexia? Moreover, whether straight or gay, everyone faces moral choices over options that include abstinence, promiscuity and permanent commitment. It therefore behooves us all to discern biblical mandates and priorities, critically evaluate and learn from the natural revelations of science, regard one another with love and grace, and learn from one another through open, honest dialogue.

---

[4]Robert Gagnon's detailed critique of my book, *The Christian Case for Gay Marriage* (with Letha Dawson Scanzoni), is available at <www.westernsem.edu/media/pub_article/rreview/autumn05>, along with my reply.

WHAT PSYCHOLOGICAL SCIENCE
AND FAITH SHARE IN COMMON

To conclude, psychological science and the spirit of faith share similar ideals: humility before nature and skepticism of human presumptions. Psychological science enlivens ancient biblical wisdom about human nature. Psychological science documents the corrosion of family values and the toxic effects of that corrosion for children and civic life. Psychological science has shown the correlates between an active faith and human health and happiness. And psychological science challenges us to revisit certain assumptions, mindful that all truth is God's truth, and therefore, truth is to be welcomed rather than feared. This is not to say that psychological science, value-laden and limited as it is, should ever be the final word. Rather, by often affirming and sometimes challenging our prejudgments, it helps keep alive that "ever-reforming" Reformation spirit.

In that spirit, we in this book lay our tentative and still-forming thoughts before one another, welcoming one another's reflections and critique. My surest conviction is that some of my ideas err. And that is why I welcome the correction and admonition of my esteemed colleagues.

REFERENCES

Banks, A. (2008). Think you know what Americans believe about religion? You might want to think again. The Pew Forum on Religion and Public Life <http://pewforum.org/news/display.php?NewsID=15907>.

Batson, C. D., Schoenrade, P. A., & Ventis, W. L. (1993). *Religion and the individual: A social-psychological perspective.* New York: Oxford University Press.

Benson, H., Dusek, J. A., Sherwood, J. B., Lam, P., Bethea, C. F., Carpenter, W., Levitsky, S., Hill, P. C., Clem, D. W., Jain, M. K., Drumel, D., Kopecky, S. L., Mueller, P. S., Marek, D., Rollins, S., & Hibberd, P. L. (2006). Study of the therapeutic effects of intercessory prayer (STEP) in cardiac bypass patients: A multicenter randomized trial of uncertainty and certainty of receiving intercessory prayer. *American Heart Journal, 151,* 934-42.

Chase-Lansdale, P., Cherlin, A. J., & Kiernan, K. E. (1995). The long-term effects of parental divorce on the mental health of young adults: A developmental perspective. *Child Development, 66,* 1614-34.

Cherlin, A. J., Chase-Lansdale, P. L., & McRae, C. (1998). Effects of parental divorce on mental health. *American Sociological Review, 63,* 239-49.

Cherlin, A. J., Furstenberg, F. F., Jr., Chase-Lansdale, L., Kiernan, K. E., Robins, P. K., Morrison, D. R., & Teitler, J. O. (1991). Longitudinal studies of effects of divorce on children in Great Britain and the United States. *Science, 252,* 1386-89.

Cherlin, A. J., Kiernan, K. E., & Chase-Lansdale, P. L. (1995). Parental divorce in childhood and demographic outcomes in young adulthood. *Demography, 32,* 299-316.

Colasanto, D., & Shriver, J. (1989, May). Mirror of America: Middle-aged face marital crisis. *Gallup Report, 284,* 34-38.

Darley, J. M., & Batson, C. D. (1973). From Jerusalem to Jericho: A study of situational and dispositional variables in helping behavior. *Journal of Personality and Social Psychology, 27,* 100-108.

Dawkins, R. (1995). *River out of Eden: A Darwinian view of life.* London: Phoenix.

———. (1997, January/February). Is science a religion? *The Humanist,* p. 26 <www.thehumanist.org/humanist/articles/dawkins.html>.

———. (2003). From *A devil's chaplain: Reflections on hope, lies, science, and love.* Boston: Houghton Mifflin. Quoted by H. Allen Orr in *New York Review of Books,* February 26, 2004.

Dawson, D. A. (1991). Family structure and children's health: United States, 1988. *Vital and Health Statistics, Series 10: Data from the National Health Survey, No. 178.* Hyattsville, MD: National Center for Statistics, U.S. Department of Health and Human Services, DHHS Publication No. PHS 91-1506.

Freud, S. (1964). *The future of an illusion.* Garden City, NY: Doubleday. (Original work published 1928)

Gagnon, R. A. J. (2002). *The Bible and homosexual practice: Texts and hermaneutics.* Nashville: Abingdon.

Gallup, G., Jr. (1984, March). Commentary on the state of religion in the U.S. today. *Religion in America: The Gallup Report, 222.*

Greeley, A. M. (1976). Pop psychology and the gospel. *Theology Today, 23,* 8.

Greenwald, A. G. (1980). The totalitarian ego: Fabrication and revision of personal history. *American Psychologist, 35,* 603-18.

———. (1984, June 12). Quoted by D. Goleman, A bias puts self at center of everything. *New York Times,* pp. C1, C4.

Haldane, J. B. S. (1971). *Possible worlds and other papers.* Freeport, NY: Libraries Press. (Original work published 1928)

Harris, S. (2006). *Letter to a Christian nation.* New York: Alfred A. Knopf.

Hitchens, C. (2007). *God is not great: How religion poisons everything.* New York: Twelve.

Hooykaas, R. (1972). *Religion and the rise of modern science.* Grand Rapids, MI: Eerdmans.

Inglehart, R. (1990). *Culture shift in advanced industrial society.* Princeton, NJ: Princeton University Press.

Johnson, W. S. (2006). *A time to embrace: Same-gender relationships in religion, law, and politics.* Grand Rapids, MI: Eerdmans.

Kierkegaard, S. (1944). *For self-examination and judge for yourself* (W. Lowrie, Trans.). Princeton, NJ: Princeton University Press. (Original work published 1851)

Koenig, H. G. (1997). *Is religion good for your health? The effects of religion on physical and mental health.* Binghamton, NY: Haworth.

Lewis, C. S. (1947). *Miracles.* New York: Macmillan.

———. (1960). *Mere Christianity.* New York: Macmillan.

MacKay, D. M. (1984, December). Letters. *Journal of the American Scientific Affiliation, 237.*

Matthews, D. A., & Larson, D. B. (1997). *The faith factor: An annotated bibliography of clinical research on spiritual subjects* (4 Vols.). Rockville, MD: National Institute for Healthcare Research and Georgetown University Press.

Merton, R. K. (1970). *Science, technology and society in seventeenth-century England.* New York: Fertig. (Original work published 1938)

Myers, D. G. (1991). Steering between the extremes: On being a Christian scholar within psychology. *Christian Scholar's Review, 20,* 376-83.

———. (1992). *The pursuit of happiness.* New York: William Morrow.

———. (1994). *Exploring social psychology.* New York: McGraw-Hill.

———. (1995). Teaching, texts and values. *Journal of Psychology and Theology, 23,* 244-47.

———. (1996). On professing psychological science and Christian faith. *Journal of Psychology and Christianity, 15,* 143-49.

———. (2000a). The funds, friends and faith of happy people. *American Psychologist, 55,* 56-67.

———. (2000b). *The American Paradox: Spiritual hunger in an age of plenty.* New Haven, CT: Yale University Press.

———. (2008). *A friendly letter to skeptics and atheists: Musings on why God is good and faith isn't evil.* San Francisco: Jossey-Bass.

———. (2010). *Psychology* (9th ed.). New York: Worth.

Myers, D. G., & Jeeves, M. A. (2002). *Psychology through the eyes of faith* (Rev. ed.). San Francisco: HarperOne.

Myers, D. G., & Scanzoni, L. D. (2006). *What God has joined together: The Christian case for gay marriage.* San Francisco: HarperOne.

Packer, J. I. (1961). *Evangelism and the sovereignty of God.* Downers Grove, IL: InterVarsity Press.

Pascal, B. (1965). *Thoughts.* (W. F. Trotter, Trans.) In M. Mack (Ed.), *World masterpieces.* New York: W. W. Norton. (Original work published in 1670)

Peterson, J. L., & Zill, N. (1986). Marital disruption, parent-child relationships, and behavior problems in children. *Journal of Marriage and the Family, 48,* 295-307.

Polkinghorne, J. (1986). *One world: The interaction of science and theology.* London: SPCK.

Rogers, J. (2009). *Jesus, the Bible, and homosexuality: Revised and expanded edition.* Louisville, KY: Westminster John Knox Press.

Schwartz, P. (1995, April 4). When staying is worth the pain. *New York Times,* p. C1.

Smith, T. W. (1996). American sexual behavior: Trends, socio-demographic differences and risk behavior. National Opinion Research Center GSS Topical Report No. 25.

Solomon, S., Greenberg, J., & Pyszczynski, T. (1991). A terror management theory of social behavior: The psychological functions of self-esteem and cultural worldviews. *Advances in Experimental Social Psychology, 24,* 93-159.

Thompson, K. S. (1996, November-December). The revival of experiments on prayer. *American Scientist,* 532-34.

Tolstoy, L. (1904). *My confessions.* Boston: Dana Estes.

Wilson, G. D., & Rahman, Q. (2005). *Born Gay: The Biology of Sex Orientation.* London: Peter Owen Publishers.

Zill, N. (1988). Behavior, achievement and health problems among children in stepfamilies: Findings from a national survey of child health. In E. M. Hetherington & J. D.

Arasteh (Eds.), *Impact of divorce, single parenting and stepparenting on children*. Hillsdale, NJ: Erlbaum.

Zill, N., Morrison, D. R., & Coiro, M. J. (1993). Long-term effects of parental divorce on parent-child relationships, adjustment and achievement in young adulthood. *Journal of Family Psychology, 7*, 91-103.

An Integration Response to Levels of Explanation

Stanton L. Jones

IN THIS ESSAY, I WILL USE THE FOLLOWING to define how we integrate Christianity and psychology: It is our Christian responsibility to live out of the lordship of Christ over all of existence by giving his special revelation (God's true Word) its appropriate place of authority in determining our fundamental beliefs about and practices toward all of reality—which includes our activities as research scientists and applied psychologists. The cognitive content—the truth assertions—of our faith, particularly the teachings of Scripture, should structure our beliefs and assumptions as we approach the empirical reality we study in psychological science, and it should also shape our practice as psychologists.

Sometimes this integration will lead us to conduct and consume "secular" psychological research with appreciation and largely without revision. At other times, it will lead us to explore alternative methodologies more appropriate to our subject matter given what we believe as Christians about that subject matter (i.e., humanity). It may lead us to explore whether there are alternate ways to understand our subject matter that may lead to alternative research questions. Faith may, in other words, lead us as Christians to be sometimes appreciative recipients of good psychological research (like David Myers), but at other times, faith may lead us to think differently about humanity, to pursue other methods, to challenge the status quo of secular thought.

The great strength of Myers's approach is his enthusiasm for good science. In my chapter on integration, I argue that Christians should delight in and celebrate good science. Why? Because while God has revealed in Scripture the great truths central to life, he has not chosen to reveal *everything* that it is good and useful to know in Scripture alone, but he has instead made us rational beings in his image, capable of pursuing and discovering truth as we engage the world (including ourselves). And because all human beings are created in the image of God, and because of God's "common grace" that allows all humans to see some facets of his truth through the world around us, all people, regardless of faith, can know some aspects of truth. To echo Myers, God has made a real world and given us the capacity to discover truth about it. Our capacity to do science is one of God's good gifts to us. But what does it mean to do good science?

Myers makes a key concession in his chapter that suggests the validity of the integration approach in relating psychology and Christianity. Myers acknowledges the inescapable role assumptions play in shaping empirical research, stating emphatically that *"belief guides perception"* (p. 54, emphasis in original). He goes on to say that "our preconceived ideas and values guide our theory development, our interpretations, our topics of choice and our language" (p. 54), and in table 1, under "expressing faith-rooted values," he writes, "Like everyone, we infuse certain assumptions and values into our teaching writing, research and practice" (p. 57).

It is (a) the recognition that, because "belief guides perception," "we infuse certain assumptions and values into our teaching, writing, research and practice" and (b) one's intentional commitment to having distinctively *Christian* beliefs guide, infuse and shape our work as psychologists that together define the integration approach. While Myers acknowledges and endorses these commitments, he never develops these tantalizing concessions. The only example he offers of what he means by allowing beliefs to guide our work is when he notes in table 1 that he "writ[es] for Christian and secular audiences."

Myers not only fails to develop this key admission but he actually seems to contradict it. After stating that "belief guides perception," he makes the critical move that characterizes the levels approach, saying "Being mindful of hidden values within psychological science should motivate us to clean the cloudy spectacles through which we view the world" (p. 54). In other words, instead of building on the recognition that it is not a matter of *whether* beliefs will shape our work but rather a question of *which* beliefs will shape our work, Myers retreats by treating assumptions as nuisances to be wiped away by improved scientific inquiry. He argues that "we can steer between the two extremes of being naive about a value-laden psychology that pretends to be value-neutral, and being tempted to an unrestrained subjectivism that dismisses evidence as nothing but collected biases" (pp. 54-55), but his own approach of cleaning "the cloudy spectacles" suggests that his approach to psychological research leans in the value-free direction.

It is here that the unsatisfactory nature of the levels approach is revealed. The levels argument only makes sense if the psychological view and the theological/spiritual view are truly distinct—particularly if the psychological view (the view of psychological science) is actually value-free and all about facts, while the theological/spiritual view is all about subjective values and not about facts at all. But this is a dichotomy that Christians must reject. As I argue in the integration chapter, the two are intertwined: Christianity includes assertions of fact, and science always involves matters of theology and values. Myers briefly admits the latter, as I noted above, but he never explicitly admits the former, nor does he come to grips with what this means for bringing psychology and Christianity together. Even so, in his discussion of the "big ideas" of human nature, we can see how he begins to address this intersection.

I found Myers's discussion of some of the big ideas about human nature from social psychology to be intriguing. I largely agree with Myers's assessment of these specific issues. For instance, I concur that Scripture and psychological science agree that there are both rational and irrational elements to human nature. But it is vital to note that this presentation, by itself, can create an impression that the contribution of biblical teaching is always of an indecisive, inconclusive, "on the one hand X, but on the other hand Y" nature. I agree with Myers that biblical revelation does, indeed, present a complex, somewhat paradoxical picture in the four areas he addresses. But there are other areas where biblical revelation is much more forceful, clear and demanding. For instance, I think it conclusive that Scripture demands a view of human freedom that does not allow us to reduce our understanding of humans to that of determined, conditioned robots who are simply living out the predetermined courses charted for us by our nature and nurture. Similarly, I think the biblical teaching on sexuality presents a clear picture that allows us to know what is and is not in God's will for our sexual lives.

In fact, Myers's discussion about sexual orientation is a great case example of how, as Myers admits, our assumptions and beliefs always shape our approaches to science. He suggests that his engagement with science has led him to reform his moral views about sexual orientation, but he offers no compelling scientific evidence for his moral acceptance of homosexual conduct. We will look briefly at several of his key assertions.

First, he asserts that "there is no known parental or psychological influence on sexual orientation" (p. 72). To start with, note that Christian belief does not demand psychological (nurture) causation of homosexual orientation over biological (nature) causation, and Myers never informs us why this psychological causation issue is of any moral or theological consequence. Rather, Christian belief centers on the biblical teaching that homosexual conduct is immoral, hence that the condition of desiring homosexual intimacy is somehow a distortion of God's intent for human life.

Further, in claiming that there is no known parental or psychological influence on sexual orientation, Myers ignores numerous studies that indicate some contribution of family and environment to the development of homosexual orientation (see Jones & Yarhouse, 2000; Jones & Kwee, 2005). Recently, two enormous and sophisticated studies involving tens of thousands of subjects have suggested that familial socialization (Bearman & Bruckner, 2002) and familial instability (Frisch & Hviid, 2006) make statistically significant contributions to the development of same-sex attraction.

Then Myers makes a second problematic assertion: that "biological factors are looking more and more important," specifically that "biological siblings of gay people, especially their identical twins, are somewhat more likely than people without gay relatives to themselves be gay" (p. 73). I have argued consistently that we Christian researchers should be open to the contribution of biological variables to the development of the homosexual condition. Even so, the magnitude of the biological contribution is regularly exaggerated. (I discuss this research in the integration chapter.) In fact, the best identical twin evidence shows no significant genetic contribution.

Finally, Myers argues that the research shows that "efforts to change a person's sexual orientation usually (some say, virtually always) fail" (pp. 73-74). I provide evidence in the integration chapter that both the biological causation and impossibility of change arguments are unsupported by the best science. So in at least these three areas, Myers claims to be responding to the best science but offers nothing compelling from science itself.

To end with, then, Myers indulges in a questionable moral conclusion from his portrayal of the state of the science: "To suggest that sexual orientation may be disposed rather than chosen leaves moral issues open"

(p. 74). In other words, Myers believes that the evidence of science requires a reconsideration or reformulation of the church's moral disapproval of homosexual practice. This is precisely the kind of reasoning that I find so uncompelling and argue against in my chapter.

In conclusion, I would argue that this essay by Myers helps to establish the validity of the integration approach and undermines his own levels approach. By admitting that "belief guides perception," Myers legitimates the consistent Christian bringing his or her biblical understandings to the work on psychological science and practice. Moreover, Myers's analysis of sexual orientation serves as a case study to demonstrate that even the person who is committed to objectively following the findings of science wherever they may lead ("If God is the ultimate author of whatever truth psychological science glimpses, then I can accept that truth, however surprising or unsettling," p. 51) still engages science through the grid of assumptions and commitments that they bring to their work. In this case, the problem is not that Myers is not allowing his theological and moral assumptions to ground his scientific understandings—he clearly is—but rather that Myers's moral understandings are at variance with the clear and consistent teaching of Scripture on the morality of homosexual conduct. Myers's analysis of sexual orientation should provoke us to ground our work as psychologists explicitly, thoughtfully and rigorously in the authoritative teaching of the Bible.

I close with an affirmation of Myers. What he and I share that sets us both apart from the approaches advocated by Robert C. Roberts and P. J. Watson or that advocated by David Powlison is a passionate enthusiasm for good psychological science and a belief that that science can inform our theological understandings as well.

REFERENCES

Bearman, P. S., & Bruckner, H. (2002). Opposite-sex twins and adolescent same-sex attraction. *American Journal of Sociology, 107*(5), 1179-1205.

Frisch, M., & Hviid, A. (2006). Childhood family correlates of heterosexual and homosexual marriages: A national cohort study of two million Danes. *Archives of Sexual Behavior, 35*(5), 533-47.

Gagnon, R. A. J. (2001). *The Bible and homosexual practice.* Nashville: Abingdon.

Jones, S. (2006). Study guide and response to Mel White's *What the Bible says—and doesn't say—about homosexuality* <www.wheaton.edu/CACE/resources/booklets/StanJones ResponsetoMelWhite.pdf>.

Jones, S., & Kwee, A. W. (2005). Scientific research, homosexuality, and the church's moral debate: An update. *Journal of Psychology and Christianity, 24*(4), 304-16.

Jones, S., & Yarhouse, M. (2000). *Homosexuality: The use of scientific research in the church's moral debate.* Downers Grove, IL: InterVarsity Press.

A Christian Psychology Response to Levels of Explanation

P. J. Watson

PSYCHOLOGY, DAVID MYERS REMINDS US, is typically defined as *"the science of behavior and mental processes"* (p. 49). He then places emphasis on the fact that "psychology is a *science.*" Christians must appreciate the essential role of science in nurturing "a *curiosity* and a *humility*" that encourages humanity to put its sometimes wrongheaded notions about existence to an empirical test. A Christian psychology response to the levels-of-explanation view would rest on three concerns about this definition.

First, this definition of psychology is problematic not for what it includes but rather for what it leaves out. Where does such a definition come from? To necessarily oversimplify a long and complicated story, Christian psychology would stress that this definition reflects nonempirical modernist presumptions that are at the foundation of contemporary psychology.

Modernism can be interpreted as an attempt by the West to overcome the religious violence associated with the Reformation (see, e.g., Stout, 1988). Catholics and Protestants could not resolve their disagreements through appeal to a shared understanding of God, so widespread death and destruction was the result. Early modernists essentially sought to cope with the threat of cultural disintegration by finding resources within Christian traditions that could help the West reestablish peace. If Catholics and Protestants could not agree on exactly how to understand God, then at least they could agree that God was associated with "truth" and that he created "nature" in ways that reflected his laws. Both "truth" and "nature," presumably, could be noncontroversially (and nonviolently) discovered with the development of the right use of reason and empirical methods. The way out of violence was to discover indisputable rational and scientific foundations of common purpose.

Descartes (1998/1637) illustrated the hope. With appropriate methods, he argued, reliable knowledge could be created. Such methods would include, among other things, reduction and then induction. Complex phenomena should be reduced to the simplest elements that can be clearly and distinctly known without controversy. Then, higher levels of organization could be described by using inductive reason to combine clear and distinct elements into more complex structures of explanation. Human understanding could thus have indisputable foundations in the "elements" of existence. The way out of violence would rest on agreements produced through the right use of science and reason.

The problem, of course, was that the modernist hope of eliminating conflict failed. As the twentieth century made clear, modernist methods did not eliminate the violence. They merely made the killing more technologically efficient (Hart, 2009). Psychology and other forms of human endeavor must, therefore, avoid the illusion that science alone can ever overcome the problem of human conflict. The levels-of-explanation definition of psychology is too reductionistic and leaves something essential out. From the perspective of Christian psychology, psychology is defined most generally as a *science that studies the behavior and mental processes of persons.*

The necessary additional point is that every understanding of "persons" is invariably a cultural construct that cannot be reduced to clear and distinct observations about behavioral and mental "elements." To omit the word *person* from the definition of psychology reflects an, at least, implicit refusal to confront an unavoidable problem that has no easy scientific solution. This problem is unavoidable not only in psychology but in the wider culture, where our conflicts over abortion supply, perhaps, the easiest example to understand. When does a "person" begin? Well, it all depends on our (usually unarticulated) definition of the person. The pro-life definition essentially assumes that persons begin at conception, and abortion can thus be described as murder. The pro-choice definition does not work from such an assumption, and instead interprets abortion as a rational medical procedure. For each side, the issue is not primarily about empirical evidence pertaining to the behavioral and mental elements of the person or "tissue" carried by the mother. Rather, the empirical evidence is interpreted relative to some broader system of meaning that can neither be confirmed nor falsified through science. Similarly, all work in psychology operates within some, often unacknowledged, definition of the "person" as interpreted by a system of meaning that can find no indisputable foundations in science itself. Examples include evolutionary psychology, psychoanalysis, various forms of biological reductionism, behaviorism, commitments to an essentially metaphysical vision of artificial intelligence and humanistic psychology, to mention only a few. The argument of Christian psychology is that all psychologists should develop increasingly more honest definitions of psychology that forthrightly acknowledge the unavoidable nonscientific dimension of their work. For Christian psychologists, this means psychology is a *science that studies the behavior and mental processes of persons as understood in Christian texts and traditions of interpretation.*

Where does the Christian-psychology definition of psychology come from? Postmodern critiques have undoubtedly been influential. David Myers dismisses postmodernists because they "often resist psychological science" (p. 53), and he goes on to complain that postmodernists unacceptably dismiss "truth" as a culturally constructed fiction. This interpretation, nevertheless, oversimplifies the complexities of postmodernism, which Rosenau (1992) describes as containing two different streams of thought. Skeptical postmodernists essentially maintain the position that David Myers rightly rejects. Rosenau also describes, however, an "affirmative postmodernism" that doubts the often-implicit presumptions of modernists to achieve objectivity and value neutrality. In explicit opposition to such pretensions, Rosenau (1992) emphasizes, "Positive value orientations and specific normative goals openly guide the affirmatives' version of social science" (p. 23).

Christian psychology uses the position of "affirmatives" to move beyond postmodernism and toward a social science that forthrightly includes Christian norms about how to define the person in the social scientific process itself. Modernists and fundamentalists falsely presume that the text of the world and of the Word can be reduced to clear and distinct elements that can easily resolve conflict. However, the very act of "reducing" a text to its elements will necessarily begin with values that are clear and distinct only within a particular community of interpretation. How a secular humanistic community, for example, interprets that "text" of a self-actualized self will be, at least, somewhat different from the interpretation of a Christian community (Watson, Milliron, Morris & Hood, 1995). Any process of reduction will, therefore, be contestable from the outset. Ideally, a Christian psychology would join advocates of atheist, Jewish, Muslim, New Age and all other perspectives in using the presumed humility and curiosity of science to better understand the opportunities and limits of agreement among perspectives.

Second, from a Christian-psychology perspective, the levels-of-explanation view is far too optimistic about the "humility" of science. David Myers appreciatively quotes sociologist Andrew Greeley as reflecting a presumably scientific acknowledgment that psychology can never fully explain the purpose and meaning of human existence. That Andrew Greeley says such a thing is unsurprising, not because he is a sociologist but rather because he is a Catholic priest. A Marxist sociologist or a Darwinian social scientist would surely present a very different evaluation of the possibilities.

Indeed, the sciences are full of perspectives that lack "humility." Within the biological level of explanation, for example, the eliminative reductionist does not merely study how the body functions in order to explain the operations of the mind, but instead argues that all scientific language about the mind can be completely eliminated and reduced to scientific language about the body (e.g., Churchland, 1986). A person, in other words, is *just* a body. Within psychology, the stimulus (S) response (R) perspective of radical behaviorism denies that concepts of meaning and purpose refer to anything other than epiphenomena that occur between environmental events and the consequent reactions of organisms (see, e.g., Skinner, 1971). An epiphenomenon exists as an effect only and assumes no real causal significance. Hence, a person is *just* a collection of behaviors (R), and behaviors are *just* a product of the environment (S). In short, a concern of Christian psychology is that the levels-of-explanation definition of psychology is far too optimistic about the humility of science and fails to include conceptual resources that can challenge the imperializing tendencies that sometimes exist within the contemporary sciences. Adding "persons" to the definition of psychology would help address this problem.

Third, and finally, the levels-of-explanation definition of psychology does not adequately describe the excellent work of David Myers. His chapter is *not* most importantly about behavior and mental processes as understood by (modernist) social science but rather about a Christian interpretation of various scientific findings. The levels-of-explanation view presents a model of what Christian psychologists could embrace as a plausible, though preliminary, Christian understanding of what the sciences could aspire to be as long as the nonscientific dimensions of all such endeavors were forthrightly acknowledged. Science could indeed operate as a hierarchically organized form of human understanding characterized by curiosity and humility in the search for "truth" and the laws of "nature." Christian psychologists and advocates of all other value perspectives should join together as scientists who forthrightly and humbly work from their own normatively determined definitions of the person. Conflicts of interpretation are an empirical reality both within and outside the sciences. True "objectivity," therefore, requires the development of social scientific methods that include conflicts within the methods of science itself. Anyone interested in how this might be possible could usefully begin (but not end) by examining the exemplary model defined by David Myers himself.

REFERENCES

Churchland, P. (1986). *Neurophilosophy.* Cambridge, MA: MIT Press.

Descartes, R. (1998). *Discourse on method and meditations on first philosophy.* Indianapolis: Hackett Publishing Company. (Original works published 1637 and 1641)

Hart, D. B. (2009). *Atheist delusions.* New Haven, CT: Yale University Press.

Rosenau, P. M. (1992). *Post-modernism and the social sciences.* Princeton, NJ: Princeton University Press.

Skinner, B. F. (1971). *Beyond freedom and dignity.* New York: Knopf/Random House.

Stout, J. (1988). *Ethics after Babel.* Boston: Beacon Press.

Watson, P. J., Milliron, J. T., Morris, R. J., & Hood, R. W., Jr. (1995). Religion and the self as text: Toward a Christian translation of self-actualization. *Journal of Psychology and Theology, 23,* 180-89.

A Transformational Psychology Response to Levels of Explanation

John H. Coe and Todd W. Hall

As with the other authors of this volume, David Myers gives clear evidence of an authentic and insightful attempt to understand the relationship of psychology and Christianity. As with the other views, there is sufficient insight and understanding in his approach that has attracted a large following of Christians doing psychology, therapy and research at a professional level. In general, Myers provides an account that, perhaps more than all the rest, gives full expression to the benefits of taking psychology seriously enough to do the firsthand work of observation and reflection, and to not merely giving a passing nod to psychology while gleaning more from the data of faith.

According to Myers, psychology provides a particular "level of explanation" viewpoint on the person, which complements the various other understandings of the person from theology, biology, physiology, neuroscience and so on. We cannot affirm Myers too highly for the rigor that his life's work has demonstrated in actually doing the first handwork of psychology. However, on closer reading, we have four general contentions with his version of doing psychology.

1. This approach does not sufficiently distinguish between ontological and epistemological ways of thinking of "levels of explanation," which results in a truncated view of the object of investigation and not merely complementary viewpoints. This truncated approach to the science of the person is fine as long as the researcher admits to the truncation and the need for a fuller view of the person as a unitary vision in science.

2. This approach only provides complementary views of an object of study with no articulated way to critique each other, no agreed on methodology between the various viewpoints (e.g., a materialist physicist, a reductionistic-materialistic psychologist, a theologian, etc.). Thus, this approach provides no robust science of the person that can adjudicate matters of controversy and difference.

3. This view adapts itself too closely without critique to the modernist approach to "science" and "psychology," which results in an inability to break from this truncated methodological approach in order to produce its own unique, thoroughly Christian version of the science of the person. This results in adopting a view of science that is incapable of addressing spiritual and mental phenomena and values, which are at the heart of ancient and biblical models of doing psychology.

4. This view also adapts itself to the modernist approach to science that is purely descriptive, excluding the prescriptive (values, character and morality) from the purview of science and from the wisdom that it could discover. As a result, this modernist view of science fails to provide a "scientific" grounding for psychotherapy, which necessarily addresses issues of values (health and unhealth). In contrast with the levels view, our hope is to put forth a premodern view of science that would provide a rigorous methodology for doing what Myers already affirms and does in a casual way by insisting that the various truncated sciences complement one another.

Our first contention is that Myers's levels-of-explanation view fails to sufficiently distinguish between an ontological (the nature of being) and epistemological (the nature of knowing) understanding of the person. When he accepts Polkinghorne's statement that "reality is a multilayered unity," we need to clearly distinguish this as an epistemological claim and not an ontological one. That is, although we can study and know elements of the person from different vantage points of investigation, the truth of the person's ontological unity necessarily makes it such that these vantage points do not provide a view to the whole. So in a levels-of-explanation view, theorists on each level must be straightforward and honest that their understanding of the person is incomplete, and if their view is overemphasized to the exclusion of the others, it may actually skew a view of the person. Unfortunately, however, addressing this truncation is not built into the levels view.

Further, because reality is unified, the goal of science should be to develop a methodology that can provide a unified vision of the person that reflects the reality of the person as a whole. The transformational model would permit modern scientific work while insisting that there is a fuller approach that provides a methodology for bringing together these complementary works of science. And Myers has given us no argument for why his view of science should be accepted and not replaced with this more robust, unitary vision that has ancient roots.

The second limitation of the levels-of-explanation approach is that, while it allows for complementary views between the various approaches to the person, it provides no rigorous, articulated way to critique differing views or adjudicate between various vantage points. That is, if the theologian, physicist and psychologist disagree about the nature of consciousness, mental experiences, dreams or teleology, there is no agreed-on methodology between them to resolve such matters. We need an approach to science that is capable of doing this, insofar as reality is unitary and discernible as God's created order—although philosophical naturalists and secularist approaches to science will not agree with our conclusions.

Our third contention is that the main weakness of the levels-of-explanation view is that it accepts without argument the modernist approach to "science" and "psychology," which is naturalistic and reductionistic in orientation. Our transformational approach provides a unitary vision of the person that takes into account all reality in God, yet it allows for criticism and adjudication while still making room for the detailed (yet truncated) views of the specialist who is still functioning on the old modernist model.

The successes of astronomy in measuring observables, their movements and relationships to one another (the appeal to efficient and physical causes for explanation) was so successful that moderns in the seventeenth and eighteenth centuries wanted to make this the chief language of physical knowledge, if not of all knowledge. Thus science adopted a method of measuring physical bodies and their movement, called *quantification*, which involved observation of bodies in motion and their causal relationships to other bodies. This was clearly successful in some fields of investigation, and was soon adopted as the universal way to do science for *all* objects and fields of study. On this model of science, you begin the scientific investigation with a universal method of measuring repeating observables, which predetermines what kinds of objects are possible to discover and investigate by that method. However, major problems resulted from this commitment for both science and psychology, which Myers's levels of explanation exemplifies.

The particular difficulties encountered have to do with the kind of knowledge-language that can be used to explain (1) spiritual reality and nonphysical phenomena and (2) ethics. Under the modernist view of science, it is not at all clear what knowledge-language can be used to intelligibly talk about "objects" that have neither extension nor movement that can be measured (things that include, arguably, God, angels, souls or minds, numbers, ideas, propositions, dreams, consciousness, mental images, personal agency, first-person identity, and experiences of feelings and thoughts). Interestingly, Myers defines psychology as "the science of behavior and mental processes" (p. 51), yet he provides no explanation of how "mental processes" can be studied by a methodology of measurement that inherently applies only to physical objects in space (some form of quantification).

Second, the scientific method of quantification is purely *descriptive* and no longer addresses prescriptive realities—such as morality (right and wrong), values (good and bad) and character (virtue and vice)—which were grounded in ancient classical-realist science and natural-law theories going back to the ancient Greeks. But psychotherapy depends on understanding values such as psychological health and pathology.

The question that confronts the Christian psychologist today is (1) whether and to what degree a legitimate psychology can address Christian realities or (2) whether the Christian psychologist is doing something other than "psychology" or science when relating psychology and Christianity.

The tension involved is clear: it is not legitimate for modernist science to include Scripture as legitimate data for psychology, nor is it legitimate to address immaterial objects, sin, life in Christ or values. However, the Christian would include Scripture as a legitimate source of knowledge and is compelled by Scripture, as well as by reflection on human nature, to address realities (such as "mind" and values) that are inherently unquantifiable. This is clearly expressed in Myers's view that Christians who accept the modern view of science (which he affirms) need to ask the nonscientific question of how a scientific psychology can be reconciled with one's commitment to the Christian faith. But we suggest that this modernist view of science and Christianity will always require an artificial, secondary process of bringing together different "levels of explanation" into a whole that is necessarily truncated.

We believe that there exists an alternate, classical-realist approach to science, affirmed by the ancients, that is capable of providing a foundation for developing holistic vision for understanding the person in light of all reality, particularly the Christian realities. It turns out that the classical and medieval thinkers represented in the ancient Near Eastern wise men (sages), the Old Testament sage, the Greeks in Plato and Aristotle, the Stoics and numerous medieval thinkers had an entirely different approach to scientific method than that of modernity. According to the modernist "new science," you begin scientific investigation with a universal method of measuring repeating observables, which predetermines the kinds of objects that are possible to discover and investigate by science. The classical realist approach reverses this process: the object of investigation determines the methodology, which involves the following:

1. Science begins with a casual *acquaintance* of the object

2. for the purpose of learning more about the *nature* of the object,

3. which allows *the object of investigation to determine* the best way to further investigate it,

4. resulting in the development of a *method of study* best suited to the object.

On this view, *reality* determines *methodology* and the way of knowing, rather than allowing a predetermined way of knowing to determine what is real and what counts as knowledge. To put it differently, ontology determines epistemology; a presupposed epistemology does not determine ontology. According to the ancients, one cannot know what is the best way to study what exists until one is adequately acquainted with what exists. This premodernist scientific methodology involves an honest, pretheoretical openness or acquaintance with what is real. On this view of science, the psychological health of the scientist to remain honest and open to reality is central to doing science well, which is foundational to our transformational psychology model. On this model, mental phenomena, God, Scripture and human values are all legitimate data of science insofar as they are real and relevant to understanding the person. No a priori methodology precludes this.

Finally, our fourth contention is that the levels-of-explanation view's failure to critique the modernist approach to "science" and "psychology" results in science being purely descriptive and unnecessarily excludes the prescriptive (values, character and morality) from the purview of science and all the wisdom that is discoverable from nature. As a result, the modernist approach to science has never been able to provide a clear "scientific" justification and understanding of what is going on in psychotherapy, which necessarily addresses issues of values (psychological health and unhealth). The levels view sees itself as supportive of ancient wisdom but doesn't have a sufficient methodology to provide this wisdom.

However, our transformational psychology adopts the Old Testament sage's view of science that insists that it is possible to discover wisdom and prescriptions for living from a study (observation-reflection) of human nature and behavior, along with the wisdom gained from Scripture and experiences of God. Of course, this transformational model's view of science is ultimately grounded in the transformative psychologist who preserves the integrity of this process by being as open as possible to what is real and true about understanding the person. This is precisely what the Old Testament wise man was pursuing. This is, ultimately, a methodological and existential model for what the levels view wants to do in bringing together complementary views into one gestalt.

A Biblical Counseling Response to Levels of Explanation

David Powlison

ON THE SURFACE IT MIGHT APPEAR THAT David Myers and I operate on opposite ends of a spectrum and never the twain shall meet.

Myers is a researcher, specializing in social psychology while paying attention to neuropsychology. I am a pastoral theologian and counselor. While I give some ongoing attention to research studies, I generally find other sources of knowledge far more significant for understanding and helping people. Myers works with populations, reveling in the correlations that good statistical data can reveal. I work with named individuals, reveling in the connections and patterns that organize the teeming details of personal and interpersonal life. Myers pursues quantitative information that can lead to generalized nomothetic knowledge. I pursue qualitative, idiographic knowledge of persons, and the pastoral wisdom that helps a person change by the grace of Christ into someone of greater wisdom and love.

Given such differences in social location, life purpose, practical emphasis and intellectual attention, it might surprise some readers to hear that I actively appreciate the sector of psychology in which David Myers specializes. As an undergraduate, I majored in social psychology at Harvard, studying under Roger Brown, one of the icons in the field. My Ph.D. studies in history of science and medicine focused on the social and behavioral sciences, as well as on psychotherapy and psychiatry. I own Myers's textbooks, *Psychology* and *Social Psychology,* and have read them (some parts twice!) with both pleasure and profit. For example, his provocative discussion of self-serving bias in the latter book gave me a metaphor for sin that I use in my chapter on the biblical counseling view. As Myers says, our self-serving bias illustrates how "self-righteous pride is the fundamental sin, the original sin, the deadliest of the seven deadly sins" (p. 59). In principle, the differences mentioned in the previous paragraphs are complementary, not antithetical: "different types of analysis can fit coherently together" (p. 52).

But there are significant differences between our views. I will respond to Myers's chapter in two ways. First, I will locate his specialty within the categories I use in my chapter. Second, I will note several substantive differences between Myers's levels-of-explanation view and my biblical counseling view. I believe that Myers's approach fails to understand people in the end, because he does not go deep enough—not because he is a social psychologist but because he does not think Christianly enough about people.

First, though, let me locate his work. At the heart of my chapter is a metapsychology, a perspective on the whole. I seek to orient us to an overarching Christian gaze regarding how we understand people, problems, and cures in our time and place. To that end, I deconstruct the word *psychology* into six different (though related) sectors of meaning. It helps to keep those different meanings in mind, so that it is clear what we are talking about at any particular moment. As a coherent outlook, Christian faith interacts in a somewhat different way with each of those six sectors. I specifically discuss psychological research as one part of the sector of psychology that I call Psych-2. The pursuit of organized knowledge includes both social psychology (nurture factors) and neuropsychology (nature factors). You will also notice that both of my lengthy case studies ("Stuck in traffic" near the beginning and "Clyde" at the end) call attention to nature and nurture variables, seeking to accurately weigh them in relation to other factors.

I can understand why Myers calls his sector of psychology the "mainstream." But as a pastoral theologian and historian of science, I view his sector's current fecundity and intellectual dominance partly as a product of our culture's overextended faith in science. To put psychological research in a wider perspective is not to discredit the genuine achievements. It is simply to keep things in perspective. Myers and I agree on the need to "bear in mind psychology's limits" (p. 53) as part of identifying its strengths, though no doubt we come to different conclusions as we each do our calculus of relative strengths and limitations.

Second, I do differ with David Myers in significant ways. I will interact with three of his "pairs of complementary truths."[1] I love Myers's metaphor of two ends of one rope dangling down into a deep well and our need to

---

[1]In the previous edition of this book, I critiqued his view of homoeroticism as an example of both bad science and bad theology.

grip both ends if we are to climb out of the well. This picture of the relationship between complementary truths is profoundly right. But from the well in which I sit, Myers's set of paired terms reaches only twenty feet down an eighty-foot hole. Most of what he describes consists of superficial parallels between generically "religious" notions and psychological ideas. He rarely mentions vigorous Christian realities. The parallels he notes are like the parallels between Christianity and Islam. Both are monotheistic religions; both meet in a house of worship; both take cues from a scriptural document; both have an ordained leader in the community; both believe in conversion. Such parallels dangle down only twenty feet, while the really interesting and decisive things happen deeper down.

RATIONALITY AND IRRATIONALITY

Myers believes that irrationality is typified by the fact that "we are swayed more by vivid anecdotes than by statistical reality" (p. 58). But surely it is significant that God himself chooses to redeem the world by vivid anecdotes. The Lord sways us from death to life by living and telling a true story, inviting us to join him, not by citing statistical realities. Sinfulness distorts how we use anecdotes *and* statistics; grace redeems our use of both. Statistics are not epistemically truer than stories. In my anecdotal experience, statistics are often interesting, but they never uncover what is decisive in any person's life. They describe, often helpfully, but they do not explain, weigh, prescribe or motivate.

Similarly, Myers's example of rationality is charming but equally ambiguous on closer inspection. Operating as an intuitive scientist, I may be able to explain my world efficiently and with enough accuracy for my daily needs. But if the God and Father of Jesus Christ in fact is providing every bite I eat, and if my daily needs also include all the other things mentioned in the Lord's Prayer, then whenever I am not consciously dependent and thankful, I show myself to be an irrational fool. The intuitive scientist is in some manner practicing pseudoscience, however efficiently and accurately life seems to be working out. It takes a Christian gaze to see all this. Research psychology, denying that gaze, wades in shallower water.

SELF-SERVING BIAS AND SELF-ESTEEM

Myers rightly likens our self-centered filter to the deadliest of deadly sins.

But do self-esteem, self-affirmation and affirmation from others build a solid foundation for being delivered from such sins—for psychological flourishing, for loving God and neighbor, and for entering eternal life? Are such things psychology's parallel to the goods of divine grace? Or are they counterfeit goodies that substitute for grace? They might make a person happier and more self-confident, but that person remains trapped in a self-referential, other-referential and futile self-salvation project, without hope and without God. Similarly, by definition, a psychotherapist's "unconditional positive regard" views people as intrinsically acceptable and able to learn how to feel good about themselves. But the divine grace of our Savior's blood, sweat and tears rescues the intrinsically unlovable. He makes us joyous and grateful. He establishes a different basis of confidence. To know that you are truly loved is rather different from believing that you are innately loveable. The former looks to the one who loves and loves in return; the latter never stops obsessing about self.

PERSONS AND SITUATIONS

This is the Achilles' heel of research psychology. The tangled workings of human intentionality—hopes, goals, expectations, motivated choices, reality map, schemata, desires (some good, some evil, some mixed; some conscious, some unconscious, some semi-conscious)—are a very deep well. Introductory psychology texts largely focus on what scientific method can best access: the relationship between nature and nurture variables, that is, the relationship between neuropsychology and social psychology. In other words, they mostly study the impact of *situations,* what the old philosophers and theologians called "material cause" and "efficient cause." But "final cause" is the Holy Grail for understanding persons in general and any person in particular. While older personality theories tried to make sense of our desires, to probe and explain the heart, their efforts degenerated into endless bickering. They couldn't go deep enough, because they would not listen to Christian insight into persons as moral agents. The Bible teaches us to understand how the mundane operations of the human heart are always God-referential, either consciously turning toward him or blindly turning away from him to some other object of our affections.

Myers largely ducks both the problematic nature of inner motives and the distinctives of a Christian understanding. In discussing the contribution of the *person,* he says, "Facing the same situation, different people may react differently, depending on their personality and culture" (p. 61). This choice of words is revealing: personality contains a significant nature component, and culture is entirely a nurture variable. Neither word says very much about the person (compare, by contrast, my two case studies). In his paragraph illustrating the effects of the personal factor, Myers repeatedly chooses examples where the person "sometimes" affects a choice. But in the Christian view, even our mundane unconscious conformity to culture and personality says something about what misrules our hearts. The personal factor is not sometimes significant, other times not; it *always* affects whatever we do, think and feel. The personal factor vis-à-vis God is final cause. Only Christian faith makes sense of the personal factor, because only Christian faith sees *how* actual behavior and mental processes are intrinsically relational and religious.

Scientific psychology is rich in describing nature, nurture and persons, but it is impoverished in accounting for the actual person who lives life physically embodied and socially embedded. So while psychological research can be interesting and informative, Christian faith is deep wisdom. When Myers attempts to correlate the two, he largely reverts to a generic religiosity that has little depth of moral understanding and no power to explain and save actual persons enslaved to deadly things.

3

An Integration View

Stanton L. Jones

Recently I stood in the Museum of Fine Arts, Boston, before impressionist Paul Gauguin's 1897 masterpiece *Where Do We Come From? What Are We? Where Are We Going?* Whatever one thinks of Gauguin's provocative work, we must agree that his title has forcefully formulated the great questions every human being faces: Where *do* we come from? What *are* we? Where *are* we going?

The integrative approach, in order to understand the relationship of psychology and Christianity, takes as one of its founding notions, that psychology as a science and as professional practice can never escape such questions; both psychological science and professional practice are shaped and molded by the answers to such ultimate questions that the psychologist favors as she or he pursues scientific or applied practice.

Further, as Christians, we believe God has given us answers to these ultimate questions through his gracious intervention in human life, even as we acknowledge that our grasp on his answers is fragmentary and incomplete. We believe that Jesus Christ is Savior and Lord of all of life. We believe that no aspect of life is outside of the scope of his sovereignty. Therefore, an integrationist believes the Christian psychologist should draw on the resource of God's answers to these ultimate questions as the foundation both for how we engage the science of psychology and how we structure our practice in the profession of psychology. The integrationist also surmises that Scripture does not provide us all that we need in order to understand human beings fully, and that there is a legitimate and strategic role for psychology as a science and as a profession in giving us intellectual and practical tools for understanding and improving the human condition.

To preview where we are heading, here is a working definition of "integration": *Integration of Christianity and psychology (or any area of "secular thought") is our living out—in this particular area—of the lordship of Christ over all of existence by our giving his special revelation—God's true Word— its appropriate place of authority in determining our fundamental beliefs about and practices toward all of reality and toward our academic subject matter in particular.*

The word *integration* is legitimately criticized for what it fails to capture and communicate about the complex relationship of faith and "secular thought." For instance, some critics claim that the term wrongly implies having to artificially mix together two things that do not naturally belong together (like oil and water). Others complain the term suggests an undesirable end product of an unpalatable "psychotheology" or "Christopsychology," which degrades both of its two constituent elements. Such complaints take the term in directions its users do not intend. Still, no one has yet come up with a better summary label for this complex approach. What matters ultimately is not the word, but what the term summarizes— the complex understandings and commitments to living out our faith with integrity. We seek to integrate because, in a perfect world, that which would go together seamlessly is now, in this world, dis-integrated and fragmented. Call it anything you like; at stake in this discussion is not the term, but one's *fundamental stance as a Christian* as one engages the entire world of learning and action.

A PERSONAL JOURNEY

I was first drawn to an integrative approach as a student at a major public university. As an undergraduate psychology major, I was captivated by the field. While I encountered remarkable and delightful opportunities to grow in my understanding of human persons in ways that seemed perfectly compatible with my commitment to Jesus Christ and his truth, as a student (and later as a psychologist) I was also confronted with tension and incongruity between the voices of psychology and of my Christian faith.

I felt this tension as an undergraduate student, but did not understand it well when, for example, I finished an entire semester of studying personality theories and research and realized we had utterly neglected the moral and religious dimension of human existence. The basic assumptions of some of these personality approaches added up in complex ways, and when stated directly, some of these assumptions seemed in tension with a biblically grounded understanding of our human nature, especially when my professors engaged in reductionism by insisting that our human experience is *nothing but* the basic constituent elements of behavior (nothing but operant learning, or neurons firing, or cognitive processing).

The concept of integration seeks to understand, address and partially resolve these tensions. In grappling with these conflicts early on, one line of advice I encountered was to keep my religious faith and my engagement with science separate. The university environment, overall, communicated a powerful message that "facts" and "values" were separate and noninteracting realities; science dealt with facts but religion with values. "So relax," I was told. "Though those two perspectives seem to conflict, they really are nonoverlapping, distinct perspectives that provide complementary snapshots of the human condition. Science is about facts and religion about meaning. Just keep the two views separate and live with the tension, and you will have an enriched, multifaceted portrait of the human condition." Somehow, this advice did not sit well.

As I struggled with these tensions, I encountered the beginnings of the biblical counseling movement in the early writings of Jay Adams (1970). Adams argued first that psychology was always founded on presuppositions and that the presuppositions shaping secular psychology were invariably in conflict with a Christian understanding of the person. For example, Adams pointed out that many of the assumptions that grounded humanistic psychology were contrary to Christian conceptions of the person—humanistic concepts as exemplified by Carl Rogers, Abraham Maslow and others, that human beings are basically good, that dysfunction is the result of the socializing environment and not of the person, and that the core human motivation is that of seeking self-actualization.

Second, Adams proposed that biblical teaching could replace everything that psychology had to offer. I met Adams in 1977 at a seminar on biblical counseling. I asked him what I could do to glorify God in my training as a clinical psychologist who was dedicated to remaining faithful to the clear teaching of Scripture. "Drop out of your training," he replied, "because (1) psychology has nothing to offer the faithful Christian, and (2) everything needed for formulating an utterly comprehensive understanding of the human person and our problems can be found in or deduced from the Bible." I walked away deeply confused, because I was indeed intent on being faithful to Scripture but (2) I could not see how the Bible could possibly provide all counsel on every issue, and (1) I found myself learning much of value about the human condition in my studies in psychology.

So in my first year of graduate school I found myself positioned, almost without knowing it, as an integrationist. I found myself in this position by exclusion, unable to embrace either of the two options. On the one hand, I was unable to accept the supposition that the fundamental nature of the relationship between psychology and Christianity is one where they provide separate, complementary truths, and where the Christian faith did not have the potential to deeply engage and change how I do psychology. In some deep way, I felt that the fundamental beliefs of a Christian about the human experience and condition should be profoundly shaped by Scripture. On the other hand, I found value in the work of the discipline of psychology and was also unconvinced that Scripture alone could provide every need for the understanding of persons, their problems and their resolutions.

Within weeks, I encountered a then-new book, Gary Collins's *The Rebuilding of Psychology* (1977), that sketched an extraordinary integration vision that I found compelling. Collins called for Christians to draw on all the riches of Scripture to develop, in as much depth as possible, a fundamentally Christian understanding of the human condition, and then seek to engage and rebuild psychology in a way that honors God and functionally places Jesus as Lord over our work as psychologists. Over the next decade and more, a series of important books elaborated roughly the same vision (e.g., Carter & Narramore, 1979; Collins, 1981; Evans, 1982, 1989; Van Leeuwen, 1985), and it has been a delight to participate in advancing this integration movement. A new volume edited by Stevenson, Eck and Hill (2007) brings together in one place many of the most formative and vital articles of the integration movement over the last forty years, and it is a great starting point for further study of this movement.

GOING DEEPER

Embedded in this account are a number of core issues that beg for elaboration. Most basically, the question before us might be phrased "How is it that we understand science, on the one hand, and Christianity, on the other hand, such that the two can interact in profound and substantive ways?" This leads to another question, in some ways the mirror opposite, "If the two entities—science and Christianity—can interact in profound and substantive ways, why is it that one cannot subsume the other?"

Why science and Christianity? Note that in framing these questions, I have used the terms *science* and *Christianity* to designate the entities we seek to integrate. The former choice of term is easy to explain. Psychology is both a science and a profession (Jones, 1994). Many discussions about integration start with a discussion of clinical or professional concerns, but here I focus on integration with the scientific aspects of the field for two reasons. First, while not every profession is scientific, in the contemporary world most of the respected human service professions derive their legitimacy by relying on the scientific method to define the core practices of the discipline. Psychology as a profession certainly bases its core legitimacy on the body of knowledge called psychological science. Further, it is common today to view science in such a way that religious faith of any kind can have no impact on science or interaction with science, so by focusing on the relationship of Christianity with science, we are deliberately taking on the hardest challenge. If we succeed in justifying why and how Christianity can interact with the science of psychology, we will have also established the basis for how it must also interact with the profession of psychology.

Why focus on Christianity in particular, rather than on the broader concept of religion? As I have discussed elsewhere (Jones, 2000), to utilize an abstraction like *religion* forces one to pare away the particularities and distinctives of specific faith traditions in order to wind up with a shared core that all faith traditions hold in common—and in the end, this leaves us with too little. Using such a method, Stephen Jay Gould (1999) developed a working definition of religion as "all moral discourse on principles that might activate the ideal of universal fellowship among people" (p. 62). Can a case be made that all religions share these few characteristics? Perhaps. Certainly Christianity involves moral discourse, and in some ways, it shares an ideal of universal fellowship among people.

The problem is that these elements are embedded in and only make sense in the context of the broader contours of Christian belief in a personal, triune God who, in the person of the Son, comes to earth, dies and rises to new life on our behalf. To limit Christianity to its "value" elements is to strip it of its core characteristics. We believe in a God who speaks and acts in history in distinct and surprising ways, and morality and fellowship are more byproducts than the major focus of true Christian faith. There are times for Christians to speak in terms of generic religion (as I did in Jones, 1994). Here, though, I am arguing for something much more specific, powerful and focused; I am arguing for how Christian faith, in all its particularity, can and should relate to science in general and psychological science in particular.

So why not focus more specifically on "the Bible" or "Christian theology," rather than Christianity? Because it is the personal faith convictions and commitments of individual psychologists that can and will shape their scientific and professional work, not the teachings of the Bible that are supposedly disconnected from the person nor the abstract discipline or body of Christian theology (Evans, 2005). It is *one's own* interpretation of and commitment to biblical truth, and *one's own* embrace of certain theological principles that will shape one's own work. So we focus here on integrating science and "Christian faith."

Understanding science and Christianity. How is it that we can understand science and Christianity so that the two can interact in profound and substantive ways? The definitions we choose are crucial. Gould (1999) offered us a clear and provocative model with which to interact in clarifying our thinking. He began with simple working definitions of science and religion:

> Science tries to document the factual character of the natural world, and to develop theories that coordinate and explain these facts. Religion, on the other hand, operates in the equally important, but utterly different, realm of human purposes, meanings, and values—subjects that the factual domain of science might illuminate, but can never resolve. Similarly, while scientists must operate with ethical principles, some specific to their practice, the validity of these principles can never be inferred from the factual discoveries of science. (pp. 4-5)

Gould then went on to declare science and religion to be "Non-Overlapping Magisteria" (NOMA), and he specifies the proper relationship between the two:

> [The] magisterium of science covers the empirical realm: what the universe is made of (fact) and why does it work this way (theory). The magisterium of religion extends over questions of ultimate meaning and moral value. The two magisteria do not overlap. . . . To cite the old clichés, science gets the age of rocks, and religion the rock of ages; science studies how the heavens go, religion how to go to heaven. (p. 6)

Later, reinforcing his point, Gould declared that science and religion "remain logically distinct and fully separate in styles of inquiry" (p. 59). Many make similar claims. In 1981, the U.S. National Academy of Sciences passed a resolution (in reaction to a trial on teaching creationism in public schools), stating, "Religion and science are separate and mutually exclusive realms of human thought whose presentation in the same context leads to misunderstanding of both scientific theory and religious belief" (NAS, 1984, p. 6). Many share this fundamental premise.

In perhaps the most telling application of his scheme, Gould is crystal clear in specifying the implication NOMA has for the belief in miracles embedded in many religions (but particularly in Judaism and Christianity):

> The first commandment for all versions of NOMA might be summarized by stating: "Thou shalt not mix the magisteria by claiming that God directly ordains important events in the history of nature by special interference knowable only through revelation and not accessible to science." In common parlance, we refer to such special interference as "miracle"—operationally defined as a unique and temporary suspension of natural law to reorder the facts of nature by divine fiat. . . . NOMA does impose this "limitation" on concepts of God. (pp. 84-85)

Gould apparently thought that his conclusion here—that we need to give up any idea of God intervening in the world—is a small price to pay for putting religion and science in their proper places. Christians should disagree.

Gould defined science and religion tightly and compactly, and then declared the two to have no relationship, because no relationship is possible between two such fundamentally disparate entities. Christians should not passively accept such definitions or the implications that flow from them, but rather challenge them in pushing for better understandings.

There are, as implied earlier, those who go in the opposite direction of Gould, embracing definitions of either science or of Christianity that are so expansive and broad that they have radically different implications for the interrelationship. Logical positivism, an approach to thinking about knowledge that was prevalent fifty years ago (though still present in certain circles) declared that true knowledge only took two forms: analytic truths that were logically true by definition (e.g., the logical law of identity, mathematical truths like 2+2=4) and empirical truths established by observation. By this understanding, religious truths are not just another or even a deficient type of truth, but literally are nonsensical and meaningless. Logical positivism collapsed for many reasons, including the recognition that the core claims of the approach themselves qualified as neither analytic nor empirical claims, and therefore were themselves meaningless. On the other hand, some religious irrationalists so elevate religious forms of knowledge that they see little contribution of science or human rationality to the true knowledge that comes from their religious sources. We here reject such all-encompassing understandings.

We must also reject the overly restricted definitions that Gould offers for both science and religion, and embrace understandings broader than he would favor. So what is Christianity? And what is science?

Defining Christianity. Gould proposed a much more restrictive view of religious faith in general, and of Christianity specifically, than do most Christian proponents of the levels-of-explanation view of the relationship of Christianity and psychology (see pp. 49-78). Still, what is consistent across such views is the claim that the exclusive (or for some, the primary) contribution that religious faith provides is its contribution of a perspective on *meaning, values, significance, ethics, morality* or *ultimacy*. Faith, they say, has no important contribution to make to our factual understanding of the reality before us; that factual understanding is the province of science and is one to which religious faith can make no substantive contribution. Only when we move to interpreting the meaning of what we have studied can religious belief have much to say.

Gould's abstract understanding of "religion" does not work for Christianity. Christian faith is not just about a "religious slant" on empirical reality. Rather, Christians have affirmed their shared belief in a God who has intervened (yes, miraculously!) in our empirical reality again and again, and also a God who speaks truthfully to his people through special revelation in the Bible about how they are to understand him, themselves and the world around them.

Some want to claim that the stories of God's mighty acts in human history are less about real, historic events, and more myths that embody religious truth. It has been a staple of liberal Christianity, for example, to deny the claim that Jesus' dead body was actually resurrected after three days in the grave, in favor of believing that something spiritually significant (but somehow nonhistorical) happened with profound religious implications for all of humanity. In contrast, orthodox Christians believe that God's interventions were factual, historical events (1 Cor 15:12-19[1]): a chemist could have done before and after analyses of Jesus' water-turned-to-wine miracle and documented the empirical realities of the change; a video recorder properly placed would have captured the resurrection of Jesus Christ from death to life.

But chemists and video recorders were not present, and so these events and others cannot be studied as science because they are not events subject to repetition under controlled conditions suitable for scientific study. These were the contingent acts of a living God, not the inevitable outworking of a mechanical universe operating according to universal causal laws. In the same way that the contingent acts of individual human beings in history are empirically real and yet cannot be subjected to empirical scientific analysis, so also are the personal acts in history of the triune God of Christian faith empirically real but cannot be studied scientifically. We can study scientifically why, on average, girlfriends break up with their boyfriends, but we cannot study in a way that is remotely scientific why a certain woman broke up with a certain man one hundred years ago.

Just as these historically real events are not just about significance, so also God's words to us are not just "values perspectives." Christians have believed that the revelation of his truth in Scripture is completely trustworthy. They are truths as stable and enduring—or more so—than any mere empirical generalization. Scriptural teachings, such as that human beings are made in the image of God, that we are both physical and

---

[1]All Scripture references used in this chapter, unless otherwise indicated, are taken from The Holy Bible, English Standard Version.

spiritual/soulish beings, that it is "not good that the man should be alone" (Gen 2:18), that we have all sinned and fallen short of the glory of God, and that adultery and murder are immoral, all are absolute and are all absolutely trustworthy truths about the human condition.

So those who claim religion only provides a values/meaning/significance perspective on empirical reality understand too little of what God has provided. We must assert that God has intruded on empirical reality both by his acts and by his revelation of truth as he perfectly knows it. We further believe that we must take this truth into account, indeed take it as foundational to our understanding of the human condition.

Why then do we need science at all? Because by his sovereign choice, God's acting and speech are limited. Further, he has created humans as rational beings capable of knowing more and more about reality around them through the exercise of their reason and curiosity. Let's explore the former point first. We have argued previously that

> while the Bible provides the most important and ultimate answers as well as the starting points for knowledge of the human condition, it is not an all-sufficient guide for the discipline of counseling. The Bible is inspired and precious, but it is also a revelation of limited scope, the main concern of which is religious in its presentation of God's redemptive plan for his people and the great doctrines of the faith. The Bible doesn't claim to reveal everything which human beings might want to know. (Jones & Butman, 1991, p. 27)

Christians believe that we find revealed in the Bible everything necessary to a full life in Christ, because the Scriptures direct us truthfully to him who is the source of all goodness and mercy: "His divine power has granted to us all things that pertain to life and godliness, through the knowledge of him who called us to his own glory and excellence" (2 Pet 1:3). But this does not mean that everything we want to know can be found in the Bible, including everything we want to know about child development, human personality, schizophrenia or depression (Jones, 2001).

Further, we need to be realistic about the precision with which we can claim to know precisely what the Scriptures are teaching us about human nature. Two quick examples:

1. The scriptural teaching that human beings are made in the image of

God (the *imago Dei*) is utterly foundational to a Christian understanding of persons. But there is ambiguity about what this doctrine means. Students will encounter individual writers who state with confidence the precise meaning of this truth, but historical study reveals variation in possible meanings. A number of authors (e.g., Beck & Demarest, 2005) have classified the different answers in three basic categories: substantive, functional and relational. The substantive understandings of the *imago Dei* focus on what we *are;* they say that humans are made in God's image in that they are made of or possess a substance (such as spirit) or a capacity (such as reason) that is distinct from the rest of the created order. The functional understandings of the *imago Dei* focus on what we *do;* they say that humans are made in God's image in that we relate to the rest of the created order in a way that represents or reflects God, such as God's command to humanity to exercise "dominion" over creation as God's stewards and representatives (Gen 1:28). The relational understandings of the *imago Dei* focus on our *unique relationship to God:* "to be in the image of God is to be related to God in the way that other creatures are not, and so related to the other creatures differently from the way in which they are related to one another" (Gunton, 2002, p. 42). These are not mutually exclusive options; they may all be true. But our point is that even for this most central of doctrines about what it means to be a human being, ambiguity remains about the exact meaning of this key concept.

2. Similarly, Scripture presents us with some challenges in understanding the basic constituent elements of human nature, the substance(s) of which we are made. The basic options boil down to three: monism, dichotism and trichotism (see Beck & Demarest, 2005, pp. 119-41). Monists believe that humans are made of one substance, with some believing we are exclusively physical beings and others some form of spirit. Dichotomists believe we are composed of two substances—our physical bodies and some type of nonphysical soul/spirit. Trichotomists believe, on the basis of such Scriptures as 1 Thessalonians 5:23 that speak of our "spirit, soul and body," that soul and spirit are different substances, distinct from the physical and from each other, so we are rightly understood to be composed of three substances. There are good arguments, grounded in Scripture and in human rationality, for each of the positions, and no one answer has dominated in church history. When we add in other passages that speak of four

elements (heart, soul, mind, strength in Mark 12:30) or note the flexibility with which Scripture often speaks about psychological phenomena (invoking psychological functions of the heart, bowels, kidneys and so forth; see, e.g., Genesis 43:30 KJV), we are driven to be cautious in advancing dogmatic, scientifically precise formulations of biblical teachings about our constituent elements.

It is for this basic reason that, while I believe that every Christian psychologist should strive to have their work reflect the distinctives of Christian views of the person, I am neither an advocate of "Christian psychology" nor of "biblical counseling" as formulated, respectively, by my friends Robert Roberts and David Powlison. However hard it is to close in on the true meaning of what it means (for instance) to be made in the image of God, I do affirm that this teaching is foundational to a Christian understanding of persons. While there may be some latitude in understanding what this means, this belief has profound implications for how we approach the study of persons. But in the same way that different denominations hold differing, distinct emphases and understandings on a number of different matters while agreeing on fundamentals, so also I think there is room for well-meaning Christians to disagree on the application of biblical teaching to psychological study. This will result in an entire family of approaches reflecting different understandings of what Scripture teaches about humanity (Jones, 1996), and it leaves wide room for the utility of the discipline of psychology to enlarge and challenge our understandings about human experience.

It is relevant to mention the positive role Christian belief has played in the development and advancement of science itself. Brooke (1991) argues that Christianity facilitated the rise of modern science by providing presuppositions supportive of science (such as belief in the uniformity, rationality and contingency of nature), and by providing personal motives for scientists—such as improving the world to bring glory to God or helping to provide rational evidence for God's existence. Far from answering all our questions for us and smothering the intellectual quest, Christian belief supports the quest for truth, and provides foundational truths about the nature of humanity that can undergird and direct inquiry fruitfully but in a way that does not decisively answer every question we have. Even as we seek to be profoundly and deeply Christian in the understandings we bring to the field, we can look hopefully to science to expand those understandings further.

Defining science. How we understand "science" is just as critical to a proper understanding of the integrative task as is our definition and understanding of "Christian faith." If science is the purely objective enterprise Gould (1999) depicted ("Science tries to document the factual character of the natural world, and to develop theories that coordinate and explain these facts" [p. 4]), we might have a hard time seeing how Christian faith can "integrate" with it. I have previously (Jones, 1994) summarized a positivistic conception of science as one that (1) construes science as grounded in brute facts that present themselves to the scientist uninterpreted and fixed in meaning; (2) scientific hypotheses and theories are derived from these facts by strictly logical processes of induction or deduction; (3) hypotheses and theories are retained based on confirmatory evidence or rejected through falsification from experimental tests; and (4) science progresses by the gradual accumulation of facts and confirmed theories.

This is the way many view science, but this is not how science really operates; contemporary scholarship paints a considerably more complex picture of science as a human enterprise. Four key points in defining science have emerged from contemporary reflection on the nature of science (Jones, 1994):

- *All data are theory-laden.* "Facts" are not quite as simple as they seem. Even a rat's lever-press in a Skinner box means nothing until we join the brute fact that the rat's paw pressed the lever *with* the concepts of operant behavior, reinforcement and so forth, and so suddenly we see the *fact* that reinforcement increases the frequency of operant behavior. We always see or interpret facts in science through the grid of some orienting theory or conceptual scheme.

- *Scientific theories are underdetermined by facts.* (a) Theories never leap full-formed from the data, but involve the creativity and imagination of the scientist. (b) It is always the case that more than one theory can explain the facts before us; facts never arrange themselves into theories. (c) Theories can never actually be proven to be true. Evidence amasses in favor of a theory, or theories are challenged by contradictory findings that seem to disprove them, but in the end scientific theories advance or

fall based on human judgments by scientists about their veracity, and
not on the basis of mechanical score-keeping.

- *Science itself is a cultural and human phenomenon.* Studies in the history,
  sociology and philosophy of science show that science often reflects prevailing cultural ideas and values in ways that suggest that science is not
  the utterly objective undertaking some maintain. Reflect, for example,
  on the reality that Freud's psychoanalytic psychology of a century ago
  utilized as a metaphor the cutting-edge technology of the day (hydrau-
  lics), cognitive science from the 1970s similarly reflected current technology (the computer), and contemporary narrative approaches to personality reflect the postmodern preoccupation with texts and stories.

- *Science progresses not through the accumulation of bare facts, but through
  refinement of theories and theory-laden facts, which are themselves embedded in broader conceptual webs.* The nursery-story version of scientific
  progress pictures science advancing as facts are collected. Indeed, the
  accumulation of new knowledge is critical, but science only advances
  through the complex relationship of facts, theories and efforts to evaluate all of that.

The picture that emerges is that science draws not just on facts but on
the entire complex array of human experience. Indeed, science is the study
of the natural world (including humans), and science is a unique human
endeavor that proposes theories and seeks to evaluate the evidence for and
against them in a way that is challenging, self-critical, progressive and
objective. Even so, all kinds of philosophical and theological beliefs frame
our engagement with science, especially in the human sciences, as was
discussed in an important article series (Nelson & Slife, 2006). Our methods and the ways we construe our subject matter are shaped by our metaphysical and epistemological assumptions. It is this reality that offers us
the chance to be *Christian* scientists—Christians who allow (even insist)
that our fundamental convictions as believers shape our work as scientists,
even as we maintain a scientific commitment to strict accountability to
empirical evidence.

Browning and Cooper (2004) have argued rightly that psychological
science (particularly applied to humans and particularly with the clinical
psychologies) "cannot avoid a metaphysical and ethical horizon" (p. xiv).

Every meaningful research question in psychological science presumes some understanding of what we are (metaphysics) and how we should be (ethics). Just think of psychological concepts we so often presume to be objective and scientific, such as adaptive and maladaptive, mature and immature, functional and dysfunctional, competent and incompetent, and so forth. To label any behavior as "adaptive" is to say it works; to say it works is to answer "to what end or purpose?" and to value certain outcomes over others, which is an ethical judgment.

To get beyond the most primitive description of raw behavior ("the child moved his arm and hand against the face of the other child with force sufficient to move the other's head three inches") and begin to study something meaningful, we must utilize metaphysically and ethically loaded concepts ("the child engaged in an act of *aggression*"). The various ways psychologists conceptualize human behavior are rarely neutral, and often Christian faith that is thoughtfully and richly developed has something to say about how we understand human behavior. It is in developing and applying such Christian conceptions that we are doing integration.

Science ultimately is a public enterprise; it is about proposing hypotheses and theories, testing those hypotheses and theories against the "facts" of the world, and revising or rejecting our hypotheses and theories in favor of improved ones. Science, at its best, is indeed progressive: we are able to rule some ideas out (or adjust them) because they do not accord with the facts, and thus contribute to a progressively improving body of knowledge about the natural world. Christians should be in the thick of psychology, contributing their ideas, submitting their hypotheses and theories to the test.

WHAT DOES INTEGRATION LOOK LIKE?

Earlier, I offered a working definition of *integration:* Integrating Christianity and psychology is living out of the lordship of Christ over all of existence by giving his special revelation—God's true Word—its appropriate place of authority in determining our fundamental beliefs about and practices toward all of reality, and toward our academic subject matter in particular. I trust that, like my friends Robert Roberts and David Powlison, I demonstrate a passionate resolve to be firmly and thoroughly biblical in my understanding of persons, and further believe, like Roberts and Powlison, that such a grounding will affect the way I do psychological science.

This understanding of integration does not require one to be in tension with all aspects of secular psychology. There are many topics to which Scripture does not speak—how neurons work, how the brain synthesizes mathematical or emotional information, the types of memory, or the best way to conceptualize personality traits. There are also many areas of psychological study where the most basic construals that nonbelieving scientists make about their subject matter are roughly in accord with how Christians might view the same subject, and so there is generous overlap in the basic understandings that all bring to the subject. There are many areas of psychology where Christians can explore and celebrate the fascinating fruits of psychological exploration and encounter no apparent tension between Christian and "secular" belief. I share in my friend David Myers's enthusiasm for the fruits of psychological science that can inform and challenge my understandings of persons.

There are no concrete steps to integrating Christian thought and scientific exploration, but to try to give a clearer picture, here are several elements that I consider as marking an integrative approach:

- We begin here, as in all of life, by anchoring ourselves in biblical truth, rigorously and self-critically pursued. We should be students of the Bible and of theology. We should seek to be clear about our fundamental loyalty. We should embody a complex stance of confidence in biblical truth with humility that can help to ensure that we are not pressing God's Word to say things that it does not say.

- We must be methodologically rigorous in the conduct of our science and in our rational argumentation. There is a lot of good science out there; there is also a lot of sloppy or incomplete science. Christians should be committed to the highest scientific standards possible in their work. Know the tools of scientific inquiry.

- We should pay attention to the tension between what we seem to be learning from our psychology and what we derive from our Christian faith. Such tension may be illusory, the result of poor science and sloppy reasoning, or it may be the result of sloppy biblical analysis and theological reasoning on our parts. But that tension also may be substantive and call on us to stand for biblical truth because the secular field of psychology is not looking at its subject matter properly.

- We should seek to conduct our science and profession of psychology in a way shaped first and most foundationally by our Christian convictions.

- We should be tentative, patient and humble. Humanity has been striving toward improved understanding since it was created.

Integration is a recursive process of expanding understanding, but always with our most fundamental loyalty being to the true teachings of the special revelation of the Bible. Integration is ultimately the task of the Christian person whom God has led to be a student or scholar of some facet of psychology, with the true teachings of special revelation as the guiding framework for how that person structures his or her deepest beliefs and loyalties. Hathaway (2004, 2005) has expounded a similar understanding of the integrative undertaking under the concept of integration as "faithful understanding."

There are a number of tangible examples of credible integrative work. In contrast to my days as a student, when religion was neglected by psychologists, today we have had an explosion of discussion about the vital role of faith, spirituality and spiritual development in human life. Rich resources are now available that present reflections on the role of religion and spirituality in human life. Christians readers must note, though, that the conceptions of religion in such volumes often do not reflect orthodox Christian faith. In a book addressing Judeo-Christian themes in psychology, Miller and Delany (2005), for example, present an extremely diverse group of scholars in terms of religious and theological tradition, all reflecting on spirituality in psychology.

Another example of the influence of integrative scholarship is the explosion of interest in, research into and application of the topic of forgiveness. Forgiveness was hardly on the map in mainstream psychology through much of the twentieth century. Thanks, in part, to Christian scholars who understood forgiveness as central to understanding our relationships to others and to God, researchers have begun to reflect on how this neglected dynamic of human relationships might be studied and facilitated. One of the most important pioneers in this field of forgiveness studies has been Everett Worthington (e.g., 1998, 2001, 2005), a Christian scholar whose personal vision for the study of forgiveness in human development and relationships has helped to spark an outpouring of reflection on forgiveness across an array of Christian (e.g., Shults & Sandage, 2003) and other religious and nonreligious perspectives (e.g., McCullough, Pargament & Thorsen, 2000).

I close with discussion of my own efforts in two integrative areas; I beg the reader to excuse my self-reference in this discussion, but since it is my own work I know best, it is here that I focus.

ENGAGING PSYCHOTHERAPY THEORIES CRITICALLY AND CONSTRUCTIVELY

There have been many positive examples of Christian integrative reflection on the conduct of psychotherapy and counseling, including Collins (1988, 1993), McMinn (1996), and McMinn and Campbell (2007). In Jones and Butman (1991) we survey the major contemporary secular approaches to psychotherapy and appraise each from the perspective of Christian belief. Our goal is to assist the Christian counselor to ground her work in biblical truth, to appropriate the creative and helpful aspects of secular approaches to psychotherapy in a way consistent with biblical truth, and to approach the practice of psychotherapy in a way that has Christian integrity.

We systematically review the philosophical assumptions that shape each model of psychotherapy, the fundamental contours of the views of personality and personhood, of the views of health and abnormality for each approach, of the core ideas about how the psychotherapeutic intervention should be conducted, and finally, we examine the evidence for the effectiveness of each approach. Our assumptions are that each approach has legitimate insights into, and questions and challenges to pose to, the human condition, and that Christians can learn useful things from how each approach construes and engages the human situation.

But we assume also that a Christian understanding of persons will lead us to stand in some contrast to and tension with each approach. We urge an engagement with these approaches, where we first seek to understand accurately the approach, and then we critique it in order to understand what we must reject from or revise of it because of our beliefs but also seeking to understand what we may embrace and learn from it. For instance, a Christian will applaud the raw effectiveness of behavioral interventions with pervasive developmental disorders of childhood (e.g., autism) and thus be compelled to use such approaches, but a Christian must question, challenge and modify the broader conception of persons in which the approach is embedded because of its atomistic, reductionistic and deterministic understanding of persons. Studying such approaches can help us understand how basic learning processes are foundational and how to incorporate such understandings without contradicting our Christian commitments.

We also discuss the reality that the practice of psychotherapy is never completely determined by the explicit dimensions of the psychotherapy theories. Psychotherapists have complex human relationships with their clients, and the concerns presented by those clients often push the practitioner beyond the limits of what their "theory" can tell them. "Given that research supplies only a small fraction of the information needed to completely understand the psychotherapeutic process, we are often compelled to rely on our tacit, background metaphysical notions" (O'Donohue, 1989, p. 1467). Browning and Cooper (2004) argue that approaches to psychotherapy necessarily go far beyond the limits of what could be called scientific theory in order to answer questions that must be framed in the context of ultimate meaning. Any system of thought or practice that is used as a guide to shape, heal or reform human life cannot avoid reliance on an extensive set of ethical and metaphysical commitments, and so they argue that psychotherapy approaches are forms of religious thinking because "they attempt to answer our insecurities, give us generalized images of the world, and form the attitudes we should take toward the value of life, the nature of death, and the grounds for morality" (2004, pp. 108-9). We always do much more in psychotherapy than what is dictated by our theories.

An integrationist, then, argues that our fundamental loyalty as Christians is to the Lord Jesus Christ, and so we ought to frame our broader understandings of the client in terms of the Christian understanding of our nature, purpose and calling. Evans (2005) argues correctly that a Christian cannot be limited only to what psychology can provide for understanding as she approaches her relationship to her client, as there is incredible wisdom in Scripture and an enormous Christian tradition of helping people, which are available to inform and shape her understanding (something the Christian psychology approach rightly emphasizes). A Christian integrationist's approach to psychotherapy will be shaped profoundly by his or her Christian convictions, but will also be shaped by a critical but appreciative appropriation of the wisdom of secular approaches. In the end, clinical integrationists will use secular conceptions and methods selectively and cautiously, striving all the while to reflect first the character of Christ and their grounding in a profoundly Christian view of persons. They will not all look the same. Subtle differences of emphasis on different parts of the biblical witness will lead to different theoretical alignments; there are Christian integrationists who are psychodynamic, cognitive-behavioral, systems and other orientations.

SEXUALITY AND HOMOSEXUALITY

The second example I present here is one of working through and with the tension created when scientific findings are applied to argue that the church's historic sexual ethic is wrong or outmoded. Many today argue that we cannot maintain our historic ethical stance in light of the new knowledge being contributed by science about sexuality in general and sexual orientation in particular. Those who believe science and religion address independent magisteria would simply deny any possibility of overlap here; those who believe the Bible tells us everything we need to know about human life might simply dismiss all of science as having anything useful to tell us about sexual orientation. As an integrationist, I approach this complex topic believing that the Bible and Christian tradition are normative and foundational for my understanding of human sexuality, but also that science can provide much useful information about human sexuality.

The Christian Scriptures present a positive and cohesive portrait of our sexuality (see Jones & Hostler, 2005): (1) Our physical bodies are good. God made us as physical beings. We do not just *have* bodies, we *are* bodies, though we are *more* than just bodies. (2) God made us sexual beings, male and female, and our sexuality is good. Genesis 1–2 depicts God creating two types of human beings, male and female, both made in the image of God and both declared to be very good. (3) We are made for relationship; in Genesis 2:15-24 we learn that even the perfect man is insufficient by himself, even in the perfect environment and in perfect relationship with God himself. God declares that it is not good that the man be alone; human beings are made for relationship with a complementary version of human being, a man for a woman and a woman for a man. (4) Humans are created capable of "becoming one flesh" through the joining of their bodies, and the resulting capacity for reproduction in marriage is blessed by God and a blessing from God. (5) Humanity rebelled against God, and in the process broke God's beautiful gift of sexuality, along with all of his other gifts to us. As a result, we are rebellious, broken, twisted. (6) God is at work redeeming our sexuality in two crucial ways: God has revealed his standards or rules for how we are to conduct our sexual lives (and his laws are for our own good; Deut 10:12-13). God has also offered us a living relationship with him through the death and resurrection of his Son, Jesus Christ, so that we are actually capable of living our lives in a way that gives him pleasure and moves us toward the blessedness he intended for us. (7) The Scriptures reveal to us that sexual intercourse has a meaning fixed and determined by God: it creates a one-flesh union between a man and a woman, a union that is to knit them together in a way that's supposed to remain permanent through life (and thus this teaching is the foundation for Jesus' condemnation of divorce in Matthew 19 and Paul's condemnation of sexual immorality in 1 Corinthians 6).

Scientific investigation of human sexuality has tremendous potential to enrich human understanding. Sadly, though, the supposed scientific findings about sexuality—particularly about sexual orientation and homosexuality—are often misunderstood or misapplied to the theological and moral issues facing the Christian church. Despite reading the scientific literature for over three decades, I have found little that confounds or refutes the traditional Christian sexual ethic. Most crucially, it is commonly believed today that science has somehow discredited the traditional Christian teaching that homosexual conduct is immoral. The research on the causation of homosexual orientation is at the center of this debate. Many well-meaning people reason something like this: "The Bible condemns homosexuality, but science has proven that homosexuality is genetic. Something that is genetic is not voluntary, and if it's not voluntary it can't be a sin. Therefore the Bible and the traditional Christian sexual ethic are simply wrong."

This argument is wrong logically and it's wrong scientifically. It is wrong logically because the Bible does not condemn "homosexuality" but condemns homosexual acts. Those acts are voluntary (unless homosexual persons are deterministic robots driven uncontrollably by their impulses, which they are not). In any case, Christian theology has never made "voluntariness" a condition of sin; all of us are sinful and prone to sin as part of our basic condition and natures. We cannot choose otherwise; we cannot choose not to be sinful (Hays, 1996, makes this point in his chapter on homosexuality in a book on New Testament ethics). The research may suggest or even prove that individuals develop certain desires or proclivities outside of their conscious choice, but the focus of Christian morality is on how we act in response to God's moral law.

This argument is also wrong scientifically. The public believes homosexual orientation is genetic, but is it? Many studies have claimed to validate this conclusion, but we have reviewed this evidence and shown that the actual results are much more inconclusive than many imagine (Jones & Yarhouse, 2000; Jones & Kwee, 2005). Let us focus, for example, on the behavioral genetics study by Bailey and Pillard (1991), the single study that seemed to do the most to establish the broad belief that homosexual orientation is genetically determined.

The basic logic of behavioral genetics is that if a behavioral or psychological pattern is influenced by genetics, then individuals who are more genetically similar should also be more similar behaviorally/psychologically than are individuals who are less similar genetically. To gauge the impact of genetics on sexual orientation, Bailey and Pillard gathered a sample of gays and their siblings, and they looked at the degree of concordance (or matching of sexual orientation) according to different degrees of genetic similarity. They found for male homosexuals a higher (52 percent) concordance between identical twins (who share 100 percent of their genes) than between fraternal twins, regular brothers and adopted siblings. This is roughly the pattern that you would find if there is a genetic component to homosexuality: the more genetic similarity, the more orientation similarity. This study received enormous publicity when it was published and, ever since, has contributed strongly to the public perception that homosexuality is genetic.

However, there were multiple problems with this study (discussed in Jones & Yarhouse, 2000), but the major flaw was their sampling methodology. To generate a valid estimate of genetic influence in a population, you must have a truly representative sample of that population, but their samples were gathered in a way likely to result in volunteer bias. Bailey realized this might be a problem, and did a study (Bailey, Dunne & Martin, 2000) that corrected this problem by obtaining a more representative sample through the Australian twin registry. The result? The original finding was erased. Their core finding was that of twenty-seven identical twin pairs where one twin was gay, in only three cases (about 10 percent of the pairs) was the other twin also homosexual. Probandwise concordance for identical twins thus dropped to only 20 percent. Bailey et al. (2000) were precise about the implications of this new research, commenting that this study "did not provide statistically significant support for the importance of genetic factors" (p. 534) for homosexual orientation. A brand new study (Långström et al., 2008), with the largest and most representative sample ever gathered, examined this question and has produced results almost identical to Bailey's (2000) later study: of seventy-one male, identical twin pairs where one twin was gay, in only seven of the seventy-one pairs was the second identical twin also gay. It is important to note that, whereas the original findings from 1991 received enormous media attention, the new findings refuting the earlier findings have been largely ignored by the media, as well as by textbooks and scholarly discussions about this topic.

These results are typical of the research findings for biological causation of homosexuality in general. Those results suggest a modest role at most for biological causation of homosexual orientation. To be clear: science does *not* disprove that genetics, prenatal hormones, brain structure or any of a number of other biological factors have something to do with sexual orientation. Our biology, including our genes, likely *does* influence our sexual orientation, but this is only one among a set of factors. There is also research, ignored by many, suggesting that family and experience are powerful influences on the development of same-sex attraction (Jones & Kwee, 2005).

Similar to faulty discussions about causation, faulty discussions about possibilities for change of the homosexual condition are often presented as if they refute the traditional, Christian sexual ethic. Science has proven that change is impossible, it is argued, and therefore the Christian sexual ethic is invalid and cruel. Again, this argument is wrong both logically and empirically. Logically, the Christian sexual ethic claims that Scripture teaches it is immoral to engage in homosexual intercourse (1 Cor 6:9-10) and that some who once engaged in such behavior were freed from their bondage to that sinful pattern (1 Cor 6:11). The passage is unclear whether these were homosexually oriented persons who became heterosexuals or who became celibate. In either case, the change allowed them to live lives pleasing to God and evidencing his transforming grace. The change required by God is that of eschewing sexually immoral conduct.

But what about scientific evidence regarding the possibility of sexual-orientation change? First, it is often argued that science has proven sexual-orientation change is impossible, but this is an empty assertion because it is impossible to conceive of a definitive study that could ever prove that change is impossible. Any number of anecdotes or studies showing that change did not happen for one or several persons can never add up to *proving* change is *impossible;* as a logical parallel, centuries of anecdotal and even scientific evidence that human heart transplant was impossible did not, in the end, mean that it was actually impossible.

Second, considerable scientific evidence exists that sexual-orientation change sometimes occurs. Jones and Yarhouse (2007) summarize scattered scientific studies over decades, reporting that change occurs for some through psychotherapy and through religious interventions. Criticisms that these studies were inconclusive or methodologically inferior mean that such claims must be interpreted cautiously, *not* that change is impossible. New studies manifesting improved rigor suggest that change in orientation sometimes does occur: A new and respected study following a group of female nonheterosexuals over a decade found dramatic changes in some, including lesbians becoming heterosexual (Diamond, 2007). Our own longitudinal study (Jones & Yarhouse, 2007, 2009) of ninety-eight homosexuals seeking change in sexual orientation through involvement in a group of Exodus International Christian ministries found that three years after beginning the change process, roughly one-third of the remaining sample either reported successful change by becoming heterosexual (15 percent) or by becoming chaste (23 percent). The findings of the outcomes at six years were even slightly more positive: of sixty-one cases still in the study at the six-year mark, 53 percent reported some version of success, either having experienced what they regarded as a full conversion to heterosexuality (23 percent) or as a successful adjustment to chastity (30 percent). Our study does not give us grounds to draw firm conclusions on how often change may be possible through involvement with Exodus ministries, but it does, we argue, suggest that meaningful change of sexual orientation is possible for *some*.

What does this all mean in terms of ethics? We all inherit inclinations that reflect our brokenness and sinfulness. The core ethical question is not "Why do I want to do the things that I want to do?" The core ethical question is "Should I do the things that I want to do? How should I behave given the claim that God has on my life?" God has given us our sexuality as a gift and has given us his rules for our good. Modern science has produced nothing that seriously challenges that ethic. Anyone who is a follower of Jesus must count it as a blessing, though a challenging blessing, to live by this ethic. Our Lord said, in John 14:15, "If you love me, you will keep my commandments."

Our commitment to integration should lead us to form our understanding of sexuality around the biblical witness. The tension we experience when science is cited as contradicting biblical teachings then leads us to approach the scientific evidence not dismissively, but with a respectful commitment to the highest empirical standards. We seek to clarify why the tension exists, and in this brief example, we have seen that it is misinterpreting incomplete results that has created that tension. We have not explored here other aspects of integrative engagement with sexuality. Our Christian convictions, for example, lead us necessarily to view homosexual conduct, and hence the desires that give rise to such conduct, as distortions of God's will and of our intended human natures. The work of Yarhouse and Tan (2004) exemplifies how careful reflection on a biblical understanding of sexuality can yield new understandings of orientation and identity that hold promise for future scientific and clinical exploration.

CONCLUSION

Integration means approaching the discipline and profession of psychology with a commitment to having one's Christian convictions shape every aspect of one's work. Because Scripture and the accumulated wisdom of the church in theology leave many areas of uncertainty in understanding and helping humanity, we approach psychology expecting that we can learn and grow through our engagement with it. Because all psychology is infused and shaped by metaphysical and moral presuppositions, we also expect that we may need to modify and reshape what we learn from psychology in light of our Christian beliefs. Because integrationists differ among themselves in their reading of Scripture and the Christian tradition, and in their reactions toward different psychological systems, the work of integrationists will manifest diversity, though all of us are attempting to be faithful first to Christian truth.

REFERENCES

Adams, J. E. (1970). *Competent to counsel.* Grand Rapids, MI: Baker.

Bailey, J. M., Dunne, M. P., & Martin, N. G. (2000). Genetic and environmental influences on sexual orientation and its correlates in an Australian twin sample. *Journal of Personality and Social Psychology, 78*(3), 524-36.

Bailey, J. M., & Pillard, R. C. (1991). A genetic study of male sexual orientation. *Archives of General Psychiatry, 48,* 1081-96.

Beck J. R., & Demarest, B. (2005). *The human person in theology and psychology: A biblical anthropology for the twenty-first century.* Grand Rapids, MI: Kregel.

Brooke, J. H. (1991). *Science and religion: Some historical perspectives.* Cambridge: Cambridge University Press.

Browning, D. S., & Cooper, T. D. (2004). *Religious thought and the modern psychologies* (2nd ed.). Minneapolis: Fortress.

Carter, J. D., & Narramore, B. (1979). *The integration of psychology and theology: An introduction.* Grand Rapids, MI: Zondervan.

Collins, G. R. (1977). *The rebuilding of psychology.* Wheaton, IL: Tyndale House.

———. (1981). *Psychology and theology: Prospects for integration.* Nashville: Abingdon.

———. (1988). *Christian counseling: A comprehensive guide* (Rev. ed.). Dallas: Word.

———. (1993). *The biblical basis of Christian counseling for people helpers.* Colorado Springs: NavPress.

Diamond, L. (2007). A dynamical systems approach to the development and expression of female same-sex sexuality. *Perspectives on Psychological Science, 2*(2), 142-61.

Evans, C. S. (1982). *Preserving the person: A look at the human sciences.* Grand Rapids, MI: Baker. (Original work published 1977)

———. (1989). *Wisdom and humanness in psychology: Prospects for a Christian approach.* Grand Rapids, MI: Baker.

———. (2005). Integration and Christian psychology: Rivals or friends? *Edification: Newsletter of the Society for Christian Psychology, 1*(2), 3-5.

Gould, S. J. (1999). *Rocks of ages: Science and religion in the fullness of life.* New York: Ballantine.

Gunton, C. E. (2002). *The Christian faith: An introduction to Christian doctrine.* Malden, MA: Blackwell.

Hathaway, W. L. (2004). Expanding horizons for Christians in psychology. *Journal of Psychology and Theology, 32*(3), 210-20.

———. (2005). Scripture and psychological science: Integrative challenges and callings. *Journal of Psychology and Theology, 33*(2), 89-97.

Hays, R. (1996). *The moral vision of the New Testament.* San Francisco: HarperCollins.

Jones, S. (1994). A constructive relationship for religion with the science and profession of psychology: Perhaps the boldest model yet. *American Psychologist, 49*(3), 184-99.

———. (1996). Reflections on the nature and future of the Christian psychologies. *Journal of Psychology and Christianity, 15*(2), 133-42.

———. (2000). Religion and psychology: Theories and methods. In A. Kazdin (Ed.), *Encyclopedia of psychology* (Vol. 7, pp. 38-42). Washington, DC: American Psychological Association; New York: Oxford University Press.

———. (2001). An apologetic *apologia* for the integration of psychology and theology. In T. R. Phillips & M. R. McMinn (Eds.), *The care of the soul: Exploring the intersection of psychology and theology* (pp. 62-77). Downers Grove, IL: InterVarsity Press.

Jones, S., & Butman, R. (1991). *Modern psychotherapies: A comprehensive Christian appraisal.* Downers Grove, IL: InterVarsity Press.

Jones, S., & Hostler, H. (2005). The role of sexuality in personhood: An integrative exploration. In W. R. Miller & H. D. Delaney (Eds.), *Human nature, motivation, and change: Judeo-Christian perspectives on psychology* (pp. 115-32). Washington, DC: American Psychological Association.

Jones, S., & Kwee, A. W. (2005). Scientific research, homosexuality, and the church's moral debate: An update. *Journal of Psychology and Christianity, 24*(4), 304-16.

Jones, S., & Yarhouse, M. (2000). *Homosexuality: The use of scientific research in the church's moral debate.* Downers Grove, IL: InterVarsity Press.

———. (2007). *Ex-gays? A longitudinal study of religiously mediated change in sexual orientation.* Downers Grove, IL: InterVarsity Press.

———. (2009). "Ex-gays? An extended longitudinal study of attempted religiously mediated change in sexual orientation." Paper presented for the symposium "Sexual orientation and faith tradition—A test of the Leona Tyler principle" (A. Dean Byrd, chair) at the American Psychological Association Convention, Toronto, Canada.

Långström, N., Rahman, Q., Carlström, E., & Lichtenstein, P. (2008, June 7). Genetic and environmental effects on same-sex sexual behavior: A population study of twins in Sweden. *Archives of Sexual Behavior,* e-publication, PMID: 18536986.

McCullough, M. E., Pargament, K. I., & Thorsen, C. E. (Eds.) (2000). *Forgiveness: Theory, research, and practice.* New York: Guilford.

McMinn, M. R. (1996). *Psychology, theology, and spirituality in Christian counseling.* Wheaton, IL: Tyndale House.

McMinn, M. R., & Campbell, C. D. (2007). *Integrative psychotherapy: Toward a comprehensive Christian approach.* Downers Grove, IL: IVP Academic.

Miller, W. R., & Delaney, H. D. (Eds.). (2005). *Human nature, motivation, and change: Judeo-Christian perspectives on psychology.* Washington, DC: American Psychological Association.

National Academy of Sciences. (1984). *Science and creationism: A view from the National Academy of Sciences.* Washington, DC: Author.

Nelson, J. M., & Slife, B. D. (Eds). (2006). Special issue: Philosophical issues in psychology and religion. *Journal of Psychology and Theology, 34*(3), 191-291.

O'Donohue, W. (1989). The (even) bolder model: The clinical psychologist as metaphysician-scientist-practitioner. *American Psychologist, 44*, 1460-68.

Shults, F. L., & Sandage, S. J. (2003). *The faces of forgiveness: Searching for wholeness and salvation.* Grand Rapids, MI: Baker Academic.

Stevenson, D. H., Eck, B. E., & Hill, P. C. (Eds.). (2007). *Psychology & Christianity integration: Seminal works that shaped the movement.* Batavia, IL: Christian Association for Psychological Studies, Inc.

Van Leeuwen, M. (1985). *The person in psychology.* Grand Rapids, MI: Eerdmans.

Worthington, E. L., Jr. (Ed.) (1998). *Dimensions of forgiveness: psychological research and theological perspectives.* Philadelphia: Templeton Foundation.

———. (2001). *Five Steps to Forgiveness: The Art and Science of Forgiving.* Grand Rapids, MI: Crown.

———. (Ed.). (2005). *Handbook of forgiveness.* New York: Brunner-Routledge.

Yarhouse, M. A., & Tan, E. S. N. (2004). *Sexual identity synthesis: Attributions, meaning-making, and the search for congruence.* Lanham, MD: University Press of America.

A Levels-of-Explanation Response to Integration

David G. Myers

I HAVE A LONG-STANDING RESPECT FOR Stanton Jones's brilliance and grace, and so am not surprised to find myself admiring his chapter for this volume. Among the chapters in this volume, I also find myself most attuned to its perspective, which engages rather than dismisses the psychological science world of today's colleges and universities.

Jones begins by assuming that both psychology and Christianity cannot escape being shaped by their answers to ultimate questions such as "Where *do* we come from? What *are* we? Where *are* we going?" (p. 101). God has given us answers, albeit fragmentary answers, to such questions, says Jones. Although science can help complete the answers, the integration of Christianity and psychology will give *"special revelation—God's true Word—its appropriate place of authority"* (p. 102).

If "all truth is one," says Jones, then the Christian scholar can feel called to work at the task of seamlessly integrating special (biblical) and general (natural) revelations, while respecting each. This task differs from the idea, embodied in this volume's other chapters, that psychological science should be dismissed and overwritten by one's Christian presumptions.

Although Jones rejects the complete separation of science and religion (as proposed by Stephen Jay Gould and the National Academy of Sciences), he also rejects, as do I, "definitions of either science or of Christianity that are [overly] expansive and broad" (p. 108). For both of us, science is an instrument of God's revelation. Its tools for exploring reality become another means by which we can worship God with our minds as well as our hearts. God "has created humans as rational beings capable of knowing more and more about reality around them through the exercise of their reason and curiosity" (p. 110). Not "everything we want to know about child development, human personality, schizophrenia or depression" is found in the Bible, Jones notes (p. 110). About "many topics"—"how neurons work, how the brain synthesizes mathematical or emotional information, the types of memory"—Scripture does not speak (p. 116). Thus

Jones and I agree in advocating neither "Christian psychology" (Roberts/ Watson) nor "biblical counseling" (Powlison).

What Stan Jones perhaps overstates is the extent to which scriptural truths are "as stable and enduring—or more so—than any empirical generalization" (p. 109). Scriptural teachings, such as that "we are both physical and spiritual/soulish beings . . . are all absolutely trustworthy truths about the human condition" (pp. 109-10).

But does that fail to appreciate the extent to which biblical interpretation is a human activity that has changed over time? Yesterday's absolute biblical truths about race and gender and sexual orientation, or about what it meant to be stewards of the creation, have all been revisited by more recent biblical scholarship. So have the dualistic Platonic (and unbiblical, say some) idea that humans possess undying disembodied souls (whose immortality is guaranteed with or without God).

Mindful of our human fallibility, even when interpreting Scripture, Jones advises and models "humility that can help to ensure that we are not pressing God's Word to say things that it does not say" (p. 116). This is good advice, because historically there are many examples of people cherry picking and interpreting the Bible in ways that make it say what they believe, thus self-justifying their own ideas.

Jones offers himself as a helpful model of "working through and with the tension created when scientific findings are applied" in ways that contradict the church's historic teachings—as in the example of tensions regarding sexual orientation (p. 120). He approaches this topic "believing that the Bible and Christian tradition are normative and foundational for my understanding of human sexuality, but also that science can provide much useful information about human sexuality" (p. 120).

So far, we have no argument. Our debate is joined at two levels: biblical and scientific. One concerns what norms the Bible actually would commend for those naturally disposed to feel an attraction to others of their own sex. Would it suggest that, for all people, love, sex and marriage should go together . . . or only for heterosexual people?

Here I would only note that serious biblical scholars, including some associated with evangelical traditions, are wrestling with differing understandings. On the conservative side, Robert Gagnon has written at length in support of Jones's perspective. On the more progressive side, former

Fuller faculty members Lewis Smedes and Jack Rogers, and Princeton Seminary theologian William Stacey Johnson, have offered a very different exegesis of the few pertinent biblical texts.

When Jones challenges the evidence that "homosexual orientation is genetic" (he finds the evidence inconclusive), my response, at one level, is to want to offer the rapidly expanding body of neuroscience and behavioral evidence that convincingly refutes the idea (especially for males) of "a modest role at most for biological causation" of sexual orientation. Moreover, his own well-intentioned study of participants in the Exodus ex-gay ministry program suffered a low rate of participation, many dropouts, likely reconstructed memories and, even so, only two dozen or so people in the entire nation who claimed (without confirming behavioral evidence) to have reversed their sexual orientation.

But this debate is for another time, and I raise our difference only to make my concluding observation: Stan Jones and I can have a spirited debate about these matters precisely because he and I (unlike the other contributors to this volume) are playing the same game. He alone takes a position on a specific issue, identifies pertinent scientific evidence to support his understanding and then connects it to his biblical understanding. That's the vocation to which I feel called. And that is why, our differences on this issue aside, I feel an underlying kinship with Jones as we both seek to engage and process insights from psychological science and integrate such with our respective Christian perspectives.

A Christian Psychology Response to Integration

Robert C. Roberts

DESPITE THE FACT THAT THE WORD *integration* stems from the Latin adjective *integer*, meaning "whole" or "entire," the concept of integration as deployed in Stan Jones's discussion is essentially a *dualistic* concept. Integration, for Jones, is apparently a process of "integrating" two very different things, two things not previously bound together; namely, psychology on the one hand and Christianity on the other. The single "whole" thing that results is presumably some modified form of modern psychology. Thus we might have a Christianized cognitive-behavioral psychology, a Christianized family therapy, a Christian reading of the data about homosexual orientation and behavior, a Christianized Rogerian psychotherapy, a Christianized Freudian personality theory, etc. The integrative model, then, starts with *two* things that are pretty strange to one another and makes *one* thing out of them, and that one thing would appear to be a standard sort of modern psychology from which the explicitly anti-Christian elements have been expunged.

By contrast, those who, like P. J. Watson and me, have advocated a Christian psychology *in contradistinction from an integrative model* have pointed out that Christianity and psychology are not necessarily two things in quite the way the integration model supposes. From its inception, Christianity has had views about what makes for a healthy soul and why people are so messed up, and has proposed actions that may help to put people back on the road to mental health. So psychology is not the special province of twentieth and twenty-first-century therapists and experimenters, but it has had many homegrown Christian variants throughout the history of the church. Furthermore, the church's views about psychology have flowed directly from what it believes about the nature of God and of human beings as God's creatures, as well as about God's saving work in Jesus Christ. These are not independent views about the psyche that need to be "integrated" into the church's faith and practice.

Christian psychology stresses the antecedent presence of psychological

truth and insight in the Christian tradition and in the Bible. Integrationists generally emphasize "control beliefs" but tend to think that modern
psychology provides the properly psychological insights and data. Integrationists tend to think that the Bible is a source or handbook of *theology*
while secular psychology provides the *psychology* to be integrated with that
theology. We think that division of labor is misguided.

However, Christian psychology as we understand it does not eschew
"integration" or the importance of scientific work in psychology. Since I
began advocating Christian psychology in the early 1990s, I have affirmed
both the possibility and the value of integrating into Christian psychological thought and practice some of the insights, techniques and research
procedures of establishment psychology (the kind of psychology that dominates the American Psychological Association and the psychology departments of the major universities of the world). (See Johnson and Jones,
2000, pp. 135-40; and Roberts, 1993, the first half of which is integration,
the latter half is Christian psychology.) We do not think that integration
is either impossible or necessarily a bad thing. But I have come to think it
is more difficult to do well, and more dangerous to do badly, than most of
its advocates suppose.

Using the results of meta-analyses of scientific studies of therapeutic
effectiveness, in combination with the widespread documentation of psychotherapy's deleterious effects on character (Vitz, 1977; Lasch, 1979;
MacIntyre, 1981; Bellah, 1985; Cushman, 1995), I have argued for a mor-
atorium on the integration of establishment techniques and explanatory
frameworks into Christian thought and practice until we Christians have
a firmer understanding and appreciation of the psychology of our own
tradition. Only such deep understanding can protect us from promoting
the narcissism, individualism, consumerism, egoism, emotivism, instru-
mentalism, victimism, irresponsibilism and atheism that the modern therapies tend to promote (for some details, see Roberts, 2001). But a morato-
rium is not a rejection. Here, in advocating Christian psychology as distinct
from integration, I am commending an *order of priorities*.

Furthermore, it should be evident from Watson's and my chapter in this
volume that we don't deny the importance of scientific work in psychology.
We do think, however, that scientific work *as it is practiced in the psychological establishment* is often methodologically flawed, and that psycholog-

ical science is virtually always affected by nonscientific metaphysical, normative or ideological presuppositions that may be more or less appropriate for Christian purposes. That is why we call not only for a retrieval of the Christian psychologies of the past but also for scientific investigation based in the metaphysics and ethics that are suitable for Christianity—that is, a Christian *science* of psychology (see, for example, my comments on the psychology of happiness in Johnson & Jones, 2000, pp. 88-95).

In the present volume, Jones defines integration as follows:

> Integration of Christianity and psychology (or any area of "secular thought") is our living out—in this particular area—of the lordship of Christ over all of existence by our giving his special revelation—God's true Word—its appropriate place of authority in determining our fundamental beliefs about and practices toward all of reality and toward our academic subject matter in particular. (p. 102)

It is interesting that, in this definition, all the authority seems to be on the side of Christianity. But, to warrant giving scientific and professional psychology such pride of place as to require *integrating* the two, we would want some account of the authority of scientific and professional psychology. In the eyes of laypeople, scientific and professional status lends tremendous prestige to establishment psychology. But it is arguable that the professional status of psychology derives from its scientific status, and its independent status as science is a holdover from its positivist past—the time in the early- to mid-twentieth century when psychologists thought their discipline was value-neutral and without metaphysical presuppositions (control beliefs) but just pure, observational truth. To the extent that Jones's own postmodern understanding of the science of psychology (which he shares, by the way, with Watson and me) prevails, the very independence of the science of psychology that the integration project presupposes is undermined. On the postmodern view there is no longer any such thing as *the* science of psychology (though many in the psychological establishment would like you to think so); instead there are multiple scientific psychologies: Christian scientific psychology, Darwinian scientific psychology, materialist scientific psychology, Buddhist scientific psychology, etc.

With a serious adoption of the postmodern, nonpositivist conception of science, the notion of integration undergoes a sea change: psychological science is no longer an independent discipline, handing down its own in-

tegral brand of truths to be somehow accommodated to a Christian outlook and practice. Instead, on the new model of science, the Christian
outlook and practice take up residence *inside* science and *coopt* it. The science—the psychology in this case—becomes Christian. In other words,
with the adoption of a postmodern view of science (Jones, 1994), the integration movement shifts decisively in the direction of Christian psychology. The shift is already present—though not complete—in the integrationists' notion of control beliefs.

Of course, the Christian's version of such psychological science will
bear some resemblance to, and to some extent be an heir of, some non-
Christian science, and will be to that extent also an "integration." Christian thought has always been heir to paganism. The apostle Paul interacts
with pagan philosophers, theologians and poets (see Acts 17), adopting
and adapting some of their language and thought. Augustine of Hippo
took over some ideas from Stoicism and Plato and used them in his mature
Christian thought about God, the world and the human psyche. The medieval church regarded the pagan Latin poet Virgil as an important source
of ideas. Thomas Aquinas formulated his theology and psychology in intense interaction with Aristotle, and the results bear some of the marks of
Aristotle. So a "Christian" psychology cannot mean a psychology influenced in *no way* by any non-Christian ideas. Does it not follow that all
Christian psychology is the result of integration?

In one sense, it does. But we must qualify this admission with three
points. First, the people whose "integrative" Christian thought has come
down to us as orthodox and excellent knew the Christian tradition extremely well and were conceptual geniuses, and thus were more discerning
interlocutors with pagan thought than most of us are. Most of us who try
to "integrate" Christianity and secular psychology are only modestly tal-
ented, and in most cases our primary training is in the secular models and
methods. What we know best is the establishment psychology. That is our
starting point for "integration." We are not well grounded in the biblical
psychology itself, nor have we been deeply trained in the traditional psychology of the church. At best, we have an amateur acquaintance with the
Bible and the Christian tradition. Second, what has come down to us has
been sifted by history: the false starts and bad jobs have fallen into historical oblivion. We do not have that advantage with respect to the false

starts and bad jobs of contemporary integrative psychology. And third, even the greatest of Christian thinkers made mistakes consequent on their dependence on paganism.

These, then, are the major differences between the orientations known as "the integration view" and "Christian psychology."

1. Christian psychology stresses the antecedent presence of psychologies in the Christian tradition prior to the twentieth century, and thus does not identify psychology with the scientific and professional psychology of the twentieth century.

2. Christian psychology insists on the priority of a deep knowledge of the psychology that is distinctive of Christianity as a prerequisite to the integration of modern professional and scientific psychologies into Christian thought and practice.

3. Christian psychology insists on a distinctively Christian science of psychology.

REFERENCES

Bellah, R. (1985). *Habits of the heart: Individualism and commitment in American life*. San Francisco: Harper & Row.

Cushman, P. (1995). *Constructing the self, constructing America: A cultural history of psychotherapy*. Upper Saddle River, NJ: Addison-Wesley.

Johnson, E., & Jones, S. (Eds.). (2000). *Psychology and Christianity: Four views*. Downers Grove, IL: InterVarsity Press.

Jones, S. (1994). A constructive relationship for religion with the science and profession of psychology: Perhaps the boldest model yet. *American Psychologist, 49*(3), 184-99.

Jones, S., & Butman, R. (1991). *Modern psychotherapies: A comprehensive Christian appraisal*. Downers Grove, IL: InterVarsity Press.

Lambert, M., & Bergin, A. (1994). The effectiveness of psychotherapy. In A. Bergin and S. Garfield (Eds.). *Handbook of psychotherapy and behavior change* (pp. 143-89). New York: Wiley.

Lasch, C. (1979). *The culture of narcissism: American life in an age of diminishing expectations*. New York: W. W. Norton.

MacIntyre, A. (1981). *After virtue*. South Bend, IN: Notre Dame University Press.

Roberts, R. (1993). *Taking the word to heart: Self and other in an age of therapies*. Grand Rapids, MI: Eerdmans.

———. (2000). A Christian psychology view. In E. Johnson and S. Jones (Eds.). *Psychology and Christianity: Four views*. Downers Grove, IL: InterVarsity Press.

———. (2001). "Psychotherapy and Christian Ministry." *Word and World, 21*, 42-50 <www.luthersem.edu/word&world/Archives/21-1_Therapy_Theology/21-1_Roberts.pdf>.

Vitz, P. (1977). *Psychology as religion: The cult of self-worship*. Grand Rapids, MI: Eerdmans.

A Transformational Psychology Response to Integration

John H. Coe and Todd W. Hall

STAN JONES IS ONE OF MANY INTEGRATIONISTS who has been thinking Christianly about psychology and science for years, and he has helped advance the discussion of how to better understand psychology and faith. When working as a Christian scientist, his basic intuitions serve his theorizing well, which is a sign of his own psychological integrity and health. However, his metareflections on methodology and science reveal the very heart of the conundrum of why and how integration itself is its own problem.

We will limit our discussion to the following three general responses to Jones's view of integration and its implied theoretical and methodological commitments.

1. We will discuss the startling but explainable fact that integration lacks a clear methodology.

2. Because of this lack of methodology, integrationists adopt an inadequate model for the science of the person, which produces an unwarranted bifurcation of fields of inquiry and an inability to scientifically ground the insights of various forms of psychotherapy.

3. We further suggest that there is a need to reclaim the nature of doing science in faith, which (a) captures the best of what integration has been doing all along and (b) makes integration unnecessary except as a second enterprise of dialogue with secular, naturalistic approaches.

METHODOLOGY

It is deeply revealing of integrationism's problems that it has no real methodology—other than what a thoughtful Christian would intuitively do when looking at psychology and faith. Jones readily admits, "there are no concrete steps to integrating Christian thought and scientific exploration" (p. 116). According to Jones, there are only "elements" that he considers as marking an integrative approach: being anchored in biblical truth that should shape one's work, being methodologically rigorous in doing science, being open to the tension between the two fields, and being humble and open to this process. These are good intuitions to have about doing psychology in faith—ones that our transformational model suggests are part of doing the *science* of psychology in the Spirit. However, the fact that there is no clear methodology to integration is the result of integrationists' accepting a problematic view of science.

WHAT COUNTS AS "SCIENCE"?

Integrationists have been hindered by failing to adequately criticize a wrong view of science, which excludes the study of faith, values and all that addresses the "spirit" of the person. This has, in turn, fostered the development of a nonscientific methodology called "integration" in order to bring these two fields together.

Since Descartes's time, there developed a long story in the history of science about why the study of the person has been so theoretically problematic, particularly for modern and contemporary psychology. The difficulty has to do with modern science's commitment to a universal method of quantification or measurement of bodies and their (efficient) causal relations to one another. The successes of astronomy in measuring observables, their movements and relationships to one another (the appeal to efficient and physical causes for explanation) was so successful that moderns in the seventeenth and eighteenth centuries wanted to make this the chief language of knowledge of the created world, if not of all knowledge. Thus science adopted a method of measuring physical bodies and their movement, called *quantification,* which involved observation of bodies in motion and their causal relationships to other bodies. This was clearly successful in some fields of investigation, and was soon adopted as the universal way to do science for *all* objects and fields of study. On this model of science, you begin the scientific investigation with a universal method of measuring repeating observables, which predetermines what kinds of objects are possible to discover and investigate by that method. However, major problems resulted from this commitment for both science and psychology. The particular difficulties encountered have to do with the kind of knowledge-language that can be used to explain (1) spiritual and nonphysical objects and phenomena and (2) ethics.

First, under the modernist view of science, it is not at all clear what knowledge-language can be used to intelligibly talk about nonphysical objects that have neither extension nor movements that can be measured (things including God, angels, souls or minds, numbers, ideas, propositions, dreams, consciousness, mental images, personal agency, first-person identity, and the experience of feelings, emotions, and thoughts), phenomena that were formerly understood to be real and knowable.

Second, the new scientific method of quantification is purely a descriptive method for measuring objects in space and their extension (or movement). In that case, this purely descriptive science can no longer provide a science of values or the understanding of prescriptive realities—such as morality (right and wrong), values (good and bad) and character (virtue and vice)—which were grounded in natural-law theories going back to the ancient Greeks. Thus the new science could no longer provide a ground for psychotherapy and its concepts of health and unhealth.

The questions that confront the Christian psychologist are (1) whether and to what degree a scientific psychology can address Christian realities, mental objects and values, and (2) whether the Christian psychologist is doing something other than "psychology" or science when relating psychology and Christianity? The tension involved is clear: on the one hand, it is not legitimate for modernist science to include Scripture as a legitimate datum for psychology, nor is it legitimate to address immaterial objects, such as sin, values and life in Christ. However, the Christian psychologist would include Scripture as a legitimate source of knowledge and is compelled by Scripture, as well as by observation and reflection on human nature, to account for such realities as mental objects and values, which are inherently unquantifiable.

So it seems clear that Christians adapting to a modernist view of science will always have a bifurcated world of that which science can address and that which can only be addressed by theology and philosophy. This was, in fact, Descartes's solution. As a result, bringing together these two worlds will require the artificial, nonscientific and secondary process called "integration." Our transformational psychology, on the other hand, insists this problem could have been avoided by rejecting modernity's limited view of science and retaining a more holistic, ancient classical-realist view of science.

CLASSICAL-REALIST SCIENCE

There exists an alternate approach to science affirmed by the ancients that is capable of providing a foundation for a holistic vision for understanding the person in light of *all* reality, particularly Christian realities. The classical and medieval thinkers represented in the ancient Near Eastern wise men (sages), the Old Testament sage, the Greeks in Plato and Aristotle, the Stoics, numerous medieval thinkers, Aquinas and so on[1] had an entirely different approach to scientific method than those of modernity. According to the modernist "new science," a person begins scientific investigation with a universal method of measuring repeating observables, which predetermines the kinds of objects that are possible to discover and investigate. The classical-realist approach reverses this process: the object of investigation determines the methodology, which involves the following elements:

1. Science begins with a casual *acquaintance* of the object

2. for the purpose of learning more about the *nature* of the object,

3. which allows *the object of investigation to determine* the best way to further investigate it and all relevant phenomena,

4. resulting in the development of a *method of study* best suited to the object.

Rather than allowing a predetermined way of knowing to determine what is real and what counts as knowledge, this view of scientific method allows *reality* to determine *methodology*. To put it differently, ontology determines epistemology, and a presupposed epistemology does not determine ontology. According to the ancients, one cannot know what is the best way to study what exists until one is adequately acquainted with what exists.[2] On this view of science, the psychological health of the scientist to remain honest and open to reality is central to doing science well, which is foundational to our transformational psychology model.

---

[1]For more on this classical-realist model of science, its history and the issues that emerged in the history and philosophy of science, see Brant, E. (1996). *The foundations of modern science in the Middle Ages.* Cambridge: Cambridge University Press; Leijenhorst, C., Luthy, C., & Thijssen, J. M. M. H. (Eds.). (2002). *The dynamics of Aristotelian natural philosophy from antiquity to the seventeenth century.* Leiden, U.K.: E. J. Brill; Coe, J., & Hall, T. (2010). *Psychology in the Spirit: Contours of a transformational psychology.* Downers Grove, IL: IVP Academic.

[2]For a good discussion of these methodological matters—of, for example, how methodology is determined by acquaintance with the object of knowing—see Willard, D. (1984). *Logic and the objectivity of knowledge.* Athens: Ohio University Press.

Thus a transformational psychology rejects the truncated modernistic method and advocates this more commonsense, premodern approach to the study of the person with dramatic implications for scientific methodology and scope. If this classical-realist methodological approach to science were taken seriously today, psychology as science would include as legitimate all objects of investigation relevant to understanding human phenomena, including mental phenomena, Scripture, God and values, as well as all relevant methodologies for doing science, such as introspection and relational interaction in therapy and normal human life—rather than relegating these to philosophy and theology and some further study of integration.

In the case of the study of consciousness, for example, one certainly would be interested in brain research and its correlates to mental phenomena. However, more central would be introspection and acquaintance with mental objects, including private, first-person experiences, third-person experiential reports, observations of correlate behavior, and rational reflection on experience in order to determine what is the best way to study these mental phenomena. In the case of morality, values and character, reflection on our conscious and immanent teleology, as well as reflection on human flourishing in general, would be appropriate science. This would form the foundation for developing a full-blown, natural-law science or approach to investigating ethics and the person, which grounds psychotherapy. Finally, the classical-realist scientist would include faith in Scripture and God as legitimate data and methodology from which to understand the person in light of the realities of creation, the Fall and redemption. Of course, much work would need to be given to developing justificative and adjudicating procedures in this science.

In general and in contrast to integration, a transformational psychology attempts to develop a single, unified vision of reality in faith and the Spirit. It attempts to provide a comprehensive and coherent scientific methodology that is capable of relating psychology to faith, of doing a psychology of Christian realities, and of providing the wisdom and insight necessary for a robust understanding of therapy. In turn, this transformational psychology is ultimately grounded in the transformative psychologist, who preserves the integrity of this process by being as open as possible to what is real and true about understanding the person. In that case, "integration" would be rightly reduced to a secondary scientific enterprise of open and critical dialogue with other scientists whose reflections stem from a truncated, bifurcated or even prejudicial view of what can be included as legitimate data in the science of the person.

In sum, our transformational psychology model proposes a return to an older, timeworn methodology (a classical-realist science) as the foundation for knowing ethics, God and mental objects, and for reintroducing these subjects and various, legitimate scientific methodologies back into the world of "science." The result is the development of a full-orbed psychology that is capable of studying all realities relevant to understanding the person, a task dear to well-meaning integrationists. This seems to be in harmony with Jones, who admits at the end of his discussion that "the picture that emerges is that science draws not just on facts but on the entire complex array of human experiences" (p. 114), admitting further that a whole host of metaphysical and epistemological assumptions, theological and philosophical beliefs frame and shape our methods and ways of doing science. If that is the case, then it is no longer clear why Jones would bar *any* realities from science as long as they have to do with the real world.

A Biblical Counseling Response
to Integration

David Powlison

STAN JONES'S CHAPTER IS THOUGHTFUL AND LUCID, evidencing the humility and balance that adorn Christian faith. For example, in discussing the adequacy of the term *integration,* he expresses one of those bits of almost off-hand wisdom that so improves the quality of conversations: "Call it anything you like; at stake in this discussion is not the term, but one's *fundamental stance as a Christian* as one engages the entire world of learning and action" (p. 102). This comment actually applies equally to each of the five views, not just integration. Labels are not the issue. What fundamental stance best expresses our Christian faith?

In Stan Jones's core definition, integration means

> our living out . . . of the lordship of Christ over all of existence by our giving his special revelation—God's true Word—its appropriate place of authority in determining our fundamental beliefs about and practices toward all of reality and toward our academic subject matter in particular. (p. 102)

Again I think that these deft words describe the aspiration of each of the five views. Our differences turn on how we actually understand and work out Scripture's "appropriate place of authority." I would also insert one significant phrase into that definition. A wide spectrum of important matters lies in between "all of reality" and "academic subject matter." I think it helpful to name at least one of those intermediate terms: "toward all of reality, *and toward how we understand and help human beings,* and toward our academic subject matter in particular."

Understanding and helping people is at stake. Numerous academic disciplines—arts, sciences, humanities, divinities—seek to make sense of life. How to engage psychology is the immediate but not the final subject of this book. What is at stake is understanding all that people are and do, and curing all that ails us. Current wisdom, current knowledge and current practice in various academic and professional disciplines, whether secular or theological, may help—and, if we are incautious, will certainly hinder—our growth toward true understanding and helpfulness.

The authority of Scripture is not the issue. We agree. Scripture is authoritative. Whether or not Scripture contains all necessary information and directly answers all our questions is not the issue. We agree. Of course Scripture does not contain all information and answer all questions. That's why we open our eyes, ask questions, listen, think, read, write, converse and learn from experience. But *how* is Scripture authoritative? Or better, *how* is the Bible relevant and what is the *scope* of relevance? "Practical theology" is the technical term for asking and answering these questions.

Much of Stan Jones's article defends the importance of a thoughtful Christian appreciation for science. Biblical counseling has always agreed. But when he easily segues, without argument or defense, from considering secular science through Christian eyes to assuming the validity of professional psychotherapy, he performs an intellectual sleight of hand. The questions surrounding professional practice are different from the questions surrounding science. For decades, proponents of the integrationist view have used an epistemological argument (the usefulness of science for studying what is) as if it also implicitly justifies professional psychotherapy (interventions to change what is). That is like using Marxist sociology (often very perceptive) to justify Marxist politics (always very problematic).

Describing a person accurately, explaining a person truly and changing a person into what a person is meant to be are three different things. The first is the forte of psychological science (up to a point as the descriptions do not go deep). The second is the fatal flaw in both research psychology and the personality theories: they cannot explain why people do what they do, because they exclude the truth à priori and elevate secondary factors to primary significance (see my response to David Myers's levels-of-explanation view). The third is the fatal flaw in the psychotherapies. For all their care and skill, they do not reorient strugglers to reality, and the deeper they probe into a person, the more misleading they become. The more a psychotherapy does orient to reality, the more it moves in the direction of biblical counseling. This is not to deny common-grace goods (see my discussion of Psych-2, 4 and 5 in my chapter). It is simply to recognize that the validity of any causal explanation, interventive strategy, dynamic of change, definition of success or social structure for delivering care cannot be established by anchoring it in science.[1]

---

[1]For further discussion, see my "Cure of Souls (and the Modern Psychologies)," appendix 3 in *The Biblical Counseling Movement: History and Context* (Greensboro, N.C.: New Growth Press, 2010).

This is what I hear the integrationist view saying about the scope of Scripture's relevance to psychological matters. From the Christian side of the discussion, Jones gives examples of what our faith positively contributes:

- ultimate answers and starting points for knowledge
- faith, spirituality and spiritual development as topics for study
- forgiveness as a topic for study
- the ethics of homosexuality
- image of God
- constituent elements in the soul

In effect, the impact of Christianity is restricted to what we might call narrowly religious topics. Scripture is a resource that generally orients us (God's redemptive plan, the great doctrines of the faith), but doesn't give us detailed insight into how people work and how intentional conversations ought to proceed.

In my thirty years of doing, teaching and writing about biblical counseling, I have never mentioned or discussed any of the examples Jones cites. Never. I have thoughts on what the Bible teaches about these matters, but the foreground conversation is filled with how our faith is immediately relevant to all kinds of things that Jones does not mention.

From the science side of the discussion, Jones gives these examples: child development, how to conceptualize personality traits, schizophrenia, depression, how neurons work, how the brain synthesizes information, the workings of memory and pervasive developmental disorders such as autism. Psychology's impact is illustrated by what we might call overtly scientific topics. These examples tend toward the biological/nature end of the spectrum (though, especially in the first four, other factors—functional, moral, personal, situational—are also very significant).

In my thirty years in biblical counseling, I've been glad to know whatever I've picked up on these topics. But such information has never been decisive for what counseling does. Never. The foreground conversation is filled with details of human experience that Jones does not mention. So what is the middle ground between the narrowly religious and the overtly scientific? It is the broad, deep, teeming, complex, tumultuous arena where most of significant life is lived: the topics that preoccupy counseling conversations.

Counseling largely picks up on "functional" matters: what's going on, how you're doing; what's happening to you; how you're reacting; how you treat people; how they treat you; and how what you want, expect, fear, and believe animates every emotion, thought, choice and reaction. People seek counseling or are pressured into it (or a counselor seeks them out, which is something unique to a biblical vision) because they are unhappy, loveless, anxious, resentful, despairing, hurting, lonely, troubled, troublesome, internally conflicted, interpersonally alienated, betrayed, bereaved, addicted, confused, willful, overwhelmed, faithless . . . or even because they are happy and self-confident when they shouldn't be! Neither the overtly scientific nor the narrowly religious is much help in this arena, but this is where *every* counseling model operates. This is where biblical counseling operates. This is where the Bible operates as redemptive ministry in action, not as a mere assemblage of proof texts and great doctrines. Life lived is the scope of Scripture's immediate relevance for our developing practical theological wisdom.

Jones does not mention problems in living. But this is where our Christian faith pointedly shines. This is where the secular alternatives show themselves remarkably dull, shallow, confused and dehumanizing. In 1991 Stan Jones commented on the negative influence of secularity on Christian counseling:

> Too much of what passes for integration today is anemic theologically or biblically, and tends to be little more than a spiritualized rehashing of mainstream mental health thought.[2]

I believe he would say the same today. It is in addressing problems in living that integrationist psychology continues to have its most significant impact on the church: importing personality theories that misconstrue causality, and practicing psychotherapies that mediate such theories to struggling people. Integrationists have not seen and articulated the pointed relevance of Christian faith in the middle ground.

The descriptive case studies in my article—"Stuck in traffic" and "Clyde"—engage the person in situ because the scope of Scripture's rele-

---

[2]Stanton Jones and Richard Butman, eds., *Modern Psychotherapies* (Downers Grove, Ill.: InterVarsity Press, 1991), p. 415.

vance is easiest to see in rich descriptions of life lived. By working with "thick description,"[3] we come to understand how Scripture has "thick relevance." Seeing our faith's thick relevance, we see how psalmic faith and proverbial wisdom catch fire in a person's life. We see how Christ's person, work and word become psychologically and situationally relevant—whether in the seemingly minor struggles of "Stuck in traffic" or in the obviously life-destroying problems of a "Clyde."

Over the years I've enjoyed cordial, candid conversations with dozens of integrationist psychotherapists, I've read dozens of books and taken notes on dozens of talks. I hear their collective testimony to a Scripture with apparently thin relevance to the middle ground. Most significant human experiences seem to transpire in categories supplied by scientific psychology and the personality theories. Most counseling conversations seem to unfold in terms dictated by the psychotherapies.

It is a redemptive grace of God when professedly integrationist Christians "do much more in psychotherapy than what is dictated by our theories" (p. 119). I've witnessed such wisdom on occasion. That "much more" comes in the shape of biblical counseling—not as a label (and certainly not as the caricature). To the degree that an integrationist's approach to psychotherapy is "shaped profoundly by his or her Christian convictions" (pp. 119-20), it comes to talk and act more and more like biblical counseling. But garden-variety integrationist counseling consistently misses Scripture's thick relevance.

I do not mean that last paragraph as triumphalistic. Garden-variety biblical counseling practice often falls far short of the wisdoms dictated by our theory—and we are all garden-variety people, after all, with many shortcomings. Some Christians live better than their theories dictate, may Jesus Christ be praised. Some Christians live worse than what their theory promises, mea culpa, kyrie eleison. I am defending the biblical counseling *view*, not the degree to which any particular proponent, practitioner or institution lives up to it. On the last day, when our call to counsel one another has been fulfilled, all Christians will have become biblical counselors in the wise image of Jesus, because his purpose is to make us like himself.

---

[3]Clifford Geertz's term for detailed descriptions of behavior in context: "Thick Description: Toward an Interpretive Theory of Culture," in *The Interpretation of Cultures: Selected Essays* (New York: Basic Books, 1973), pp. 3-30.

4

A Christian Psychology View

Robert C. Roberts and P. J. Watson

ONE PSYCHOLOGY? OR MANY?

Not long ago, many people regarded psychology as a scientific discipline, fully analogous to chemistry and physics, that originated sometime in the late nineteenth century. Psychology's failure to yield a single dominant paradigm accepted by all its major practitioners was often explained by saying it was such a young discipline. Never mind that in personality psychology, situationists—who practically denied the existence of personality traits—flourished academically alongside robust trait theorists. Never mind that handbooks of psychotherapy had to survey as many as twenty distinct paradigms of intervention, each with its special way of understanding and explaining psychological dysfunctions and each with a somewhat different conception of mental health and different strategies for restoring it (for example, see Corsini & Wedding, 2007). Never mind that meta-analyses repeatedly showed that psychotherapies are all about equally effective, regardless of which paradigm of treatment and explanation one deploys, and almost regardless of how much training in "psychology" the therapist has received (Lambert & Bergin, 1994). Never mind that no one could explain with precision how neuroanatomy relates to personality. Never mind that human behavior could be predicted only in a rough and probabilistic manner. Our science is young, after all; give it time.

But times are changing. For example, in recent years, the so-called positive psychologists have begun to recognize that psychology dates back far beyond the nineteenth century, back at least to Plato and Aristotle in Greece, and similarly to ancient thinkers in China and India. In contrast to the psychology of much of the twentieth century, the positive psychologists have begun to appreciate the wealth of deep psychological reflection that is available from ancient sources, and the inseparability of psychological functioning from moral functioning (see Peterson & Seligman, 2004). They have reverted, in their psychological investigations, to the older language of happiness (not in the sense of "feeling good," but in a more or less classical sense of deep and sustained well-being dependent on character [Annas, 1993]), and above all to the language of the virtues and vices. The therapeutic orientation of Greek and Hellenistic ethics and psychology has become more evident, along with the striking similarities between some of the ancient and some of the modern therapies (Nussbaum, 1994). So psychology as a discipline of careful observation and reflection about human psychic well-being and dysfunction, and how to go about promoting the former and correcting the latter, has been around for twenty-five centuries or so.

A lesson that might have been learned from this growing historical awareness is that the concept of human psychic well-being is *essentially contested*. That is, it is not the kind of question that can be settled to everyone's satisfaction independently of metaphysical, moral and religious commitments. It is not a question that can be settled by purely empirical methods of research. This lesson might have been learned from the longer history of psychology, because in that history one can see the variety of notions of human flourishing that have arisen, and one can see that they are conditioned by the metaphysical commitments of their advocates.

For example, the Epicureans, who practiced a psychotherapy bearing some similarities to that of Freud, were eliminative atomists. That is, they thought that human beings are nothing but physical stuff, in certain arrangements that give temporary living status to beings that are constituted of the stuff. And they thought that human well-being required an absolute renunciation of long-term hope; like many contemporary therapists, they thought psychic well-being was just a matter of maximizing the pleasantness of this temporary life.

Platonists disagreed, thinking that people are more than just physical matter and their happiness more than just the maximization of pleasure. Somewhat like modern Jungians, Platonists thought that human well-being requires that we be personally in touch with something eternal, and Plato's moral therapy was thus designed to get the soul to "recollect" its eternal nature and thus to come to love what is eternally good.

Stoics and Skeptics both thought that the highest human well-being required being emotionally "undisturbed," and designed therapies that aimed to achieve this equanimity (Stoics: *apatheia* or passionlessness; Skeptics: *ataraxia* or tranquility). They had very different ideas about how to achieve this state. The Stoics, somewhat like modern cognitive therapists, thought one could achieve it by rational argument; the Skeptics thought that it required the renunciation of all belief whatsoever.

Aristotle did not agree with either the idea that happiness was pleasure-maximization or the idea that happiness was tranquility. He thought that it required excellent functioning as a rational social animal in a properly constituted community, along with contemplation of the eternal in a way reminiscent of Plato's thought. But his notion of the eternal that one needed to be in contact with for the highest happiness was quite different from that of Christians and Jews. Aristotle gives a more detailed account of the virtues required for happiness than any of the other ancient thinkers, but if one carefully compares the virtues that he describes with, say, their Christian counterparts, one begins to see significant differences.

For example, Aristotelian liberality (Aristotle, 1980, book 6.1-3), which has to do with giving away one's wealth in an appropriate way, is not quite the same virtue as Christian generosity—though each of these psychologies regards the virtue as necessary for complete human functioning. The difference is traceable to a difference in how practitioners of these two moral outlooks conceive of *people*. People, in the Christian conception, are created in the image of God, and thus have an intrinsic value or dignity or respect-worthiness. When the properly generous person freely bestows good things on the recipient, he sees himself as serving and seeking to benefit someone created in the image of God. By contrast, the person expressing Aristotelian liberality—in giving a gift to someone—is properly expressing his fullness, a kind of overflow of his own abundance (see Roberts & Wood, 2007, chap. 10). Both Christians and Aristotelians conceive of persons as social beings, so that their well-being or self-realization depends in significant part on how they relate to other persons. In the Christian view, a person could not have full well-being if she did not respect the fundamental dignity of others, simply as human beings. Since Aristotle has no conception of the fundamental dignity of persons simply as human beings, he does not have the same concept of a proper relationship between persons. This difference in the virtue(s), and consequent difference in the conception of human well-being, is traceable to a difference between the Christian and the Aristotelian metaphysics of the person, namely the answer to the question, "What, fundamentally, *is* a person?"

The positive psychologists might have learned, from their interest in the history of thought about the virtues that concepts of virtues are relative to metaphysics and that metaphysical disputes can seldom be settled by appeal to empirical data alone. But the leaders of the positive psychology movement do not seem to appreciate this point. Instead, they remain in quest of a transcultural, metaphysics-neutral conception of the virtues: a single conception that any rational and informed person could accept, regardless of his or her religious or metaphysical views about the nature of persons.

It appears that the learning from history and culture has been negligible, because the scholarship has been superficial. For example, positive psychology so far does not seem to be interested in a deep and careful exploration of the psychology of well-being that is embodied in any one of the great moral-spiritual traditions. Instead, one sees unsupported generalizations like the following: "This form of love [namely, *agape* as found in the New Testament] is present in all the major world religions, from the Jewish notion of *chesed* (steadfast love) and the Buddhist ideal of *karuna* (compassion) to rough equivalents in Islam, Hinduism, Taoism, Confucianism, and Native American spirituality" (Peterson & Seligman, 2004, p. 326).

After making such an astounding claim, the positive psychologist moves on to discuss the benefits of the trait, the potential for measuring the trait, how the trait develops, what are the trait's evolutionary origins and neurological substrata, how persons with the trait affect members of other populations, such as persons with mental disorders or cognitive deficits, etc., etc.—all without any very clear idea what the trait in question *is*. Were one to look carefully at the Christian tradition, one would find that *agape*, as it appears in its paradigm exemplars, is strongly associated with a particular conception of God, as revealed in the historical life and death of Jesus of Nazareth. In such exemplars as Mother Teresa of Calcutta, *agape* involves a disposition to see, in each of the recipients of one's love, the person of Jesus Christ. Love for the human being *is* love for Jesus Christ (Roberts, 2007a).

This is a particularity obviously lacking in any Buddhist, Islamic or Native American counterpart of agape, if there is such. But agape also has other, less historically conditioned features that may be lacking in some of the other moral traditions. The Christian psychologist Søren Kierkegaard strongly stressed that an essential feature of agape is that it is divinely commanded, and he details many ways in which the power of agape to promote the well-being of the possessor of the trait depends on the possessor's taking agape as commanded by God (see Kierkegaard, 1847/1995; also Evans, 2004). No doubt the "rough equivalents" of agape in Hinduism, Taoism and the other major religions have equally interesting psychological peculiarities that a positive psychologist would have to be clear about before he could devise an instrument for measuring that trait, or comment competently on how the trait promotes the well-being of its possessor and his or her associates.

We do not deny that virtues can be described in such a way as to make only the most minimal reference to particular views about the nature of persons, the nature of the universe in which we dwell, and the nature of God (or whatever transcendent or immanent being, if any, takes the place of God). One can describe human well-being in widely varying degrees of generality or specificity. It is probably true, for example, that courage, in all its varying forms, enables its subject to face supposed threats. Similarly, the various versions of generosity probably all have to do with giving good things as gifts (as contrasted with selling things) to others. Describing the traits in such generalities may give the impression that they are pretty much the same across metaphysical and spiritual traditions. But if one digs a little deeper into the virtue concepts, one raises questions about subtler aspects of the motivation that is normative for actions that exemplify the virtue in question.

What, for example, are the considerations that are normative for the motivation of generous actions? How does the generous person conceive the things she gives? How does she conceive the people to whom she gives? What is her attitude toward a possible grateful response from her beneficiary? The answers to these questions can vary considerably with the metaphysical background of generosity, but a psychologically competent answer to such questions is a necessary prerequisite for genuinely scientific scholarship about the trait.

One might think that these are subtleties that we can safely ignore in our psychology of human well-being, in the interest of finding virtues on which all rational persons, regardless of their metaphysics, can agree. But if we ignore them in the interest of universal agreement, we will find that our psychology of well-being is considerably less rich and less subtle than are the particular historical-cultural metaphysically grounded psychologies of well-being from which we pretend to derive our understanding. And we will find that the people who may be guided by our psychology in their quest for happiness are shaped more superficially and lead less profoundly significant lives than the practitioners of the original traditions.

To the positive psychologist who supposes (with the rest of the psychological establishment) that psychology must be a single body of thought and information equally acceptable to any rational person, regardless of metaphysical commitments, our proposal of a Christian psychology may seem parochial and unscientific. However, if the considerations we have brought forward above have force, then "parochial" may be the name of the game in a positive psychology—that is, a psychology that attempts to outline the kind of human well-being that a moral-spiritual tradition affords, and to explore ways of measuring and promoting it. Positive psychology is simply not the kind of beast that can garner universal consensus among adherents of the various religions and spiritual outlooks of the world, and any professional psychologist who thinks he has come up with such a universally acceptable psychology is looking not at reality, but at the clean, glistening walls of his academic ivory tower.

So we admit the charge of parochiality, but claim that it is inevitable for anyone who wishes to do responsible positive psychology. What about the charge of being unscientific? We admit that empirical work in psychology can be done, more or less, without metaphysical assumptions, but that the less it depends on or interacts with such assumptions, the less "interesting" it will be. Some research programs—for example, in evolutionary psychology—are highly dependent on naturalist metaphysics to the extent that they aim (interestingly!) to offer fully naturalistic explanations of human traits. But in that case, the explanations cannot themselves be fully grounded in the empirical data. They are "commitments" of the scientists and their adherents. Similarly, one can imagine a study comparing different kinds of forgiveness (say, fully Christian forgiveness and a secularized facsimile) for their effects on physiological stress markers such as heart rate, blood pressure, skin conductance and facial electromyography. If the study showed a greater effectiveness of the Christian kind of forgiveness, someone might take this as evidence for the truth of Christianity; if it showed equal effectiveness, secular psychologists might take the result as evidence for the truth of naturalism. But in either case, the data would constitute such evidence only on the basis of further assumptions, which derive from the worldview.

If the concerns addressed above are true about positive psychology, which at least possesses some awareness of the contributions of ancient philosophy and the world's religions regarding the understanding of human well-being, how much more compromised is the research of most modern psychology, which essentially ignores these matters? In light of the foregoing, Christian psychologists eschew establishment psychology's goal of a universal psychology that aptly describes all human beings generically, believing that it is less scientific than it might be. In contrast, we wish to develop a psychology that accurately describes the psychological nature of human beings as understood according to historic Christianity. Our project begins by examining the rich resources that lie within our own historical tradition. Then, in the second half of this chapter, we look ahead to consider the empirical potential of a contemporary Christian psychology based on this tradition.

STEP ONE: RETRIEVING CHRISTIAN PSYCHOLOGY

The Bible has a special and authoritative place (Johnson, 1992, 2007a; Talbot, 1997) as the fountainhead of Christian ideas, including psychological ones. Much of the foundational work in Christian psychology will therefore require a careful rereading of Scripture, in the light of some of the great Christian psychologists of the subsequent past (Augustine, Aquinas, Pascal, Kierkegaard), by people who are familiar with contemporary psychology and can therefore sniff out a biblical psychology that effectively speaks to current circumstances. This is the business of psychologically informed Bible scholars, philosophers and theologians, as well as biblically informed professional psychologists and counselors. Let us consider, as an example, a passage from Jesus' Sermon on the Mount.

The Sermon is usually classified as ethics, but it is a special kind of ethics that is closer to what we know as psychology than what we have come to think of as ethics in the late modern period (up until roughly the 1980s). In the late modern period, one thought of ethics as rules for action and social policies that promote certain actions and discourage others. The Sermon does have much to say about actions, but it is also, and more deeply, about character—about the form of persons. It is about how to live, by being a person of a certain kind of character who acts well as a part of living well. And it is about the transformation of persons from being one kind of character and living less well to being another kind who lives well. But the study of character, the aspects of well-being and the change of character for the better seem to be a sort of psychology. To further the assimilation of the Sermon to psychology, we might point out that modern psychologies and psychotherapies are, in fact, ethical systems (see Browning, 1987; Roberts, 1993;[1] Browning & Cooper, 2004). The positive psychology movement is an obvious admission of psychology's continuity with ethics.

One reason we might be surprised by the suggestion that the Sermon contains psychology is that we have come to expect a certain vocabulary to be present wherever psychology is, and most (if not all) of this expected vocabulary is absent from the Sermon. We do not find terms like *behavior, personality, dysfunction, emotion, therapy, self-object, drive, defense mechanism, schema, congruence* or *selfhood*. But these items (and many more) are elements of systems of thought and practice in which human nature is characterized; in which human actions, thoughts and emotions are explained and evaluated; and in which a change from negatively evaluated to positively evaluated forms of functioning is commended and facilitated. The Sermon certainly does not have the same conception of human nature as the psychologies that are structured by words such as the ones listed above; nor does it have the same pattern of explanations and evaluations of actions, thoughts and emotions; nor the same recommendations or strategies for change. But in the Sermon's own vocabulary—in terms such as blessed *(makarios),* poor in spirit *(ptōchoi tō pneumati),* to sorrow *(pentheō),* humble or gentle *(prays),* to comfort *(parakaleō),* pure in heart *(katharoi tē kardia),* peacemaker *(eirēnopoios),* righteousness *(dikaiosynē),* to get angry *(orgizomai),* to commit adultery *(moicheuō),* to lust *(epithymeō),* love *(agapē),* pray *(proseuchomai),* to forgive *(aphiēmi),* tres-

---

[1]Don Browning (1987) argued this point—and again in Browning and Cooper (2004)—even though he thinks of ethics as a matter of act-injunctions. Roberts (1993) made the point in a way that conceives ethics more classically, as a reflection about the virtues and vices.

pass *(paraptōma)*, treasure *(thēsauros)*, heart *(kardia)*, hypocrite *(hypokritēs)*, reward *(misthos)* and others—it offers its own conception of human nature. It also offers an ideal of personality functioning, as well as explanations and evaluations of actions, thoughts, and emotions, and it includes recommendations or strategies for change.

Overview of the Sermon as psychology. The Sermon conceptualizes "personal well-being" as comprising of the following character traits and their implied actions and attitudes: gentleness, desire for righteousness, mercy, purity of heart, being a peacemaker, being a lover of enemies, being disposed to forgive offenses, poverty of spirit, willingness to be persecuted for Jesus' sake, mourning, penitence, humility, respect for great things, self-unawareness (the opposite of private ostentation), treasuring the kingdom of God, expecting good things from God, endurance through difficulties. A person who had these traits or was disposed to these actions and emotions would, according to the psychology of the Sermon, be "mature," "perfect" *(teleios)* or "blessed," "happy" *(makarios)*, or solidly founded like a house built on a rock (Mt 7:24[2]).

The Sermon also conceptualizes *psychopathology*. It is a disposition to anger, grudge-bearing and revenge; to lust, adultery and divorce; to hatred of enemies; or it manifests itself as greed, acquisitiveness or being mastered by mammon; as hypocrisy and ostentation (both public and private); as arrogance and disrespect for what is great; as anxiety about necessities; as judgmentalism of others and blindness to one's own faults. A person who is given to or mired in such dispositions will be functioning poorly as a human being, and he or she will not be mature, happy or solidly grounded. Were we to elaborate the psychology of the Sermon, we could infer more traits of health from some of the traits of dysfunction, and more traits of dysfunction from some of the traits of health, simply by inferring to the contrary of each. (Throughout, we are assuming that the psychology of the Sermon is a consistent system of thought and practice.)

While *psychological explanation* is not as patent in the Sermon as are the pictures of personal well-being and pathology, some patterns of explanation are explicit and others can be inferred. Inwardness (e.g., lust, anger) explains actions (adultery, revenge). Certain blindnesses are explained by

---

[2]The Scripture references used here, unless otherwise indicated, are taken from the Revised Standard Version of the Bible.

perverse patterns of "treasuring," that is, caring about things. Shapes of personality ("hearts") are explained by "treasurings." Seeing God is explained by purity of heart. Hatred of God is explained by reference to being mastered by mammon. An elaborated biblical psychology would multiply patterns of explanation by exploring the system of concepts that operate in the Sermon and elsewhere in the Bible.

A number of *therapeutic interventions* (or avenues by which a person might move from pathological to healthy patterns of thought, passion and action) are rather explicit in the Sermon: be poor in spirit, mourn, behave gently, hunger for righteousness, be merciful and pure in heart, make peace, allow yourself to be persecuted for the sake of Jesus, let your light shine before people, keep the commandments, take responsibility for your own anger, take responsibility for other people's anger when you have caused offense, control your lustful eye, do not seek revenge on those who offend you, do not be ostentatious in your piety, do not fret about daily needs but seek the kingdom, focus chiefly on your own shortcomings rather than on those of others, do not hold others in contempt because of their shortcomings.

For a couple of reasons these interventions might not sound very therapeutic or very much like psychology to a contemporary person. One reason is that some of these ideas seem to go against the recommendations of well-established psychotherapies of our own day. To this we can simply reply: Yes, the Christian psychology is a different psychology. A more interesting objection would be that these "interventions" all seem to have the form of bald commandments: Just do this, or Just don't do that. But some people may be at a loss as to *how* to do what is commanded. What is needed, and what contemporary psychotherapies tend to provide, is some facilitation of the therapeutic action, some discipline by which, perhaps stepwise, a person can implement the commanded change. Here the post-biblical psychological tradition—the desert fathers, Gregory the Great, the sixteenth-century mystics and others—has responded by devising disciplines and helps that can be provided by advisors. Contemporary psychological research might add to the resources of the Christian tradition new strategies for inculcating the biblical virtues.

Comments on Matthew 5. In the rather short compass of this illustration of Christian psychology, we cannot give a full discussion of the psychology of the Sermon, even of Matthew 5. Clarifying comments will often have to take the form of suggesting directions of further thought and research.

Matthew 5:1-12. In verses 3-11 Jesus calls one or another group or kind of persons "blessed" *(makarioi)*, that is, "happy" or "well off," thus establishing an immediate connection with contemporary psychological concerns in therapy, personality and motivation. The word *happy* is a misleading translation if it suggests to modern readers a simple state of "feeling good." To be *makarios* is to be well and to be doing well, but it is compatible with suffering tribulations and obstacles. Thus the concept of well-being that drives the psychology of the Sermon is quite different from its counterpart in some of the modern psychologies. The groups that Jesus describes are certainly not "well adjusted" to their social and physical settings, nor are they contented and enjoying life, though they are free from a certain kind of anxiety (see Mt 6:25-33). Of the groups that Jesus describes as *makarioi,* the mourners and the persecuted are both obviously suffering; the rest are grouped according to their virtues: the poor in spirit, the gentle, those who hunger and thirst for righteousness, the merciful, the pure in heart, and the peacemakers.

Nevertheless, the concept of *makarios* does make a connection with psychology in our sense of the word: well-being is certainly the *form* of any goal of psychotherapy, however much the various therapies may differ in their particular conceptions of this goal (see Roberts, 1993, part one). We rarely see therapists commending gentleness or mercy or purity of heart or hunger and thirst for righteousness as strategies for psychological well-being. They tend, instead, to try to facilitate high self-esteem, contentment, individual satisfaction, individuation and a sense of empowerment.

Jesus suggests how each suffering or trait is a blessing: because of its connection with possessing the kingdom of God, being comforted, inheriting the earth, having one's desire for righteousness satisfied, obtaining mercy, seeing God, being called children of God. The Christian psychologist will want to elaborate on these explanations. From the point of view of the gospel of Jesus Christ, "happiness" is grounded in the new creation that comes in Jesus. The new order is one that supports people who are poor in spirit, gentle, who hunger and thirst for righteousness, who are merciful and so forth. The new order is one in which they can function so as to be "happy." But people live at least partially in the old order, so it is instructive for them to be reminded of their happiness and the other context (the kingdom) in which their virtues constitute a more obvious well-being. Jesus may be engaging in some "reframing" here. People who are being persecuted will not be immediately inclined to see themselves as happy, and there can be something therapeutic in having Jesus remind them that they are actually functioning better than may outwardly appear.

The Christian psychologist will want to investigate the various categories of blessedness to learn what traits are actually being commended. It is not obvious what poverty of spirit is, and some of the other categories, such as purity of heart or being a peacemaker, may not be immediately obvious either. The Christian psychologist will want to know how one becomes poor in spirit, a peacemaker and so on. What is the therapy for those who are not? How can people be helped in this undertaking? And what are the consequences of not having these traits? What kinds of things tend to go wrong in the lives of people who lack the traits? If we knew this, we would have material for some diagnostic explanations as well. The way to answer these questions may be a combination of conceptual-historical and empirical research.

Matthew 5:13-16. The disciples, says Jesus, are "salt" and "light." Each of these metaphors describes some personal orientation, set of traits, or state of life that is good and healthy. But it is good for someone other than its possessor. The salt is good, not for the salt but for those who are eating. The light is good, not for the light but for those who are making their way through the world. The disciples are expected to permeate the world, as salt does the food and light the landscape. We might say that, for Jesus, personal or psychic well-being is never abstractly or privately for the person in whom it resides. This too seems to mark a difference between the psychology of the Sermon and many of the psychologies of our day. To be *makarios*, it seems, is to possess a kind of well-being whose "wellness" belongs to others whom one affects, as well as to oneself.

Matthew 5:17-20. Jesus is not here to relax the law but to fulfill it. The Jews were very positive about the law, in part because they thought of it as a blessing to them, a guide for their lives, a guide for happiness and well-being (see Ps 1). One might say that for the Jew the law was God's psychotherapy. Jesus is claiming the same for his own teaching, and claiming a kind of continuity between the two.

Matthew 5:21-26. Jesus insists that anger itself, and not just its untoward consequences such as murder, is a problem, a barrier to well-being. Most psychologists will agree that anger can be a problem, but not all of them will explain anger's dysfunctionality in the way suggested by the Sermon. Psychologists may point out that it is bad for the subject's physical health, that it can prevent the subject from getting what he or she wants from people, that in excess it is not good for marriages and partnerships. These are all acceptable points, no doubt, but they are not the heart of the matter in Jesus' psychology: improper anger is a disruption of the spirit of the kingdom, which is one of loving fellowship with God and fellow people.

In verse 23, Jesus makes a switch that can be confusing. In verses 21-22 he has been warning against *our* anger, but in verse 23 he starts talking about what we should do if *somebody else* is angry (or, at any rate, has cause to be angry) with us. The upshot seems to be that we are not only to take responsibility for mitigating our anger at others, but also to take responsibility for mitigating others' anger at us. The well-functioning person, in Jesus' conception, is one whose general policy and demeanor is to minimize anger, both in oneself and in those with whom one has to do. This is only a general policy because Jesus himself sometimes displays anger (Mk 3:1-6), and the apostle Paul seems to have understood anger among disciples as not always inappropriate (Eph 4:26-27). Thus discernment is needed. Jesus' stress both on the spiritual significance of anger and on each person's responsibility for anger, whether his or her own or somebody else's, should be of guiding interest in our psychological work.

Matthew 5:27-32. Adultery and divorce often come up in counseling, and a psychologist's treatment (theoretical and practical) of these expresses his or her more general views about human nature, sexuality and the family.

In Jesus' discussion of adultery, as in that of anger, he stresses the inwardness that constitutes the relationship. A person whose serious sexual desires are directed to someone other than his or her spouse has already adulterated the marriage bond, because it is a spiritual thing and not just a matter of outward behavior. Christian psychologists will want to know how to manage lust. Since the therapy that Jesus seems, on a literal reading, to commend—an operation we might call auto-ophthalmectomy— will not be encouraged by most Christian psychologists, we must look for some nonliteral counterpart. To know how to help the sufferer "pluck out the lustful eye," it will be essential to know what lust is (how it differs from an ordinary, normal and acceptable attraction to members of the opposite sex, and how it compares with what our contemporaries call a sex "addiction"). We will want to know what choices, habits of life and environmental influences tend to promote it and which ones tend to mitigate it. We will want to distinguish the lust of the married from that of the unmarried. We will want to explore how lust has the alienating effect that Jesus seems to ascribe to it. And we will want to know whether and how it is connected with other sins such as greed, selfishness, pride and anger. If it is so connected, it may need to be treated in connection with other psychopathologies, or they in connection with it. Such a conception of lust will be distinctive of Christian psychology, since in most current psychologies lust is not treated as psychopathology or as the source of psychopathologies.

If the marriage bond is not to be compromised even in thought and feeling, it is certainly a great evil to break it formally and outwardly by divorce. Behind this teaching about divorce that sounds so "inhumane" to modern therapeutic ears is the Judeo-Christian concept of the marriage "self"—a psychology of marriage, if you will—that the two are "one flesh" (Gen 2:24). This thought is behind Paul's statement in 1 Corinthians 6:18 that sexual sins are unique in being against the sinner's own body (read "self"). Jesus seems to be saying that the marriage bond—the self of the one flesh—is indestructible by the formality of divorce, so that postdivorce sexual activity with a person other than the original spouse is adultery. Jesus does not proscribe divorce, though on the present reading he denies the efficacy of any such formal procedure to dismantle the marriage, so perhaps he would allow that sometimes permanent separation is an option (see 1 Cor 7:11). In the clause "except on the ground of unchastity" (Mt 5:32), Jesus seems to allow that adultery itself can destroy the bond, so that the "innocent" party's postdivorce sexual activity with a new partner can be *treated* as not amounting to adultery. Perhaps the thought is that it is as though the original partner were dead (see Rom 7:2-3). But it seems that on the "one flesh" view, remarriage even by the "innocent" party is a compromise involving "self"-damage. It seems safe to say that no modern psychological theory about sex and marriage duplicates the biblical psychology on this point.

Matthew 5:33-37. Why would it be evil to swear by something as opposed to just saying yes or no and keeping one's word? In verses 34-36, Jesus explains his prohibition by referring to the qualities of the things that people were inclined to swear by, thus suggesting that to swear by them was to slight their greatness. In other words, it is a failure of respect. It is as if one says, "If I don't keep this oath, then Jerusalem be damned. If I go back on my word, you can have my hair." On this reading, the dysfunction would be a kind of arrogance in acting as though one is lord of one's own hair or that one is in a position to say, "Let Jerusalem be damned." Or the thought might be that the act of swearing by these things casts the responsibility onto the thing and away from oneself: "If I default on my word, take Jerusalem and we'll be even." Perhaps plain swearing expresses both responsibility and respectful humility.

These virtues might be a psychological theme: There is something healthy about "healthy respect"—for the earth, for the great king and his city, for human achievements, for one's own body. People who lack such respect do seem to us to be shallow or immature and likely to make bad decisions in life. This is, perhaps, a characteristic of people who think very instrumentally about cities, paintings, forests and their own work. On the other hand, to be a person who intelligently but steadfastly keeps his word is to have personal depth and solidity. No doubt some psychopathologies, or at least problems in living, result from lack of respect and lack of responsibility for one's word. A Christian psychology will trace these out.

Matthew 5:38-42. Retaliation is basically dysfunctional and immature behavior. The contrasting actions that Jesus commends—turning the other cheek, giving more than is extorted, going the second mile—are calculated to stop cyclical retaliation and thus cyclical anger and hatred, which destroy or prevent mutual love and cooperation. These actions illustrate a style of response to offenses, and the Christian psychologist who is working with someone who has a problem with vengefulness will want to facilitate a disposition to respond creatively within the Christian style. Accordingly, the phrase "do not resist one who is evil" needs to be applied discriminately. Jesus resisted the "evil" scribes and Pharisees, though he did not retaliate. He was sometimes angry with them and did not hesitate to criticize them, even in rather colorful terms, and no doubt he made them angry. Jesus does not commend being a passive doormat.

The Christian psychologist will want to find ways to help people make needed discriminations and develop the required creativity. He or she will also want to help people recognize subtle, unnoticed retaliations that may be a chief cause of their poor functioning in relationships. The foundational commitment of Jesus' psychology is to love. The premise is that psychological and relational well-being will paradigmatically be love, a beneficent and benevolent relating in which the other is seen and treated as a brother or sister, a respected and valued fellow human being. Deviations from the paradigm, such as anger, are justified only as arising from a motivational background of love.

Matthew 5:43-48. As if we needed any more convincing that, in the Sermon, Jesus is doing, in part, the kind of thing that modern psychologists do (though admittedly in substantively different and largely rival terms), Jesus ends this pericope on loving one's enemies by exhorting the disciples to be *teleioi* as their father in heaven is *teleios*. Dictionaries offer the following as translations of this word: complete, perfect, whole, full-grown, mature. So *teleios* has intimate connections to developmental and therapeutic psychology. Jesus is suggesting that to love one's enemies is to exemplify the behavior and attitude of a mature, grown-up, properly functioning human being, and that to hate one's enemies is childish, an example of stunted growth. A person who hates his enemies is "incomplete"; a person who loves his enemies is in the likeness of his perfect heavenly Father—a complete human person.

STEP TWO: EMPIRICAL RESEARCH WITHIN THE CHRISTIAN TRADITION

So far, we have stressed the retrieval of the long tradition of Christian psychology. But Christian psychologists will have as a second important goal to investigate human beings empirically in a manner common to contemporary psychology, and to practice such research in conformity with their broader commitments. When Jesus exhorts his disciples (Mt 5:48) to be perfect *(teleios)* as their father in heaven is perfect, he is defining a maturity, perfection or ideal that is the Christian standard for evaluating human functioning. A Christian empirical psychology will be "teleological" from the outset, with that "telos" being the picture of human well-being that dominates our Christian psychological tradition (e.g., Wells, 2007).

Such an approach will pursue research strategies that differ in key respects in the assumptions and sometimes in the methods that currently dominate psychology. The often-implied goal of the psychological establishment is to be as "objective" as possible. Historically, this typically meant that any ideal of proper functioning must emerge inductively from an unbiased assessment of empirical data. But one important insight of "postmodern" thought is that the pursuit of uncontestable, worldview-neutral norms of human functioning is quixotic and necessarily beyond the reach of purely empirical methods (Smith, 2005). Psychology is essentially a normative discipline, and norms are never derivable from data alone (Watson, 1993, 2008a). A Christian empirical psychology will begin unapologetically with an explicit normative understanding of human beings and will thus be more methodologically honest than any clinical or personality psychology that even implicitly purports to be "unprejudiced" but which, in fact, must orient itself by a contestable ideal of proper functioning. Psychological research into persons-as-they-should-be cannot avoid operating within the normative framework of one worldview or another. This fact should not be epistemologically embarrassing, nor should it signal abandonment of methodological rigor. A Christian empirical psychology can and should take its place as a worthy intellectual competitor to the secular psychologies (whether naturalistic, humanistic or postmodern) with their usually unacknowledged metaphysical assumptions about human nature and flourishing.

OPERATIONALIZING THE CHRISTIAN TRADITION

On this interpretation of research, Christian psychology, like all worldview-dependent forms of empirical inquiry, will need to engage in two related tasks. First, Christian psychology will need to use well-established, social-scientific methods to examine hypotheses about persons that reflect the teleological assumptions of the worldview. In the Sermon on the Mount, seeing God is explained by purity of heart. Hatred of God is explained by being mastered by mammon. These explanations are testable. In setting up the relevant studies, however, it is crucial to pursue a conceptual analysis that makes it possible to express or "operationalize" these constructs in truly Christian terms. If we are to establish empirically whether the one does or does not cause the other, Christian investigators will need to have a clear idea about what *seeing God* and *being pure in heart* amount to procedurally, so that it can be assessed in an actual human life. This determination will require careful historical and hermeneutical analysis. A Christian psychology will therefore need to supplement standard research procedures with conceptual demonstrations of what might be called "tradition validity"—the fitness of research instruments to measure psychological realities *by the norms given in one's metaphysical/religious tradition*. Such operationalizations, in other words, will need to reflect the Christian tradition faithfully. And if the claims of the tradition seem to be disconfirmed by defensibly valid procedures, then Christian researchers will have good reason to suspect that they have misconstrued Christian psychology and that they should return to the Bible and the tradition for a better interpretation. Faith, in these instances, will use empirical methods as a stimulus for seeking deeper understanding.

Numerous studies have in fact, either directly or indirectly, advanced the distinctively Christian goals of Christian psychology. Much of this indirect work falls under the rubric of "psychology of religion," and the "tradition validity" of these studies has not always been expressed formally but can be inferred from the content of and findings for many of the measures used in this area of research. Christians, for instance, are likely to believe that prayer and meditative communion with God can have beneficial effects, and this hypothesis has received support in a variety of research projects (see Finney & Malony, 1985; Francis & Astley, 2001; Lewis & Breslin, 2008). An extensive and complex literature has also examined the overall impact of religion on psychosocial functioning (Spilka, Hood, Hunsberger & Gorsuch, 2003), and in conformity with biblical beliefs, has documented the general mental health advantages of serious religious commitments (Gartner, Larsen & Allen, 1991). More specifically, recent research has associated religion with beneficial forms of self-control and self-regulation (McCullough & Willoughby, 2009), and distinctive virtues emphasized by the Christian tradition, like hope, forgiveness and gratitude, have been linked with psychological adjustment (e.g., Worthington, 2006; Fraser, Dutton & Guilford, 2006).

More directly, empirical investigations into beliefs about sin illustrate how a more formally Christian psychology research program might develop. Secular psychological theory often stresses how beliefs in sin necessarily promote a psychopathological form of guilt. The Christian message, however, is that the problem of sin is covered by God's grace. Confirmation of the biblical perspective is suggested in procedures demonstrating that sin-related beliefs predict greater mental health when examined within the context of beliefs about grace (Watson, Morris & Hood, 1988a, 1988b). Such findings point toward a plausible Christian hypothesis. A biblical worldview may nurture development of a psychological dynamic that encourages healthier self-functioning. More specifically, beliefs in sin may promote a form of self-reflection that helps one more honestly evaluate one's needs for improvement (i.e., repentance), and this process can occur without defensiveness because truthful discovery of transgressions will be covered by God's grace. The ultimate consequence should be a lifelong process of self-maturation as defined by the Christian *telos*. Indeed, newly developed scales demonstrate even more clearly that Christian beliefs about sin (Watson, Morris, Loy, Hamrick & Grizzle, 2007) and about grace (Sisemore, Arbuckle, Mortellaro, Swanson & Santan, 2007) broadly predict better psychological adjustment.

With regard to other more formally Christian research, Johnson (1998), for example, found a distinctive pattern of complex thinking in Christian undergraduates that supports a Christian model of postformal cognitive development. And Johnson and Kim (submitted for publication) have shown that Christians can make distinctions in their self-representation that correspond fittingly to the Christian metanarrative (creation, Fall, redemption). Kwon (2009) has recently developed scales to measure wisdom from a distinctly Christian perspective, and contrasted that with a secular model of wisdom. Though such research is in its infancy, empirical tests of distinctively Christian conceptual frameworks point to the promise of Christian psychological research.

COMPARATIVE EMPIRICAL INVESTIGATIONS IN LIGHT OF WORLDVIEWS

Christian psychologists will also need to pursue a second research task. Empirical methods will need to examine issues in a comparative psychological perspective that brings the Christian worldview into explicit dialogue with the worldviews and often hidden metaphysical assumptions of establishment psychology. Such research will accomplish at least four goals.

First, it will help Christian psychology maintain a faithfully Christian sensitivity to prominent concerns within establishment psychology. An emphasis on Christian faithfulness should help highlight differences between the psychologies of the Christian tradition and the contemporary psychologies (Watson, 2008a, 2008b).

Second, we will want to use comparative methods to defend our tradition against unwarranted criticism. Comparative empirical procedures have demonstrated, for example, that research programs based on existentialist (Watson, Hood & Morris, 1988), humanistic (Watson, Morris & Hood, 1990), rational-emotive (Watson, Morris & Hood, 1993) and other (Rosik, 2007a, 2007b) ideological perspectives sometimes misrepresent the psychological implications of Christian belief. Christian psychologists will seek to eliminate such bias in their own use of empirical methods.

Third, comparative procedures could help discover commonalities across perspectives that are useful in pursuing causes of common concern. Christian communities, for example, will not be alone in their desire to nurture loving marriages, happy families and social justice.

Finally, such procedures could encourage Christians to remain open to the possibility of valid critique from other perspectives. Evidence obtained in dialogue with other psychological frameworks could suggest some incoherence within Christian understandings of an issue. In such cases, Christian researchers would once again have good reasons for suspecting that they should return to the Bible and to their tradition for deeper understanding.

In trying, particularly, to accomplish the second task, Christian psychology will need to develop methodological innovations, because Christian investigations will need to demonstrate empirically how the sometimes-unacknowledged, metaphysical assumptions of worldviews can influence empirical findings. Thus far, five procedures have been devised for this purpose.

First, *direct rational analysis*[3] may be especially useful in documenting a potential bias against Christian views in psychological research. For example, a scale was created to determine if a person avoided, in a maladjusted way, the harsh realities of life, like questions of meaninglessness, suffering and death. Correlational evidence found that using this scale will predict both sincere Christian commitments and anxiety, and will therefore, in fact, link Christian commitments with an anxious refusal to confront existential realities (Watson, Hood & Morris, 1988). However, one question within this scale that supposedly indicates "existential avoidance" is the affirmation that "God exists," and another identifies this avoidance

---

[3]Contemporary philosophers term this activity "conceptual analysis," whereas those in the human sciences label it "qualitative research" (see, for example, Creswell, 2005).

in a positive response to the belief that a person is "quite certain what happens after death." Instead of accurately measuring avoidance, these questions may merely reveal the scale's existentialist metaphysical framework, where faith is interpreted as a tendency to hide from the harsh realities of life, thus indicating maladjustment. Most orthodox Christians, assuming their theistic point of view, would regard belief in God as reflecting a healthy confrontation with the realities of existence. Using direct rational analysis, some items in the original scale were determined to contradict Christian faith (forming an "anti-Christian" subscale), whereas other items were unobjectionable from a Christian standpoint (forming a "Christian-neutral" subscale). Based on reanalysis of these subscales, the association of sincere Christian faith with "existential avoidance" was found to be limited to the *anti-Christian items,* and maladaptive existential avoidance was determined by responses to the Christian-neutral subscale. Consequently, the initial finding of a correlation between the full scale and sincere Christian commitments merely demonstrated that the original scale was biased against Christian belief in God and the afterlife. In other words, the original scale operated as a tautological empirical ambush of Christians.

A second comparative investigative strategy, *correlational marker procedures,* relies on a psychological scale that has "tradition validity" to evaluate the role of metaphysical assumptions in previous empirical research. Again, "tradition validity" for Christians is the conceptual fitness of a scale to measure variables in a way that is consistent with or valid for the Christian tradition. In one project using a largely Christian sample, researchers examined relationships between a measure of sincere religious commitments and each of 150 separate items from a humanistic self-actualization scale (Watson, Morris & Hood, 1993). Some of these items correlated positively with the religious commitment scale and thus were marked "pro-Christian," but others correlated negatively and consequently were marked as "anti-Christian." One "pro-Christian" marker of "self-actualization," for example, was, "I do not have feelings of resentment about things that are past." One "anti-Christian" marker of "self-actualization" stated, "People need not repent their wrongdoings." In correlations with other measures, "pro-Christian" statements more likely predicted adjustment, whereas "anti-Christian" items pointed toward poorer psychological functioning. Inclusion of both "pro-Christian" and "anti-Christian" items within a single scale therefore resulted

in a measure that was misleading in describing Christians with regard to the
presumed mental health of "self-actualization." Most notably, the "pro-
Christian" and "anti-Christian" items of the scale correlated negatively with
each other. This feature of the instrument was thus a violation of psycho-
metric standards of scale development, which require a strong positive relationship among all items within a scale. This humanistic measure, therefore,
not only was biased against the assessment of healthy Christian self-
functioning, but this bias created a metaphysically based internal incoherence in the instrument, at least with reference to the measurement of
Christians. More generally, such findings, therefore, illustrate how a widely
used and generally accepted psychological scale could have hidden liabilities
when administered to Christians.

Third, the *empirical translation schemes* technique examines whether the
language of a psychological worldview can be "translated" into the language of Christianity. Conflicts between worldviews may so polarize perceptions as to undermine people's sensitivity to similarities between worldviews. In defending our own perspective, for example, Christians may
mistakenly presume that another perspective is *wholly* different and *wholly*
wrong. A Christian commitment to truth would seem to require us to
explore the actual boundaries of difference by also taking care to map out
areas of possible agreement. Are assertions made in the language of one
worldview at least partially compatible with Christian beliefs? If so, then
it should be possible to show that Christian articulations of a belief correlate positively with non-Christian assertions of the analogous belief in
another psychological framework. Conversely, are beliefs articulated in a
non-Christian language radically opposed to Christian understandings? If
so, then it should be possible to demonstrate that Christian expressions of
a belief correlate negatively with the parallel non-Christian statements. In
short, the empirical translation schemes technique seeks to determine in
empirically defensible ways how agreements and differences can be translated. This procedure, therefore, makes it possible to test hypotheses about
a more truthful mapping of positions across worldviews.

For instance, both Christian and secular psychological theorists sometimes suppose that the humanistic vision of self-actualization is diametri-
cally opposed to or is wholly incommensurable with Christian assumptions. Research using the correlational marker procedures described above

already raises doubt about such a supposition (since some self-actualization items successfully measured Christian well-being), but the empirical translation schemes technique offers a way to test this issue with greater precision. For example, with the empirical translation schemes procedure, each statement of self-actualization in a humanistic psychological scale could be articulated in a number of hypothetically comparable expressions of a Christian maturational ideal. A positive correlation between the two kinds of statements then identifies some degree of conceptual overlap. One study using this procedure found that Christian communities have linguistic resources to describe something similar to what humanists call "self-actualization" (Watson, Milliron, Morris & Hood, 1995). One humanistic measure of self-actualization says, for instance, "I can like people without having to approve of them," and it was found to positively correlate with a roughly analogous Christian statement—"Christ's love for sinners has taught me to love people regardless of their background and lifestyle." The resulting *"Christian* self-actualization scale" predicted higher levels of Christian commitment and, as made apparent in relationships with other measures of healthy self-functioning, turned out to be more useful than the secular humanistic self-actualization scale in assessing Christian psychological adjustment.[4]

The empirical translation schemes technique can also be used to test hypotheses about radical incompatibilities between worldviews. The discovery of linguistic parallels between worldviews can lead in all kinds of interpretive directions. For example, discoveries that humanistic self-actualization can be rendered in roughly analogous articulations of at least some dimensions of the *Christian* maturational ideal might be treated as evidence that humanism has unacknowledged foundations in Christianity that need to be admitted and more fully understood (Ghali & Dueck, 2008). Evidence of apparent incompatibilities between worldviews might also lead to sharpened thinking about the incompatibilities that actually

---

[4]While most of the comparative procedures discussed here examine the distinguishing effects of worldviews on psychological research, the purpose of the present procedure is to demonstrate that differing worldviews are not entirely incommensurable. Notable conceptual overlap was discovered between two measures of a psychological construct, which reflect two different worldviews. However, the different forms of expression (and the low correlations obtained) also suggest that the two questionnaires are not measuring *identical* concepts, the concepts are analogous to each other, and therefore they provide grounds for communication between researchers from different worldview communities.

do exist. Then, the empirical translation schemes technique could be used to test hypotheses about how other humanistic interpretations of psychological adjustment can only be in conflict or incommensurable with other dimensions of Christian maturity. Overall, however, findings based on the empirical translation schemes procedure already suggest that Christian and establishment psychologists should consult the resources of both traditions in order to define more precisely the similarities and differences that do exist between worldviews.

Fourth, *comparative rationality analysis* requires that Christians respond to an extant psychological scale twice. First, they react to questionnaire items under standard conditions (reading them as they were intended to be read by the original investigators). Then, they respond once again, but this time by evaluating whether each scale item is consistent or inconsistent with their personal religious commitments. For example, one psychological measure of "irrational beliefs" presumes that it is psychopathological to believe, "People need a source of strength outside themselves." However, Christians with their theistic worldview will naturally evaluate this kind of statement as being quite rational and healthy, and such "dependency"-expressing beliefs have, in fact, been confirmed as predictive of greater mental health (Watson, Morris & Hood 1988c). Analysis of the Christian evaluations of these supposedly "irrational" beliefs can be used to determine how a particular psychological scale can be rescored to operationalize an empirically derived Christian perspective on what rationality and irrationality actually are within the Christian psychological framework. Comparisons can then be made *quantitatively* between the psychological establishment and Christian psychology with regard to how to define irrationality. Unsurprisingly, this comparative analysis of rationalities has demonstrated that, as made evident in patterns of relationships with other measures, a Christian rationality is relatively more valid than the psychological establishment rationality when used with Christians (Watson, Morris & Hood, 1993).[5]

Fifth and finally, *statistical control procedures* examine the relationship between Christian commitments and psychological functioning after ac-

---

[5]We recognize that empirical strategies like this one cannot obtain perfect validity in establishing norms such as rationality or mental health within a Christian worldview framework (Watson, 1993, 2008a). Such empirical work necessarily depends on the competence of the study's subjects to make valid judgments about Christian rationality or the Christian conception of mental health.

counting for possible conflicts between worldviews. In one project, numerous measures of Christian religious commitment were correlated with an array of scales assessing self-esteem, self-acceptance and self-actualization (Watson, Morris & Hood, 1987). For these scales taken together, Christian commitments were more likely to predict unhealthy than healthy self-functioning, although most relationships proved to be significant. In this study, an effort was also made to both assess self-actualization in humanistic terms that were clearly anti-Christian and then to assess Christian beliefs about sin and guilt that were clearly anti-humanistic. Statistical procedures made it possible to subtract out the influences of anti-Christian and antihumanistic language on the observed relationships. The result was that Christian commitments were overwhelmingly linked with healthy self-functioning. Definitive interpretation of these results is complex and will likely require additional research. Nevertheless, this outcome demonstrates the importance of understanding how worldviews can condition supposedly "objective" empirical assessments of Christian psychological functioning.

In short, a Christian empirical psychology will begin with a formal commitment to its own "tradition validity," the details of which will be supplied by retrieving them from the historical Christian tradition (see "Step One" above). Sometimes, this will mean that the metaphysical assumptions of Christianity will supply a conceptual foundation for articulating and then exploring explicitly Christian research hypotheses. These studies should use the full range of available social-scientific methodologies. At other times, "tradition validity" will reveal a need for procedural innovations that make it clear that worldview assumptions can never be eliminated wholly from social-scientific research and that beliefs associated with Christian and all other worldviews require a respectful attention that is factored into the research itself. We should also make clear that Christians are free to pursue investigations of countless psychological topics that are not as worldview dependent as those discussed above, for example, neuropsychology, episodic memory, cognitive development, schizophrenia and social influence—areas where faith assumptions make relatively little measurable impact on the investigations. However, our primary agenda in this chapter was to show the need for Christians to practice their psychology in light of their basic assumptions and the resources of their distinctive tradition. At the most comprehensive level, "tradition validity" for Christians will mean that the Christian worldview, which comes to us from the past, will enable us to meet the challenges of the present faithfully by rationally and empirically demonstrating how essential the love of Christ is for our future (Watson, 2008b).

THE PROMISE OF CHRISTIAN PSYCHOLOGY

Why should we pursue Christian psychology, the psychology of our faith, and not be satisfied with simply accepting modern psychology as it is? The basic answer to this question is that psychology is native to Christianity; it is already a fundamental dimension of our faith.

If the experience of churches in the past one hundred years is any indication for the future, we can expect that in the measure that we lose touch with our own psychology and replace it with the psychologies of the establishment, we will also lose touch with the apostolic faith. Ours is a psychological age, an age in which people hunger and thirst for psychology, buy self-help books that induct them into psychological patterns of thinking about themselves that are, in many ways, alien and contrary to the faith, and become formed in the image of this advice and theory. The chief impetus behind the Christian psychology model is that we cannot, in faith, simply leave our psychological thinking to be done by non-Christians, or even to be done by Christians according to the canons and methods of the establishment psychologies.

Today, many, if not most, Christians who are psychologists teaching in colleges and universities and working in clinical settings are far better versed in the establishment psychologies than they are in the psychology of their own religious tradition. Many are not even aware that their tradition *has* a psychology of its own. For them, psychology is simply the psychology of the establishment. The promise of Christian psychology is that this situation can change. All Christians who work as professionals in psychology should be at least as well versed in the thought of some great Christian psychologist as they are in their own corner of establishment psychology. What if Christians in the field were to chart a new direction in psychology, one based on the Bible and their tradition, devising new hypotheses, research programs, psychological theories, and clinical practices in areas where worldview beliefs make a difference? In addition to demonstrating the potential value of

Christian worldview beliefs for the human sciences, they could help to usher in a more pluralistic psychology. This would be a psychology that acknowledges the essential roles that worldview beliefs and interpretation play in psychological theory and research—and which welcomes worldview-explicit psychologies, along with the establishment psychologies. Such a shift would lead to a more comprehensive understanding of human beings. Such a shift would permit Christian psychologists (as well as those from other worldview communities) to teach, publish and practice in the public square according to their worldview commitments.

REFERENCES

Annas, J. (1993). *The morality of happiness.* New York: Oxford University Press.

Aristotle. (1980). *Nicomachean ethics* (W. D. Ross, Trans., J. L. Ackrill & J. O. Urmson, Eds.). Oxford: Oxford University Press.

Browning, D. S. (1987). *Religious thought and the modern psychologies: A critical conversation in the theology of culture.* Philadelphia: Fortress Press.

Browning, D. S., & Cooper, T. D. (2004). *Religious thought and the modern psychologies* (2nd ed.). Philadelphia: Fortress Press.

Charry, E. T. (1997). *By the renewing of your minds: The pastoral function of Christian doctrine.* New York: Oxford University Press.

Cole, S. O. (1995). The biological basis of homosexuality: A Christian assessment. *Journal of Psychology and Theology, 23,* 89-100.

Corsini, R. J., & Wedding, D. (2007). *Current psychotherapies* (8th ed.). Florence, KY: Brooks Cole.

Creswell, J. W. (2005). *Qualitative inquiry and research design: Choosing among five traditions.* Thousand Oaks, CA: Sage.

Edwards, J. (1959). *A treatise concerning religious affections.* New Haven, CT: Yale University Press. (Original work published 1746)

———. (1969). *Charity and its fruits.* Edinburgh: Banner of Truth. (Original work published 1852)

Evans, C. S. (1989). *Wisdom and humanness in psychology: Prospects for a Christian approach.* Grand Rapids, MI: Baker.

———. (1990). *Søren Kierkegaard's Christian psychology: Insight for counseling and pastoral care.* Grand Rapids, MI: Zondervan.

———. (2004). *Kierkegaard's ethic of love: Divine commands and moral obligations.* New York: Oxford University Press.

Finney, J. R., & Malony, H. N., Jr. (1985). Empirical studies of Christian prayer: A review of the literature. *Journal of Psychology and Theology, 13,* 104-15.

Francis, L., & Astley, J. (Eds.). (2001). *Psychological perspectives on prayer.* Leominster, UK: Gracewing.

Fraser, W., Dutton, K., & Guilford, L. (2006). Human spiritual qualities: Integrating psychology and religion. *Mental Health, Religion & Culture, 9,* 277-89.

Gartner, J., Larson, D. B., & Allen, G. D. (1991). Religious commitment and mental health:

A review of the empirical literature. *Journal of Psychology and Theology, 19,* 6-25.

Ghali, A., & Dueck, A. C. (2008). Lost in translation: A response to Watson. *Edification: Journal of the Society for Christian Psychology, 2*(1), 25-27.

Gurman, A. S., & Messer, S. B. (2003). *Essential psychotherapies.* New York: Guilford.

Johnson, E. L. (1992). A place for the Bible within psychological science. *Journal of Psychology and Theology, 20,* 346-55.

———. (1998). Growing in wisdom in Christian community: Toward measures of Christian postformal development. *Journal of Psychology and Theology, 26,* 365-81.

———. (2007a). *Foundations for soul care: A Christian psychology proposal.* Downers Grove, IL: IVP Academic.

———. (2007b). Toward a philosophy of science for Christian psychology. *Edification: Journal of the Society for Christian Psychology, 1*(1), 5-20.

Johnson, E. L., & Kim, L. (2009). Assessing the metanarrative perspectives of a Christian self-representation. Manuscript submitted for publication.

Kierkegaard, S. (1980). *The concept of anxiety* (R. Thomte, Trans.). Princeton, NJ: Princeton University Press. (Original work published 1844)

———. (1992). *Concluding unscientific postscript to philosophical fragments* (H. Hong & E. Hong, Trans.). Princeton, NJ: Princeton University Press. (Original work published 1846)

———. (1993). *Upbuilding discourses in various spirits* (H. Hong & E. Hong, Trans.). Princeton, NJ: Princeton University Press. (Original work published 1847)

———. (1995). *Works of love* (H. Hong & E. Hong, Trans.). Princeton, NJ: Princeton University Press. (Original work published 1847)

———. (1997). *Christian discourses: The crisis and a crisis in the life of an actress* (H. Hong & E. Hong, Trans.). Princeton, NJ: Princeton University Press. (Original work published 1848)

———. (1980). *Sickness unto death* (H. Hong & E. Hong, Trans.). Princeton, NJ: Princeton University Press. (Original work published 1849)

Kwon, V. (2009). An empirical exploration of wisdom from a Christian psychology perspective. Unpublished doctoral dissertation, Southern Baptist Theological Seminary, Louisville, KY.

Lambert, M., & Bergin, A. (1994). The effectiveness of psychotherapy. In A. Bergin and S. Garfield (Eds.), *Handbook of psychotherapy and behavior change* (4th ed., pp. 143-90). New York: Wiley.

Lewis, C. A., & Breslin, M. J. (2008). Prayer and mental health: An introduction to this special issue of *Mental Health, Religion & Culture. Mental Health, Religion & Culture, 11,* 1-7.

McCullough, M. E., & Willoughby, B. (2009). Religion, self-regulation, and self-control: Associations, explanations, and implications. *Psychological Bulletin, 135,* 69-93.

Maddi, S. (1980). *Personality theories: A comparative analysis.* Homewood, IL: Dorsey.

Nussbaum, M. C. (1994). *The theory of desire: Theory and practice in Hellenistic ethics.* Princeton, NJ: Princeton University Press.

Peterson, C., & Seligman, M. (2004). *Handbook of positive psychology.* New York: Oxford University Press.

Plantinga, C. (1994). *Not the way it's supposed to be: A breviary of sin.* Grand Rapids, MI: Eerdmans.

Roberts, R. (1987). Psychotherapeutic virtue and the grammar of faith. *Journal of Psychology and Theology, 15*, 191-204.

———. (1992). Thomas Aquinas on the morality of emotions. *History of Philosophy Quarterly, 9*, 287-305.

———. (1993). *Taking the word to heart: Self and other in an age of therapies.* Grand Rapids, MI: Eerdmans.

———. (1997a). Parameters of a Christian psychology. In R. C. Roberts & M. R. Talbot (Eds.), *Limning the psyche: Explorations in Christian psychology* (pp. 74-101). Grand Rapids, MI: Eerdmans.

———. (1997b). Attachment: Bowlby and the Bible. In R. C. Roberts & M. R. Talbot (Eds.), *Limning the psyche: Explorations in Christian psychology* (pp. 206-28). Grand Rapids, MI: Eerdmans.

———. (1997c). Dialectical emotions and the virtue of faith. In R. L. Perkins (Ed.), *International Kierkegaard commentary: Concluding unscientific postscript* (pp. 73-93). Macon, GA: Mercer University Press.

———. (1997d). Christian psychology? In R. C. Roberts & M. R. Talbot (Eds.), *Limning the psyche: Explorations in Christian psychology* (pp. 1-19). Grand Rapids, MI: Eerdmans.

———. (1997e). Existence, emotion and virtue: Classical themes in Kierkegaard. In A. Hannay & G. D. Marino (Eds.), *The Cambridge companion to Kierkegaard* (pp. 177-206). Cambridge: Cambridge University Press.

———. (2001). Outline of Pauline psychotherapy. In M. McMinn & T. Phillips (Eds.), *Care for the soul: Exploring the intersection of theology and psychology* (pp. 134-63). Downers Grove, IL: InterVarsity Press.

———. (2007a). Compassion as an emotion and as a virtue. In I. Dalferth and A. Hunziker (Eds.), *Mitleid* (Religion in Philosophy and Theology, Vol. 28, pp. 119-37). Tübingen: Mohr Siebeck.

———. (2007b). Situationism and the New Testament psychology of the heart. In D. L. Jeffrey (Ed.), *The Bible and the academy*, pp. 139-60. Grand Rapids, MI: Zondervan.

Roberts, R., & Wood, W. J. (2007). *Intellectual virtues: An essay in regulative epistemology.* Oxford: Oxford University Press.

Rosik, C. (2007a). Ideological concerns in the operationalization of homophobia, part 1: An analysis of Herek's ATLG-R scale. *Journal of Psychology and Theology, 35*(2), 132-44.

Rosik, C. (2007b). Ideological concerns in the operationalization of homophobia, part II: The need for interpretive sensitivity with conservatively religious persons. *Journal of Psychology and Theology, 35*(2), 145-52.

Sisemore, T.A., Arbuckle, M., Mortellaro, E., Swanson, M., & Santan, B. (2007, March). *Grace and mental health: Relationships and implications for practice.* Presentation at the Christian Association for Psychological Studies Annual Convention, Valley Forge, Pennsylvania.

Smith, R. S. (2005). *Christian postmodernism and the linguistic turn.* In M. B. Penner (Ed.), *Christianity and the postmodern turn* (pp. 53-69). Grand Rapids, MI: Brazos Press.

Spilka, B., Hood, R. W., Jr., Hunsberger, B., & Gorsuch, R. (2003). *The psychology of religion: The empirical approach* (3rd ed.). New York: Guilford Press.

Talbot, M. R. (1997). Starting from Scripture. In R. C. Roberts & M. R. Talbot (Eds.),

Limning the psyche: Explorations in Christian psychology (pp. 102-22). Grand Rapids, MI: Eerdmans.

Van Leeuwen, M. S. (1985). *The person in psychology: A contemporary Christian appraisal.* Grand Rapids, MI: Eerdmans.

Vitz, P. C. (1994). *Psychology as religion: The cult of self-worship* (2nd ed.). Grand Rapids, MI: Eerdmans.

———. (1997). A Christian theory of personality. In R. C. Roberts & M. R. Talbot (Eds.), *Limning the psyche: Explorations in Christian psychology* (pp. 20-40). Grand Rapids, MI: Eerdmans.

Watson, P. J. (1993). Apologetics and ethnocentrism: Psychology and religion within an ideological surround. *International Journal for the Psychology of Religion, 3,* 1-20.

———. (2008a). Faithful translation and postmodernism: Norms and linguistic relativity within a Christian ideological surround. *Edification: Journal of the Society for Christian Psychology, 2*(1), 5-18.

———. (2008b). Faithful translation, ideological perspectives, and Christian psychology beyond postmodernism. *Edification: Journal of the Society for Christian Psychology, 2*(1), 51-62.

Watson, P. J., Hood, R. W., Jr., & Morris, R. J. (1988). Existential confrontation and religiosity. *Counseling and Values, 33,* 47-54.

Watson, P. J., Milliron, J. T., Morris, R. J., & Hood, R. W., Jr. (1995). Religion and the self as text: Toward a Christian translation of self-actualization. *Journal of Psychology and Theology, 23,* 180-89.

Watson, P. J., Morris, R. J., & Hood, R. W., Jr. (1987). Antireligious humanistic values, guilt, and self esteem. *Journal for the Scientific Study of Religion, 26,* 535-46.

———. (1988a). Sin and self-functioning. Part 1: Grace, guilt and self-consciousness. *Journal of Psychology and Theology, 16,* 254-69.

———. (1988b). Sin and self-functioning. Part 2: Grace, guilt and psychological adjustment. *Journal of Psychology and Theology, 16,* 270-81.

———. (1988c). Sin and self-functioning, Part 3: The psychology and ideology of irrational beliefs. *Journal of Psychology and Theology, 16,* 348-61.

———. (1990). Intrinsicness, self-actualization and the ideological surround. *Journal of Psychology and Theology, 18,* 40-53.

———. Mental health, religion, and the ideology of irrationality. In D. O. Moberg & M. L. Lynn (Eds.), *Research in the Social Scientific Study of Religion.* (Vol. 5, pp. 53-88). Greenwich, CT: Jai Press.

Watson, P. J., Morris, R. J., Loy, T., Hamrick, M. B., & Grizzle, S. (2007). Beliefs about sin: Adaptive implications in relationships with religious orientation, self-esteem, and measures of the narcissistic, depressed and anxious self. *Edification: Journal of the Society for Christian Psychology, 1*(1), 57-65.

Wells, M. A. (2007). The necessity of a Christocentric anthropology for Christian Psychology: Reflections on Ray Anderson's doctrine of humanity. *Edification: Journal of the Society for Christian Psychology, 2*(2), 57-64.

Worthington, E. L., Jr. (2006). *Forgiveness and reconciliation: Theory and practice.* New York: Brunner-Routledge.

A Levels-of-Explanation Response
to Christian Psychology

David G. Myers

WHAT A GREAT IDEA FOR PHILOSOPHER Robert Roberts to combine his knowledge of intellectual history with the insights of the distinguished psychology-religion explorer Paul Watson. They offer us a model of interdisciplinary collaboration.

In this chapter, and in his previous writings, Roberts has helped us view today's psychology from the broader perspective of 2500 years of big ideas. These ideas include the teachings of Jesus, notably the Sermon on the Mount, which offers rich insights relevant to our day and our work—richer insights, suggest Roberts and Watson, than those offered by the science of today's "establishment psychology." Instead, Roberts and Watson advocate a distinct "Christian psychology" that "will therefore require a careful rereading of Scripture, in the light of some of the great Christian psychologists of the subsequent past (Augustine, Aquinas, Pascal, Kierkegaard)" (p. 155).

Like Roberts and Watson, I am inspired by Jesus' Sermon on the Mount (my favorite Scripture section). I, too, have found Pascal's wisdom, as expressed in his *Pensees*, to have remarkable foresight in anticipating some big ideas of today's cognitive science. Ditto La Rochefoucauld's *Maxims* and Francis Bacon's *Novum Organum*. All three of these works, from some three centuries in the past, anticipated modern explorations of phenomena such as self-serving bias, automatic processing and illusory thinking.

I concur with Roberts and Watson's esteem for the rich insights of the ancient philosophers, of Jesus and of theologians from Augustine to Kierkegaard, but I do so without conflating them all as psychology. By nearly all definitions, psychology is *today's* science of behavior and mental processes. So while Roberts and Watson may dismiss today's psychology—that of national psychology organizations, of leading universities, of psychology exams and of psychology texts—as mere "establishment psychology" and instead advocate Christians to gather on their own to create a different psychology, that's a bit like dismissing the American Medical Association or the National Institute of Health or university medical schools as offering "establishment medicine." So they are, but Christians are ill-advised to scorn their achievements and to absent themselves from medicine's practice and leadership.

Rather than replacing psychological science with the sages of the ages, why not respect *both* as valuable but limited? We esteem literature, philosophy and religion as distinct and valuable disciplines that ask their own questions with their own methods, and while we might relate their insights to those of psychological science, we shouldn't diffuse psychology's focus on scientific explorations of behavior and mind by equating, say, philosophy with psychology.

More so than Roberts and Watson, and this volume's other authors, I find myself intrigued by psychological science's discoveries, which the sages of the ages seem not to have anticipated, such as

- the functions of our two brain hemispheres
- the quantified heritability of a multitude of traits
- the remarkable cognitive abilities of newborns
- the extent to which peer influences trump parental nurture in shaping children's language, smoking habits and lifestyle choices
- the effects of experience at different ages on the brain's neural networks
- changes in mental abilities with aging
- how eyewitnesses construct, and reconstruct, memories
- the powers and perils of intuition
- the components of intelligence
- the effects of stress on the body's immune system
- the ways our self-concept guides our information processing
- the effects of aerobic exercise on mild depression and anxiety
- the things that do and don't predict human happiness

Psychological science is barely more than a century old. What we have learned is only a beginning and will seem as relative ignorance to our great-grandchildren. As I emphasized in my chapter, the scope of its questions and answers are limited. It offers only one perspective on life. Yet what we have learned—and my list just scratches the surface—is, methinks, worth celebrating.

If establishment psychology is indeed where significant discoveries and new understandings are emerging, do we really want to run off into the corner to create our own Christian psychology? By doing so do we not risk irrelevance? Are we not called to be in the world, if not of it? to be salt and light to the world? And do we not, therefore, need *more* Christian scholars not in the stands but down on the playing field? With an intellectual Super Bowl underway, do we not want Christians called into the game? As C. S. Lewis once declared, "We do not need more Christian books; we need more books by Christians about everything with Christian values built in." Or as Stanton Jones says in his chapter, "Christians should be in the thick of psychology, contributing their ideas, submitting their hypotheses and theories to the test" (p. 115).

Reformed philosopher Nicholas Wolterstorff said it well in urging the Christian psychologist to occupy the academy

> as a Christian who sees the world in the light of the gospel, but occupy it also as a psychologist, not as one who surveys the scene from outside and now and then makes some clucking noises, but as one who participates in the nitty-gritty of actual psychological explorations. Do not just be a critic. Be a creative initiator, faithful in your thinking as in your doing the gospel of Jesus Christ.

Our differing perspectives and callings aside, I concur with Roberts and Watson that "norms are never derivable from data alone" (p. 165). Child-rearing advice, therapy interventions, topics of investigation and even our labels for psychological phenomena all reflect our preexisting values. Is responsiveness to social influence "conformity" or is it "social sensitivity"? Is saying only nice things about oneself "high self-esteem" or "defensiveness"? Is opinion change "brainwashing" or "education"? As Roberts and Watson say, we "cannot avoid operating within the normative framework of one worldview or another" (p. 165).

Two other brief observations:

1. Roberts and Watson criticize positive psychologists for seeking a universal description of human virtues that crosses cultures and religious traditions. It's not just positive psychologists who have done so. In *The*

Abolition of Man, C. S. Lewis offered a list of universal moral teachings, which he called "natural law" or "Tao," that cross cultures and faiths. An illustration came from the 1993 World Parliament of Religion: "Every form of egoism should be rejected. . . . We must treat others as we wish others to treat us. . . . We consider humankind our family" (pp. 7, 2).

2. Roberts and Watson helpfully encourage a spirit of humility: "If the claims of [Christian] tradition seem to be disconfirmed by defensibly valid procedures, then Christian researchers will have good reason to suspect that they have misconstrued Christian psychology and that they should return to the Bible and the tradition for a better interpretation. Faith, in these instances, will use empirical methods as a stimulus for seeking deeper understanding" (p. 166). To that I say, Amen. And so it has happened as Christians have been inspired by new understandings of ecology, of race, of gender and of sexual orientation to remove the lenses of their own cultural assumptions and to take a second and deeper look at what the Bible actually teaches. As Anselm (A.D. 1033–1109) reminded us, "faith seeks understanding."

REFERENCES

Parliament of the World's Religions. (1993). Declaration toward a global ethic. New York: Continuum   <www.parliamentofreligions.org/_includes/FCKcontent/File/Towards AGlobalEthic.pdf>.

An Integration Response to Christian Psychology

Stanton L. Jones

THERE IS MUCH TO PRAISE IN THIS PRESENTATION of a view of Christian psychology. The heart of the view advocated here is summarized in a substantive paragraph that begins "In short . . ." (p. 173). This paragraph is too long to quote here, but it distills the entire argument that Christianity—indeed Christian faith—embodies or entails certain psychological views of the person that can and should have a transformative impact on our scientific and applied/therapeutic efforts. The authors continue: "The chief impetus behind the Christian psychology model is that we cannot, in faith, simply leave our psychological thinking to be done by non-Christians, or even to be done by Christians according to the canons and methods of the establishment" (p. 174). The argument is a good one, one that I have trouble distinguishing from the core of the integrationist approach. C. Stephen Evans (2005), regarded as one of the founding thinkers of the Christian psychology movement, also fails to see the sharp contrasts of the Christian psychology project with the integration movement, seeing the two instead as complementary ventures.

This chapter offers important arguments regarding how our views of the person are always profoundly conditioned from the assumptive or presuppositional framework—the worldview—we adopt as we begin to frame our inquiry. Their critique of positive psychology as an example is incisive and edifying, particularly regarding that movement's tendency to brush aside important distinctions in how different religions construe the different virtues. Roberts and Watson's argument that "the concept of human psychic well-being is *essentially contested.* That is, it is not the kind of question that can be settled to everyone's satisfaction independently of metaphysical, moral and religious commitments" (p. 150) is exactly right. Christians must approach the subject matter of humanity embracing what God has told us about what it means to be fully human first; that then is our framework for engaging psychology as a social science.

In his prior presentation of this approach in the first edition of this book, Roberts (2000) brought his argument to its conclusion by arguing that "Our task as Christian psychologists, as I see it, is in large part to retrieve the Christian psychology of the past, understand what these writers have to say, sift it for what has enduring importance and present it to our contemporaries as a form that can be understood and used" (p. 153). While arguably important as a foundation, this made the task of Christian psychology look primarily historical, lacking a rich grasp of the possibilities for constructive, prospective contribution to furthering and deepening our understanding of human psychology. That limitation has been corrected in this new presentation of the approach. Roberts and Watson propose a two-stage methodology: to first appropriate the resources of the rich, Christian psychological tradition, and then to employ it in the advance of empirical science and applied practice. They give robust examples of how Christian understandings of the person can yield verdant hypotheses that can be operationalized and tested, thus advancing human knowledge in the broader academy. This is worthy of affirmation.

With so much to praise and with which to agree, what concerns merit exploration? First, I continue to be concerned here with a seeming presumption that "Christian psychology" is a singular entity. In his original presentation of this model, Roberts (2000) explicitly suggested that there was one, singular Christian psychology. The "psychologies of the twentieth century," wrote Roberts (and note the plural reference to the various psychologies), "are all, in one way or another, rivals and alternatives to the Christian psychology" (p. 155). *The* Christian psychology (singular)? Is there only one Christian psychology?

While not as explicit or forceful in this version of their chapter, Roberts and Watson continue to suggest that "Christian psychology" is a unitary entity. There are a number of places where this presumption is manifest, but in two particular places, they write, "In contrast [to the secular psychologies], we wish to develop a psychology that accurately describes the psychological nature of human beings as understood according to historic Christianity" (p. 155). Later they argue that "psychology is native to Christianity; it is already a fundamental dimension of our faith. . . . [The Christian] tradition *has* a psychology of its own" (p. 175, emphasis in original). Has "*a* psychology of its own"? Can Roberts and Watson really cast their gaze across the Scriptures, the church fathers, Augustine, the desert fathers, the Reformation and Counter Reformation, Baxter, Kierkegaard,

Dostoyevsky and others to see *the* Christian psychology, one homogeneous and monolithic system of psychology? That would be quite remarkable, similar to casting our eyes across all of Christendom for the last two millennia and seeing *the* Christian theology. Surely there are core commitments, core similarities and consistencies, but while Christians have embraced certain core assertions of the faith, they have disagreed about many, many specifics of theology throughout history. Christians have also disagreed about the nature of Christian psychology—disagreed about virtues, vices, emotions, personality and so forth—for as long as we have been reflecting on it.

An excellent case study in such disagreement is a recent book on Christian perspectives on emotion. Elliott (2005), who actually uses Roberts's excellent philosophical work on emotion to argue for a better understanding of how emotion is understood and discussed in Scripture itself, documents how much misunderstanding and disagreement there has been about the most basic nature of emotion in the history of the church. Elliot argues that Roberts's view of emotion is the best one, but does so by pointing out how there has not been one ("the") Christian view of emotion in the life of the church. If there has not even been *one* Christian view of emotion, how can there be one, singular Christian psychology?

The integration view looks very much like the Christian psychology approach outlined in Roberts and Watson's chapter, but integrationists understand that our commitment to a biblical view of persons provides a presumptive framework, not a fully constructed system of psychology. The key difference is how much we claim we can construct of a complete psychology from the Scriptures and Christian tradition and resources.

Second, I remain unconvinced that Roberts and Watson have clearly articulated a concise summary of what it is that constitutes their Christian psychology. After critiquing positive psychology appropriately, they move to examining the psychological resources of the Sermon on the Mount, arguing, "But in the Sermon's own vocabulary . . . it offers its own conception of human nature. It also offers an ideal of personality functioning, as well as explanations and evaluations of actions, thoughts, and emotions, and it includes recommendations or strategies for change" (pp. 156-57).

I found the discussion of the "psychology" of the Sermon on the Mount to be edifying yet unsatisfying. Clearly there are a cluster of psychological insights offered there that must be formative for the Christian thinker; these are, after all, the very words of our Lord and Savior. But is what is offered here a systematic psychology? Their brief discussion of marriage and divorce from Matthew 5:27-32 may serve to illustrate the problem. The authors are certainly right that Jesus' emphasis on marriage and its inviolability should lead us to think differently about people. For example, Jesus' teaching that we become one flesh should challenge the insipient individualism that so characterizes secular psychologies.

But the authors' conclusion that "on the present reading [Jesus] denies the efficacy of any such formal procedure [i.e., divorce proceedings] to dismantle the marriage, so perhaps he would allow that sometimes permanent separation is an option" (p. 162) is questionable. The authors argue for a particular view of marriage and divorce, namely that marriage is permanent in a way that actually makes divorce impossible. This is *one* view of marriage in Christian circles: divorce is never legitimate and, in fact, impossible (they argue that a divorce proceeding fails to actually "dismantle" the marriage). But again, this is only one view among a number of options within Christian thinking (House, 1990). Other serious Christians, arguing from such vital passages as Deuteronomy 24:1-4; Malachi 2:10-16; Matthew 5:31-32; 19:3-12; Mark 10:2-12; and 1 Corinthians 7:10-17, have come to alternative conclusions that divorce may be legitimate and real in cases of adultery alone—or in the cases of adultery or desertion—but that remarriage after divorce is never legitimate. Yet still others conclude that divorce is legitimate and real in cases of adultery or desertion, and that remarriage after divorce for such specific reasons is legitimate. However, my point is not to resolve the specific case of marriage and divorce. Rather, I want to point out that Roberts and Watson here, and in other places within this brief exposition of the Sermon on the Mount, write as if quick and clear closure has been attained on this very specific meaning of Jesus' teaching. And then they extrapolate this out to a broad understanding of the Christian psychology, but I remain unconvinced. Not only have they not adequately summarized and synthesized the specific psychological issues within the Sermon of the Mount, but they have not synthesized these teachings with the other teachings from the whole of Scripture. Nor have they synthesized those teachings of all of Scripture with the psychologies that developed throughout church history.

I close by reiterating that I agree with the broad strokes of the view expressed by Roberts and Watson here; what they argue is broadly compatible with the integration view I have submitted. Our core disagreement seems to be over how much we can glean from Christian Scripture and tradition to construct a systematic psychology. I argue that what the Scriptures and tradition give us is fundamental but incomplete. Thus, as I argue in my chapter:

> It is for this basic reason that, while I believe that every Christian psychologist should strive to have their work reflect the distinctives of Christian views of the person, I am neither an advocate of "Christian psychology" nor of "biblical counseling" as formulated, respectively, by my friends Robert Roberts and David Powlison. However hard it is to close in on the true meaning of what it means (for instance) to be made in the image of God, I do affirm that this teaching is foundational to a Christian understanding of persons. While there may be some latitude in understanding what this means, this belief has profound implications for how we approach the study of persons. But in the same way that different denominations hold differing, distinct emphases and understandings on a number of different matters while agreeing on fundamentals, so also I think there is room for well-meaning Christians to disagree on the application of biblical teaching to psychological study. This will result in an entire family of approaches reflecting different understandings of what Scripture teaches about humanity (Jones, 1996), and it leaves wide room for the utility of the discipline of psychology to enlarge and challenge our understandings about human experience. (p. 112)

REFERENCES

Elliott, M. A. (2005). *Faithful feelings: Rethinking emotion in the New Testament.* Grand Rapids, MI: Kregel.

Evans, C. S. (2005). Integration and Christian psychology: Rivals or friends? *Edification: Newsletter of the Society for Christian Psychology, 1*(2), 3-5.

House, H. W. (1990). *Divorce and remarriage: Four Christian views.* Downers Grove, IL: InterVarsity Press.

Jones, S. (1996). Reflections on the nature and future of the Christian psychologies. *Journal of Psychology and Christianity, 15*(2), 133-42.

Roberts, R. C. (2000). A Christian psychology view. In E. Johnson & S. Jones (Eds.), *Psychology and Christianity: Four views* (pp. 148-77). Downers Grove, IL: InterVarsity Press.

A Transformational Psychology Response to Christian Psychology

John H. Coe and Todd W. Hall

THE CHRISTIAN PSYCHOLOGY VIEW is a thoughtful approach to understanding the relationship between psychology and Christianity, and it provides a helpful epistemic strategy given postmodern considerations for doing psychology. Robert C. Roberts and P. J. Watson articulate well the need for Christians doing psychology to become deeply versed in the Christian tradition's understanding of the person—both from a depth-understanding of the psychology in Scripture and the history of Christian thought—lest Christians look to contemporary psychology for their approach to the person and only supplement it with what they know by their faith. However, we argue that their primary strategy—bringing the Christian tradition back into the current empirical model of doing psychology and science—as creative and interesting as it is, fails to thoroughly critique the current empirical model. In other words, we believe that Christian psychology points toward but fails to create a holistic, scientific psychology that is inherently and thoroughly Christian. Our critiques are twofold:

1. Christian psychology fails to affirm what Christianity affirms of itself: that "Christian psychology" is more than just another competing form-of-life but that it can be known to be true and can be adjudicated between traditions.

2. Christian psychology's two-step approach of (a) grasping its own scriptural and historical tradition's understanding of the person and (b) using this tradition to ground and inform the current empirical work of scientific psychology does not go far enough in its critique of science. Rather, Christian psychology should provide the core of a unitary, single vision of reality in God and the love of God, which would allow for adjudication between competing ideas in psychology.

Christian psychology does not fully realize that its insights point *beyond* merely allowing the Christian view to be at the table of competing psychologies; rather we need to deconstruct and reconstruct what a science of the person should have been in the first place in God's world.

First, Christian psychology fails to provide a view of doing psychology that adjudicates between competing claims. Roberts and Watson have followed an interesting postmodern, philosophical strategy of recognizing that science and theory are embedded within metaphysical and worldview traditions, and so Christian psychology should be unashamedly explicit about this and encourage a pluralism of psychologies for mutual interaction and nonexclusion. However, we think this strategy over-depends on the concept of forms-of-life or a traditions approach to knowledge claims, which does not allow for ultimate adjudication or critique in order to get at what is real and true.

Although Roberts and Watson probably do not hold to the radical subjectivism of some postmodern critiques, nevertheless, that they employ postmodern critique, even heuristically, limits what science can and cannot do. That is, their insistence on doing science within a tradition does not allow them to arbitrate and pass judgments on conflicting viewpoints in other traditions—as evidenced in their discussion about the limits of examining comparative psychology-traditions perspectives. But, of course, this kind of relativism is not what is affirmed by the Christian tradition for which Roberts and Watson so earnestly contend.

The historic Christian tradition and concept of the person does not merely have the epistemic status of a competing form-of-life tradition among other competing, pluralistic traditions with the goal of mutual benefit yet without ultimate adjudication. This is good only if one's goal is to get a hearing at the pluralistic science table, not if one wishes to assert that Christianity's view of the person can be known as true and that there are antithetical claims that can be known to be false.

Second and most important, Christian psychology fails to go far enough in a full deconstruction and reconstruction of what science is in God's world. According to Roberts and Watson, science is still to be done "in a manner common to contemporary psychology, and to practice such research in conformity with their broader commitments" (p. 164), with the difference that Christian psychologists have the full epistemic right to do it within their Christian tradition, allowing its worldview and metaphysical assumptions to ground and inform the process. However, they fail to move beyond this epistemic strategy of making Christian psychology a viable option among many *to* a strategy of seeing what science really is in God's world. One indicator of this is that their discussion of research emphasizes quantitative methodologies and does not emphasize the rich knowledge that can be gained from less quantifiable sources, such as observation and reflection on life, relational experiences in doing psychotherapy and in conducting in-depth interviews.

However, transformational psychology intends to go one step further and bring the Christian psychology approach to its telos by doing psychology "behind the veil." That is, as a thought experiment, what would it be to rethink scientific methodology and psychology as if there were no prior "traditions" of doing psychology? What would it be to deconstruct the present modern tradition of the science of quantification as well as postmodern views of competing traditions and reconstruct a truly Christian view of science and psychology in the fullest sense of the term?

To begin with, the Christian deconstruction would reject the modernist approach to science as the model to build on in developing a Christian view. This current approach to psychology and science, apart from a mild to moderate infiltration of postmodern considerations and the quasi-relativist appeal to competing traditions, is still generally committed to a universal method of quantification—or measurement of bodies and their causal relations to one another. In this modernist model of science, one begins scientific investigation with a universal method of quantification of bodies in motion or the measuring of observables, which predetermines the kinds of objects that are possible to discover and investigate. However, major problems ensued.

The particular difficulties that science encountered had to do with the kind of knowledge and language that could be used to explain (1) spiritual and nonphysical phenomena and (2) ethics. Under the modernist view of science, it is not at all clear what language can be used to intelligibly talk about nonphysical objects that have neither extension nor movement that can be measured in space (things that include, arguably, God, angels, souls or minds, numbers, ideas, propositions, dreams, consciousness, mental images, personal agency and experience of feelings-emotions-thoughts). Furthermore, modern science's commitment to being purely descriptive can no longer provide a science of values (the good and the bad), morality (right and wrong) and character (virtues and vices), which was formerly grounded in ancient classical-realist science or natural-law approach going back to the ancient Greeks. This approach to science could no longer ground psychotherapy and its value notions of health and unhealth.

The methodological quandary that emerged for Christians was that accepting the new science meant that theology and what is most interesting about people and reality related to God and the human spirit, consciousness, experiences, emotions, thoughts, character, morality are no longer within the domain of science other than the strictly *physical* phenomena associated with the mind (e.g., behavior and the study of brain phenomena). The problem that emerges for Christians interested in understanding the person is how to hold to the integrity of being both scientific and Christian.

Roberts and Watson attempt to overcome this problem of modernity by appealing to postmodern considerations that are intended to give epistemic permission to their two-step process of (1) doing current psychology-methodology (2) within the Christian tradition, taking their place amidst the plurality of other psychologies (and their metaphysical and worldview traditions). But this is not how Christianity understands itself. The Christian psychology view, as thoughtful as it is, would have been better served to reject the modern approach to science, set aside any postmodern considerations and strategies for the sake of legitimization, and instead, *reconstruct science and psychology in the real world*—God's world. Then science and psychology would be construed not merely as contending traditions, but as what they should have been in the first place.

Our transformational approach offers a more thoroughly Christian version of science and a methodology that provides a unitary vision of the person, which investigates all relevant reality in God, is grounded in the psychologist doing science in the love of God (which allows for criticism and adjudication) and accommodates the detailed work of the specialist working in the modernist model. There exists an alternate model to science affirmed by the ancients that is better suited to be transformed into a full-blown Christian view. The ancient and medieval thinkers represented in the ancient Near Eastern wise men (sages), the Old Testament sage, the Greeks in Plato and Aristotle, the Stoics, and numerous medieval thinkers had an entirely different approach to scientific method than that of modernity. According to the modernist "new science" model, you begin the scientific investigation with a universal method of measuring bodies in motion, which predetermines the kinds of objects that are possible to discover and investigate. The classical realist approach *reverses* the process: *the object of investigation determines the method of approach*. So

1. Science begins with a casual *acquaintance* of the object

2. for the purpose of learning more about the *nature* of the object,

3. which allows *the object of investigation to determine* the best way to further investigate it,

4. resulting in the development of a *method of study* best suited to the object.

Rather than allowing a predetermined way of knowing to determine what is real and what counts as knowledge, this view of scientific method allows *reality* to determine *methodology*. To put it differently, ontology determines epistemology, and a presupposed epistemology does not determine ontology. According to the ancients, one cannot know what is the best way to study what exists until one is adequately acquainted with what exists. On this view of science, the psychological health of the scientist to remain honest and open to reality is central to doing science well, which is foundational to our transformational psychology model.

We can build on this ancient model of doing science by appealing to the Old Testament wisdom literature. The Old Testament sage is a biblical model for a science of the person; by observing and reflecting on human nature, Scripture and human experiences of God, one gains wisdom and prescriptions for healthy and unhealthy living under God. On this view, like the Old Testament sage, the scientist is capable of discovering the laws of sowing and reaping, of healthy versus unhealthy living, from Scripture and what is supplemented by observations and reflections on nature as are evident in Proverbs. This provides a rudimentary structure for developing a comprehensive and coherent scientific methodology as a unified vision of reality, which is capable of relating psychology to faith and of doing a psychology of Christian realities. In this scientific psychology all relevant reality for understanding the person would be included as legitimate data of study: Scripture, God, mental phenomena, values, teleological considerations, sin and our capacity to be indwelt by God. This provides methodological grounds not only for doing holistic science but for a science of values that further grounds a robust psychotherapy and its understanding of psychological health and psychopathology.

Finally, this re-creation of science in our transformational psychology is ultimately grounded in the transformative psychologist who preserves the integrity of this process by (1) being as open as possible to what is real and true about understanding the person; (2) loving God in the doing of psychology; and (3) contemplating the object of investigation in God. This, therefore, is not merely one more tradition competing within a plurality of traditions of psychology. Rather, this is what science and psychology should have been in the first place in God's world.

A Biblical Counseling Response to Christian Psychology

David Powlison

CHRISTIAN PSYCHOLOGY AND BIBLICAL COUNSELING sound many same or similar notes. Indeed, it might be said that biblical counseling essentially pursues the development of a full-orbed, fully Christian psychology. By that I mean a comprehensive understanding of people (a "psychology") and effective face-to-face ministry (a "psychotherapy"). *Practical theology* and *cure of souls* are terms native to our faith that describe such desirable achievements.

How do Christian psychology and biblical counseling line up? Are our aims complementary, though we pursue somewhat different priorities? What do Christian psychologists and biblical counselors need to say to each other? To hear from the other? Christian psychologists and biblical counselors look across the aisle at each other, and as we strike up conversations during coffee hour, we each come with questions in mind.

Christian psychologists come to the conversation wondering: Will biblical counseling prove to be one more reversion to pat answers and quick fixes of formulaic Bible-talk and God-talk, variously tinctured with moralism, pietism, doctrinalism or even animism? Will biblical counselors fail to understand how relationships, counseling and change are unfolding processes? Will biblical counselors talk a good game but show themselves to be another bull barging into the china shop of the human soul? How do biblical counselors treat our most unspeakable vulnerabilities—the darkest motions of our hearts and our inner experience of the assaults of a cold, dark, voracious, depersonalizing world? Will biblical counselors prove clumsy, uncomprehending, simplistic? Do biblical counselors understand how hard life is for many people, how hard it is to change? Do biblical counselors hear the Bible's call to encourage the faint-hearted, to hold on to the weak, to be patient with all, as well as hearing the call to admonish, instruct and exhort? Are biblical counselors one more reversion to clannishness and the paranoid style? Do they triumphalistically imagine that they have arrived and that others have nothing to say worth listening to?

Biblical counselors come to the same conversation wondering: Will Christian psychology prove to be one more reversion to secular psychology, where the Christianity does not run very deep? Do Christian psychologists talk a good game but in practice rehearse musty, tired truisms from the therapeutic? In one way or another do Christian psychologists communicate the following messages: "The confluence of difficult personal history and physiological defects causes your DSM-diagnosable problems. Real counseling is the province of licensed professionals. The church can provide auxiliary social support to supplement professional practice, but psychologists do the heavy lifting, and churched people are a clientele"? At the end of the day, are Christian psychologists essentially licensed professionals? At the end of the day are Christian psychologists essentially academics, intending to practice a library-based, scholarly discipline? At the end of the day, are Christian psychologists essentially scientists, intending to practice a laboratory-based empirical discipline? Do Christian psychologists think that psychologists have privileged insight into people and unique efficacy in helping? Will their scholarship and research express the wisdoms of Christian thinking and contribute to the wisdoms of ministry practice in our time and place?

I welcome this conversation, and I'm curious whether we can both prove the above suspicions to be caricatures. Let me make four comments in response to Roberts and Watson.

First, there are places that glow with the concision and freshness of a poem: for example, the opening paragraph's cascade of "Never minds" and the comparison between "fully Christian forgiveness and a secularized facsimile" (pp. 149, 155). At the outset Roberts and Watson capture well the failure of the modern psychologies to come up with a single dominant paradigm capable of unifying research, personality theory, psychotherapy and the mental health system (what I term Psych-2, 3, 4 and 5 in my chapter). But in the conclusion, when they aspire to "usher in a more pluralistic psychology," I hope they merely express a pragmatic desire to gain a place at the table (p. 175). Surely worldview diversity cannot be their actual goal. A truly Christian psychology entails an eschatology. On the last day every knee bows to a single dominant and unifying paradigm. The God who had first say in how human beings work will also get last say. The Christian paradigm will come true. Working in the light of the Christian paradigm, Roberts and Watson's case study of positive psychology is judicious both in its commendations and criticisms.

Second, I agree with the intentions driving "Step One: Retrieving Christian Psychology." But here's how I would rewrite the programmatic statement (compare with p. 155):

> Much of the foundational work in Christian psychology will require careful reading of Scripture in the light of firsthand human experience: your own life certainly, and the personal struggles and situational troubles of those whom you have come to know well, those whom you love, those whom you seek to help. Live the psalms and proverbs, in the light of Jesus Christ who lived them fully. Because Scripture *is* normative practical theology, learn how our Redeemer goes about explaining, addressing and changing people.
>
> Know the classic formulations of Christian faith, and wrestle with the implications for a God-centered understanding of persons. Read from the great Christian psychologists of the past. [I wouldn't delete names from their list, but it's noteworthy that they cite only one pastor of souls, Augustine. I would add other pastors and pastoral theologians, for example, Gregory, Luther, Calvin, Baxter, Edwards, Bonhoeffer, as I think they are more helpful—wiser—than the Christian philosophers.] Study the great hymns and liturgies of the church. They express psychological genius. Their feel for human experience in relationship to God is akin to the psalms. A true counseling model sings the same worldview that it converses.
>
> Keep current with contemporary writers in biblical counseling. They seek to articulate a biblical psychology that effectively speaks to current circumstances, persons and problems. [I can't resist a plug for bridge-building.] Maintain a working familiarity with contemporary secular psychologies. They notice things worth noticing, ask questions worth asking and tackle problems worth tackling. Their ideas, practices and structures are the cultural air we breathe, and a robust Christian psychology will produce something clearly recognizable as fresh air.

I agree that familiarity with contemporary psychology is bound to be part of the picture, but it is not the sine qua non. Familiarity with the ways of God, with the ways of people and with how to bring the two together is the decisive element.

Third, Roberts and Watson's portrayal of "human well-being" via the Beatitudes exhibits many strengths. It is a work in progress, and here are some seed thoughts that might make it even richer and clearer.

Honest, thriving humanness this side of the return of Christ has a large place for sorrow, anguish, struggle and sense of need. Consider the preponderance of minor-key psalms that wrestle with awareness of sin, with the experience of suffering and threat, with awareness of the God who promises to act. The first four Beatitudes express in various ways this psalmic sense of need for various mercies from outside of ourselves, necessities from the Father's hand, the arrival of the King. If the third Beatitude's "humble or gentle *(praüs)*" (p. 157) is given its provenance in the psalms, then it is not describing gentleness toward other people. Instead, it further describes the humility and neediness of reliance on God's mercies. A heart that has been "gentled," like a wild horse learning attentiveness to its master's voice, inherits the whole earth.

It is also worth noting that the virtues mentioned in the final four Beatitudes are specifically redemptive qualities. They are ways of going out toward people in need and into a world of trouble. Jesus lived the eight Beatitudes, both the first four minor-key expressions of need for God (faith), and the second four major-key expressions of a fruitful, purposeful life (love). So Jesus comes with generous mercies to others: he is pure in heart and intention; he works to make peace between persons and God, between person and person; he is actively righteous and boldly rejoicing. Receiving the goodness of such a Christ, we are being formed into people who relate to others in just these ways.

Throughout this section, though, I felt jarred by Roberts and Watson's use of the word *trait* to describe the quality of flourishing humanness. The eight Beatitudes strike me as *relational* realities more than character traits. The Beatitudes don't actually describe characteristics of an individual who is considered as a discrete entity. Rather, they describe how, in the context of a broken world, Jesus Christ relates to God and then to us. They picture how in Christ we come to relate to God and then to our fellow human beings. It is significant that these ways of relating always occur amid the exigencies envisioned by the Beatitudes: sinfulness, interpersonal conflict, troubles, impurity, liability to death, experience of groaning need, the everywhere-evident incompleteness of God's redemption. Isn't there a better word than *trait* to communicate the relational processes and contextual locatedness of honest human thriving amid troubles?

Fourth, I was surprised that "Step Two" consists of a proposal for redeeming empirical research. The discussion does make good sense. Imagine that, a research program freed of the constraints of dogged secularity—research finally willing to traffic with the real world instead of relentlessly suppressing reality! But it seems to me that hammering out a fruitful research program is a second-tier priority in the larger scheme of things.

The more significant proof of any of the five views presented in this book is whether or not it generates a truer understanding of actual human beings, starting with ourselves. Such understanding is the handmaiden of redemptive intervention. The fruit of such redemption is a flourishing of love that issues from a pure heart, a good conscience and a sincere faith (1 Tim 1:5). Renewed empirical research will contribute to better understanding of people, as one form of the church's flourishing. But it is an auxiliary discipline, a flying buttress attached to the cathedral wall, not the sanctuary in which the community lives.

In the conversation between biblical counselors and Christian psychologists, I'm curious how each will approach "redeemed research." Will Christian psychology coherently and consistently do such redeeming, or will it prove to be captivated by secular assumptions? Will biblical counseling value the contribution that the right sort of research can make, or will it prove to be biblicistic? Or will both parties prove to be partners engaging in the same large practical theological task?

5

A Transformational Psychology View

John H. Coe and Todd W. Hall

> For with you is the fountain of life;
> In your light we see light.
>
> PSALM 36:9

> Above all . . . God destines us for
> an end beyond the grasp of reason.
>
> THOMAS AQUINAS, *SUMMA THEOLOGIAE* IA

THE TRANSFORMATIONAL PSYCHOLOGY MODEL is an attempt to both rediscover and redesign our traditional way of thinking of psychology in relation to Christianity, as well as rethinking the very nature of science itself. The bottom line will be that doing science and, in this case, psychology is ultimately an act of love. This account may seem strange to anyone trained in typical universities today, though perhaps it would not seem so odd to a Desert Father or one of the "thinker-scientists" of the thirteenth-century monasteries. We do not often associate monks with psychology, let alone science. However, the ancient church fathers and medieval theologians and scientists may have provided an insight into the relationship between spirituality and knowing ("In your light we see light," Ps 36:9[1]) that was too quickly thrown out by the secular, modernist approach to science.

Our goal is to argue for a spiritual formation approach to psychology and Christianity, which takes the spiritual-emotional transformation of the psychologist as the foundation for understanding, developing and preserving the (1) process, (2) methodology and (3) product of doing psychology in the Spirit, which will all, in turn, open a new horizon into the doing of science in general and psychology in particular.

We will also attempt to provide the general outlines or contours for this transformational model, as well as distinguish it from previous models, showing how it accommodates the best of the other approaches, avoiding their weaknesses, while capturing and building on the insights of the new directions being taken by others. We believe these "new directions" point toward our model, in which the relating of psychology and Christianity is understood as a single act of doing "science," grounded in the spiritually transformed psychologist.

This is less a model of relating psychology to faith and more a transformation of psychology—indeed, science itself—into something that is intrinsically a single act of faith and love. This is what psychology was meant to be, whether before or after the Fall of humanity, but because sin clouds our view, it is possible to "do psychology" naturalistically in terms of methodology, manner and outcomes—outside of a relationship with God. Christians wanting to do psychology consistent with faith were faced with an existing scientific tradition that is naturalistic and reductionistic toward spiritual and nonphysical phenomena, as well as ethical values of health necessary for psychotherapy. What follows, then, is the ideal, though our frailties and sins oblige us to admit that we are capable of only approximating the *ideal* when we attempt to do psychology in God.

FOUNDATIONS OF TRANSFORMATIONAL PSYCHOLOGY

In order to understand this transformational account of psychology and science, we begin with several foundational notions about the overall vision and sources relevant to what it is to do psychology in faith

1. The person doing psychology within a history or tradition of psychology

---

[1]All Scripture quotations, unless otherwise indicated, are taken from the *Holy Bible, New International Version*®.

2. The person doing psychology anew in the Spirit

3. The person doing psychology grounded in reality, including the realities known by faith

4. The person doing psychology as one, single, yet complex, study of reality in faith (of reality observable to all and those realities known by faith)

5. The person doing psychology as a science that is both descriptive and prescriptive in nature

The focus or vision of the transformational model is for each generation and, in some sense, each psychologist to do the work of psychology afresh in the Spirit, grounded in reality and faith, open to other and earlier traditions but not in such a way that limits or hinders the personal process of doing psychology for themselves.

Doing psychology within a tradition. First, the transformational psychologist does psychology and science within a tradition or history of psychology. We use the phrase "doing psychology within a tradition" to indicate that, in reality, all scientific inquiry is done within a particular historical context of others who have done science before them; current scientific inquiry is not an activity cut off from a past consensus of what has been insightful. Doing psychology within a tradition does not mean there is no epistemological basis for truth, that truth is merely what those within a tradition agree on to be true or that truth and rationality are tradition-dependent as MacIntyre appears to believe (1984). Rather, we do science open to the truth but in a way that is mindful of the history of relevant truth claims, though not in such a way that it dominates the present doing of science.

The central vision of doing psychology anew in the Spirit. Doing psychology within a tradition should be secondary to the primary task of doing psychology anew in the Spirit. This involves the radical attempt to "get behind the veil"[2] of psychology and what tradition has told us is "good psychology." So this means that, as a thought experiment, we suspend our commitment to historical approaches to doing psychology—secular and Christian.

---

[2]Doing something "behind the veil" is a term taken from Harvard political philosopher John Rawls's (1971) thought experiment to imagine what ethics would be like prior to "tradition"— or prior to society's existing theories and conventions of ethics and manners.

This does not mean that we suspend judgment on all truth claims. Rather, it means that the transformative psychologist reserves the right to withhold judgment on accepting as true what any tradition may teach, while he or she engages in the firsthand work and methodology of psychology. Because, as helpful as traditions are, they can also be blinders, not allowing the psychologist to truly see.

Of course, it is impossible to actually do psychology anew, entirely apart from some tradition, as there is clearly a learning spiral between dependence on a tradition and learning from one's mentors versus working behind the veil and doing one's own observation and reflection. But as a thought experiment, we want to become aware of overdependence on a tradition(s). *The goal here is to learn and discover, to set off on our own course (as an individual and in community) to reexperience and redesign the process of doing psychology and its end product.* In this process, we strive to be open to study ourselves, God, others and reality, as well as to the traditions that we have become familiar with and the mentors who have led us. The goal, then, is for each generation in the Spirit to allow *reality* and *faith* to shape this endeavor, to do the work of psychology in faith and then, as a secondary task, reintegrate its findings with those truths and traditions within which it finds itself.

Thus, there is a need to imagine what it would be like to do psychology in the faith prior to adhering to the ideas of Aristotle, Aquinas, Calvin, Freud, Skinner, Ellis, Rogers, Bowlby, Winnicott or any other theorist doing psychology or relating it with Christianity. The result of looking *too intently* at prior theories is that the believer doing psychology often develops a patchwork quilt in which some theorist (e.g., Aristotle, Rogers or Freud) is artificially stitched together with certain fundamental doctrines of the Christian faith. Though there are many Christian psychologists whose work is insightful, we cannot help but wonder what their theories or their experiences in training and teaching might have been if they had more consciously studied and developed "behind the veil"—instead of primarily within the context of the accepted psychological categories of the traditions in which they were trained.

Consequently, our transformational approach is a mandate to do psychology in faith anew: to do the firsthand work of discovering a psychology of the person that is *science* open to the experience of the Spirit and open to the truths from Scripture, *as well as* open to truths from observation and reflection on ourselves, on other human beings and on what others have thought about human nature.

Doing psychology grounded in reality and the realities of faith: The relevant sources. This transformational model is an attempt to discover and practice an approach to science and the understanding of the person that is driven less by any one theory and tradition and more by the person and the process of doing psychology. In particular, this process of doing psychology anew is grounded in reality, including those realities understood by faith (e.g., original sin, the ministry of the indwelling Holy Spirit, the demonic).[3] In that case, our own history, experience and lack of experience of reality will be the limiting horizon to our work and to what we are open to discover; therefore, our work in understanding reality is only an approximation to all that is real and can be known.

We use the term *discover* insofar as reality dictates the doing of psychology and scientific methodology in general; a particular scientific or psychological methodology does not dictate reality. To say the same thing differently, ontology determines epistemology and not the reverse, as in the case of modern science. That is, we do not begin with some universal method of quantification or measurement as the universal method of science, which is true of modernity's view of science. Rather, according to the premodern view of science, the object of study and the psychologist's (or scientist's) acquaintance with reality determines the best way to study an object, which is an important distinction from the methods of modern science as well as postmodern tendencies (Coe & Hall, 2010; Willard, 1984). Consequently, the existence of God or the immaterial human spirit are not a priori ruled out of science, as is the case with the unwarranted prejudice of a naturalistic methodology. *Our transformational psychology does not relegate what is known by faith as being outside "science"* (as defined by modern science), nor does our psychology relegate a piece of theology as something to be *integrated with* science. Further, our transformational psychology does not merely *assume* certain Christian beliefs to

---

[3]What is meant by "specifically Christian realities" is those realities that can be known by observation, reason or faith but which are a priori, excluded by the naturalistic methodology of science as being either unknowable or outside the purview of science (e.g., the reality of original sin, the indwelling Holy Spirit, the human soul).

be true for the sake of constructing a coherent integrative system as in a postmodern approach. Rather, the Christian apprehends or knows these specifically Christian realities that, in turn, affect and alter the very essence of our being and communities, which are further reflected in our beliefs and psychology.

Psychology starting with the realities of faith. Central to a transformational psychology is the fact that we start with the Christian realities, for they do not merely constitute the faith as some belief system or worldview, but they are known by faith to be true and reflect the realities that constitute and ontologically ground our very existence. These beliefs and realities constitute and inform our lives as the redeemed, the beloved of God, reflecting the depth of our hearts' desire for an unbounded love. In some ways, these Christian realities are more real than that of the believer's own existence, reason and the senses (though these are also quite trustworthy), for the Christian realities ontologically ground our very existence and the use of reason and observation. These realities of the faith redeem the possibility of doing psychology according to reality and not merely the dictates of our fantasies and perceived needs. It should be clear, then, that our treatment here of a transformational psychology is not primarily written for the unbeliever; otherwise, much of what follows would require a thoroughgoing apologetic or defense.

Given that Christian realities ground our transformational model of psychology, it is our highest priority to understand these shared realities and truths of the faith that help frame both our existence as well as the contours of doing psychology. The following are some of the central realities and truths that we know by faith in experience: (1) that God exists (Heb 11:1-2); (2) that we are created in the image of God to rule, understand and properly relate to creation as fundamentally relational beings (Gen 1:26; 2:18); (3) that we are sinners saved by grace through the finished work of Christ on the cross (Rom 5:6-10); (4) that we are now a new creature "in Christ" (2 Cor 5:17); (5) so that being fundamentally relational, our ultimate end or purpose in life in Christ is loving neighbor and God, glorifying him forever "so that God will be all in all" (1 Cor 10:31; 15:28 NASB); (6) that this is only accomplished by being transformed into the image of Christ by means of the indwelling Holy Spirit, who in union with our spirits desires to fill us with the fullness of his presence (Eph

3:17-19; 5:18) so that all of life is for the sake of his glory and ends; and (7) that God has taken special care to reveal these truths in Scripture and, in part, in the believer's experience. *These tenets frame and inform our existence and the entire framework of science,* of knowing and being rightly related to reality.

The epistemic and ontological value of Christian realities to our transformational psychology. We do not want the reader to misunderstand what is meant by these shared Christian realities and tenets. We are *not* saying that these tenets or beliefs are presuppositions, if one means by "presupposition" something that I know by assuming or supposing it to be true. On the contrary, we do *not* know these Christian tenets to be true because we presuppose them. Rather, they are true because they correspond to or are born out in the experience of reality, and they are subject to scrutiny as are any beliefs. They are as certain as the knowing of my own existence and of other objects; in fact, they *condition* and *ground* my knowledge and very existence experientially and theoretically, particularly for the believer. Historically, the church has argued that we know these realities of faith by means of both (a) the ministry of the Holy Spirit in illuminating and bearing witness to the human spirit regarding the truth of these claims and realities, and (b) in harmony with the canons of knowing and rationality as well as appropriate warranting procedures as in all truth claims. However, our task in this short piece is not to provide the deep epistemology and apologetic to support these claims or defend our knowledge of these Christian beliefs.

Central to our transformational psychology is that these core realities and tenets of the faith not only inform psychology of its origins and goals, which observation and reflection on creation alone cannot grasp; *they also shape the entire process, product and person* doing psychology. Because these core spiritual realities and tenets are included in and lie at the heart of a transformational psychology, it turns out that the *spiritual-emotional development of the psychologist is foundational* to the process of arriving at deep truths about human nature (the conceptual product), and to doing this in the Spirit as an act of worship for the sake of the love of God, which is the final end of life (the embodied product). Thus, this transformational model affirms that the transformation of the psychologist is the determinative and foundational element for the process and product of doing psychology. This, in part, accounts for why our transformational psychology is a distinct, "new" (though "ancient") model, which we believe affirms the best of the other models and merely sets them in a more expansive framework.

Doing psychology as a single, unified vision of reality in faith. It should be clear from what has been said thus far, that our transformational psychology is committed to developing a science or methodology for psychology that does not exclude Christian realities from its scope of investigation. The term "Christian realities" (e.g., the existence of immaterial objects, the reality of sin, salvation, the indwelling ministry of the Spirit in transformation) is not meant to arbitrarily dichotomize religious and secular realities. Both are reality in God's world. Rather, we use the term to signify those realities that secular, modern science has excluded from investigation. The central methodological questions that confront the Christian transformational psychologist are: (1) can, and to what degree can, a legitimate psychology address these distinctively Christian realities, and (2) is the transformational psychologist doing something other than "psychology" when addressing these Christian realities and relating them to psychology? That is, is this relating of psychology/science with Christianity a "science," or is it a relating of two separate kinds of studies involving two different kinds of methodologies that are mutually exclusive, which the believer then brings together in some fashion with its own peculiar methodology (which has been called "integration," or perhaps other terms could be used)?

We argue that our transformational psychology is uniquely committed to a single, unified methodology that is capable of providing a science or "psychology" of both created and distinctively Christian realities—for it makes no distinction between them methodologically. That is, this psychology does not merely have as its data the natural phenomena of the person but includes "Christian realities" as a legitimate datum of science. These "Christian realities" are comprised of the contents of Scripture, the nature of the human spirit, values, sin, our capacity to be indwelt by God, and so on. All of these realities are within the boundaries of our transformational approach to psychological theory and research. This is a correction to a wrong turn in the history of modern science, which bifurcated the world into the "scientific" and the "ethical-religious" by means of a dichotomy between naturalistic and theological methodologies.

In that case, our transformational psychology is less about the relationship between *two distinct fields or methodologies* (science/psychology and theology) or *two distinct domains* (natural, psychological realities and "Christian" realities), and is more about doing *a single, unified—though complex—science and psychology of reality* (e.g., of human emotions, relationships as well as sin, values, and what it means to be filled with the Holy Spirit). It follows that the person doing psychology is determinative for the process and product, one who is open and not closed to all relevant realities. This model encourages the development of a new kind of psychology and psychologist, who—by virtue of being open to the Spirit and all reality—grounds the entire process and product of doing psychology. In our view, the character of the person doing psychology discovers and preserves the process and product of doing psychology by helping the said psychologist stay open to what is real and true, and minimizes any pathological need to distort reality and falsify the truth.

Commitment to a nonnaturalistic methodology in science and psychology. Because a transformational psychology is about a single, unified-though-complex science/psychology of reality in the Spirit, it clearly rejects any view of science embracing a naturalistic methodology that precludes the study of certain realities from its domain. In that sense, a transformational psychology rejects the unnecessary split between studying solely created realities in science and studying distinctively Christian realities in theology. This split has resulted in the unhelpful and false radical bifurcation of the world into a study of the secular and of the sacred, of science divorced from theology and vice versa. Rather, transformational psychology is grounded in the scientist who in faith engages in a single, unified act of studying all reality in the Spirit.

Thus, a transformational model affirms that doing science is a single, unifying act that mingles both the *act of faith* and the *act of observation-reflection* on creation into one, by loving God in the object of science and the object of science in God. This includes observing and reflecting on all sources of information relevant to understanding a particular phenomenon. One must be willing to rigorously and painstakingly observe and reflect on whatever is relevant from (1) Scripture, (2) creation, particularly the study of persons, and (3) preexisting psychological/scientific/theological reflections and theories. It is very important that the scientist and psychologist take seriously all the elements or data in doing science in order to minimize any imbalance in what material becomes central. If one of these dominates to the exclusion or lessening of the other's contribution, distortion from what it was intended to be by God will result in the person doing the science and in the process or the product.

On this view, then, the process of doing science as a Christian is *not* primarily an act of employing a naturalistic methodology of investigation to which is added a second act of glorifying and loving God from the doing of science. Rather, the very act of doing science and psychology was meant by God to be done in the love of God, contemplating and open to all relevant reality while contemplating and loving God.

Doing psychology as a descriptive and prescriptive science. Because transformational psychology is a unified yet complex science that is open to all relevant data and reality, it also rejects any a priori view of science and scientific methodology that insists on being purely descriptive in nature, prohibiting the possibility of providing facts about values and prescriptions for living. In fact, it turns out that transformational psychology rejects the following notions: (1) that Scripture is the only place for finding wisdom or prescriptions for living well in God and (2) that psychology and its scientific methodology are solely descriptive in nature.

Rather, transformational psychology affirms with Scripture that psychology as science is capable of providing prescriptions and wisdom for living. The Old Testament Wisdom literature provides a biblical model for gaining prescriptions for wisdom from doing science in the broadest and best sense of the word. That is, the Old Testament wise man (a sage) insists that it is possible to discern prescriptions or wisdom for living from observing and reflecting on creation and human persons in their complex situations in real life. This, in turn, provides a biblical justification for dialogue with the unbeliever's partially distorted wisdom. Thus, the Old Testament sage is a kind of a biblical prototype for doing psychology in God, as a science that is both descriptive and prescriptive in nature.

The Old Testament sage had the unique role of instructing or giving counsel to Israel concerning how to live well in all areas of life on the basis of his wisdom and experience (Prov 1:1-6, 8-9; 4:1; 6:20) and not solely from the prescriptions of the Torah. Of course, he recognized that the essence of this wisdom involves having a right relationship with God (Prov 1:7), who is the ultimate source of all wisdom (Prov 2:6) and who has provided wisdom in his written revelation *(Tora)*, revelation that is central to the mental health of a people for the sake of growth in God (Prov 22:17-19; 29:18).

However, of particular relevance to our discussion is the Old Testament sage's insistence that God has made available an important extrabiblical source of wisdom for living: observing and reflecting on the natural world (Prov 6:6; 30:24-28; cf. natural sciences in 1 Kings 4:29-33) and especially persons and their complex situations (Prov 24:30-34; 30:21-23). God created the world by wisdom (Prov 3:19-20) such that his wisdom is imprinted onto creation as the natural order of things (Prov 8:22-31) (Aitken, 1986). By observing these dynamic wisdom laws or ordering structures that are evident in and govern nature in general and human nature in particular, the Old Testament sage is able to *discover* and understand not only straightforward, descriptive information about human beings but also information about healthy versus unhealthy living—what it is to live well in accord with human nature or poorly against the grain of human nature. From these reflections, he is able to discover a set of wise principles of sowing and reaping to avoid folly and live a good and wise life under God in accordance with the created way of human nature (Prov 8:32-36). This is the ground for a natural-law understanding of virtue-vice, good-bad and "creation oughts" (or prescriptions for living well under God).

Thus, the Old Testament sage as protopsychologist and therapist is convinced that one can discover facts about values from facts about nature, particularly from facts about human behavioral, interpersonal and intrapsychic phenomena. For example, by observing complex situations of human communication, the sage discovers that it is generally wiser to respond to anger with a gentle answer over a harsh reply, for gentleness tends to lessen strife and harshness tends to stir it up (Prov 15:1). In general, these facts about values can take the form of a conditional "if . . . then . . ." statement, which attempts to illustrate the quasi-causal or sow-reap laws that can be discovered by observing and reflecting on human phenomena. In the case of Proverbs 15:1, the implied conditional statement is as follows: If one is to lessen strife and anger in tense situations, then one ought to respond with gentle words. This cause-and-effect structure of things is evident throughout human experience, from the complexities of human communication to the deepest intricacies of human emotions. As Old Testament theologian Gerhard von Rad (1972) insightfully points out from Proverbs 13:12; 15:13 and 17:22, "The law of cause and effect is traced right into the hidden regions of the soul" (pp. 124-25). This is the biblical basis for a natural-law theory of ethics and psychology. Of course, the sage does not explicitly record his moral observations and science of values in such a stilted form. Rather, he employs Hebrew poetry (parallel structure and imagery) for mnemonic and heuristic purposes.

Nevertheless, beneath the poetic and descriptive form in most of the Old Testament sage's proverbs lies an implied *prescription* or *natural ought* that he assumes persons are capable of discerning. The general structure of these wisdom and moral principles/laws for healthy living are captured in the following conditional statements:

Universal conditional: If person S is to live well (be successful) with respect to life in general, then S *ought* to (must, should, needs to) live in harmony with the quasi cause-effect order of things evident in the human situation.

Particular conditional: If person S is to live well (be successful) with respect to a particular task/end/goal p, S *ought* to do X.

The universal conditional reflects the natural ought or quasi-causal structure *in general,* which the sage recognizes to be governing human persons and situations relevant to believers and nonbelievers alike. The particular conditional reflects the natural ought or quasi law-like structure, which lies behind any *particular* proverb containing a piece of advice or an implicit prescription relevant to a particular aspect of the human situation. For example, the implied conditional and prescription in Proverbs 24:33-34 ("A little sleep, a little slumber, / a little folding of the hands to rest— / and poverty will come on you like a bandit / and scarcity like an armed man") is: *if* a person is to live well and avoid financial disaster, *then* that person *ought* to be diligent in work and not procrastinate. Notice that the "ought" or prescriptive element in these conditionals is grounded not in a divine command but in the ordering structure of human phenomena such that values are *discovered* by observation and reflection—not simply *derived* from Scripture or *created* by human opinions and desires. This is the nature of a "natural ought." This is entirely contrary to the modernist approach to science, which insists that facts are divorced from values and that science has nothing to do with providing ethical prescriptions for living.

Consequently, the Old Testament wise man provides a biblical precedent, justification and even mandate for the task of doing transformational psychology, for discerning wisdom for living from observation and reflection on creation and Scripture in the fear and love of God. In the case of biblical proverbs, God works through the wise man's experience to produce inspired observations and principles for living (nothing has been said here that denies or contradicts the doctrine of inspiration concerning Proverbs). While the wisdom collected in Scripture has a divine sanction and authority, the church's ongoing task or mandate to do psychology and natural-law ethics is subject to epistemological scrutiny from reason, observation and Scripture. This implies, also, that we can learn from and dialogue with unbelievers doing psychology insofar as (1) they are created in the image of God, retaining the capacity to observe and reflect on creation for the sake of gaining wisdom, and (2) to the extent that they develop this skill and openness to reality. Of course, their wisdom will be truncated in part, for only the believer has the possibility to know and live out these principles as one ought in relation to God.

THE EXISTENTIAL AND THEORETICAL FRAMEWORK FOR A TRANSFORMATIONAL PSYCHOLOGY: THE PERSON, PROCESS AND PRODUCT

This transformational psychology attempts to address the person, process and product of doing psychology in the light of faith—that is, in the light of reality, of what is real and true about God and the universe. In particular, there are a number of fundamental claims that lie at the heart of and provide the general framework for understanding this model of doing psychology in faith behind the veil.

- *The Christian final-end thesis:* We are created relational by nature, with ourselves, others and, fundamentally, with God. We are created in such a way that the ultimate end of human existence, which necessarily colors all other ends or goals, is *love*. This is made possible by union with God and filling the human spirit with God's Spirit on the basis of the work of Christ on the cross, resulting in conformity to the image of Christ, loving God and neighbor to the glory of God, all of which makes up the healthy self (Eph 3:17-19; 2 Pet 1:4; Col 1:28). If that is the ultimate human end, then by definition, all human pursuits and activities, including doing psychology, are a means to the goal of union with God by which one loves God and neighbor and glorifies God.

• *Transformational psychology thesis:* Doing science or psychology, as a fully human activity as God intended, is a means to the goal of love through union with the Holy Spirit, by which one loves God and neighbor and glorifies God. Thus, the psychologist does psychology well to the degree that

> the psychologist as a person is more and more transformed into the image of Christ by the filling of the Spirit (the *person* as foundational),

> the psychologist is using his or her abilities in God to observe and reflect correctly on the reality of the person (the *process*), and that

> the psychologist is capable of producing a body of knowledge and wisdom concerning the nature of persons, sin and well-being, for the sake of the world and the church, that corresponds to reality (the *theoretical product*), as well as for the end of the transformation of the psychologist (the *existential product*).

• *The spirituality-ethics of epistemology and science thesis:* The Christian faith and its view of creation and sin implies that science is impacted well or poorly by both the abilities *and* psychological health of the observer, depending on the development of those abilities and the openness or closedness to the realities of creation and the faith.

The Christian final-end thesis. It is clear from Scripture and the history of the church that humans are fundamentally relational in nature, and that loving God and neighbor to glorify God form a cluster of realities that combine to constitute the ultimate end or goal of the Christian life (called "constituent ends" of the Christian life). And it is the very logic of a life possessing an ultimate end that all other pursuits and goals, though perhaps good in themselves, ultimately are a means toward this final end.

Furthermore, it is central to the new-covenant teaching of the apostle Paul that this goal of conformity to Christ, which includes loving and glorifying God, is not possible in the power of the self by mere character formation. Only a person who is "in Christ," justified on the basis of the work of Christ on the cross—and whose human spirit is indwelt and increasingly filled by the Spirit of God, growing in greater union with God—is capable of experiencing this life of love and transformation of character in Christ. Thus, life in the Spirit and growth in union with God by the filling of the Spirit just *is* the life of loving and glorifying God, being conformed to the image of Christ, and loving one's neighbor, which are part of the cluster of constituent ends that make up the final end of life and the healthy self.

Transformational psychology thesis.

The transformed person as most fundamental. This thesis gets at the heart of our transformational model of Christianity and psychology. Given that the goal or end of the Christian life is relational, it turns out that doing psychology is relational and, moreover, is a means to relationship (to loving neighbor and to union with God), as well as to personal transformation. According to the church fathers and medieval theologians, to study creation or anything apart from transformation and the telos of the love of God is to commit the vice of *curiositas* (Latin for "curiosity").

In his discussion on the intellectual virtues and vices ("On Curiosity"), Aquinas (1892) notes at least two forms of the vice of curiosity (Q 166): (1) the desire to know what should not be known (e.g., "as in those who inquire of evil spirits about things to come") and (2) the desire to know something in a *manner* that it should not be known (viz., for its own sake only and not also for the love and glory of God).

Regarding this second form of curiosity, Aquinas (1892) says it is likened to

> when one seeks to learn the truth about creatures without reference to the due end, which is the knowledge of God. Hence, Augustine says: "We must not gratify a curiosity, idle and sure to be thrown away over the study of creatures; but we must make of that study a ladder to ascend to immortal and everlasting goods." (2a2ae, Q 167)

Of particular relevance to transformational psychology is this second form of curiosity, in which it is possible to exercise our intellectual capacities apart from their true telos of loving God and from "everlasting goods" in the knowing. This kind of knowing or curiosity was understood by the ancients to be an intellectual vice, a dysfunction in the actual experience of knowing, a falling short of how we were created to experience the knowing process. This vice of curiosity involves the absence of love and openness to God, which should shape all intellectual acts of observation and reflection. The result is a kind of "epistemological pathology," or distortion in knowing. Thus, psychologists, physicists and theologians can be tempted by curiosity to turn aside to lesser goals in their research and teaching, resulting in a truncated knowledge that is divorced from personal transformation and the glory of God.

Because the ultimate goal of all human activities, including the acts of knowing and doing science, is the love of God and neighbor, there is a need for a further, more inclusive model in doing psychology based on the transformed person. We do psychology well to the degree that the psychologist is more and more transformed by and open to the Spirit in the act of knowing and doing psychology—for the end of all actions, including doing psychology, is love of neighbor and ultimately the love of God. To say it in another way, doing psychology well is to do it as a form love, of contemplation and loving of God *in* the very act of studying persons. It is also a form of neighbor love in God. Anything less is a form of academic dysfunction and curiosity.

In that sense, the nonbeliever is unable *fully* to do psychology well and, thus, is in part dysfunctional as a psychologist. The reason is clear: the unbelieving psychologist does not study as he or she ought for the love of God or for the purpose of realizing his or her potential in the love of God and neighbor-love. Nor is he or she even open to understanding the person in relation to God (a point we shall discuss below). This, of course, is quite foreign to the contemporary mindset of science. Of course, the unbeliever, by common grace, is partially able to apprehend the truth of something. However, our point is that the psychological and spiritual health of the psychologist determines whether he or she does psychology well in the love of God as psychology was intended. Thus, even the experience of being parented well and having healthy ongoing relationships are important to the doing of psychology well, for formative relationships prepare the psychological-epistemological ground for doing psychology as it should be—namely, open to discovering what is real and true in the love of God and not closed due to psychopathology, being sinned against, defensiveness and sin.

The person determines the process. Second, transformational psychology insists that the state, experience and character of the person observing and reflecting in doing psychology determine the quality of the *process of psychology*. That is, the character of the psychologist grounds, develops and preserves the process of doing psychology, so long as the psychologist remains open to what is real and true without any need to distort what is discovered or experienced. In this sense, the *good* person is most able to do psychology, for good character transformed by the Spirit and other healthy relationships is the guarantor of (1) the investigator doing the work of science in the love of God (our point above) and (2) the investigator being open to study all relevant reality (internal and external) and not being closed due to some pathological need to distort or not see what is real (our point here). Because we are radically relational by nature, it follows that even the knowing experience is in some sense a way of being rightly related to what is real, while skepticism and ignorance are often ways of being unhealthily or dishonestly related to the real. Understanding this important connection between *relationality* and *knowing*, between epistemology and being rightly related to reality, is very important to our transformational approach to psychology and science in general.

Consequently, our growth in character and relationality (early and ongoing) are intimately tied to epistemology and knowing, a point we will develop further in the "Spirituality-ethics of epistemology and science thesis" section below. Of course, goodness alone does not ensure that the process of doing psychology will be done well; however, it does help ensure that it will be done for the right reason and motive in the love of God, and open to reality as it is and not as it needs to be to suit one's desires and fantasies.

The person and process determine the product. According to transformational psychology, the *person* determines the *process*, which, in turn, impacts the *product* of doing psychology. The good person who is in the process of transformation, and who has developed well his or her abilities to observe and reflect on the human condition in the love of God, has the potential to be truly open to what is real and to produce the best product or body of knowledge of psychology. Certainly this entails the training of one's abilities. Thus, doing psychology well will involve much energy, skill, training, practice in observation and reflection, and skill in communicating this product in words or in the care of others.

Nevertheless, the direction of the person's growth in God and in relationship to oneself and others will be most fundamental to doing psychology and producing a systematic body of knowledge and reflections in a psychology. Personal goodness, seeing oneself in truth, being open to one's observations in God and others—in general, being rightly related to what is real—is critical to producing a thoughtful and existentially meaningful body of knowledge and understanding of the human condition for the sake of the world and the church. Psychological unhealth results in potential blinders, prejudices, defenses and inabilities to see certain elements of reality that may be too painful or just psychologically beyond the experiential purview of the psychologist. Furthermore, psychological health advances the ultimate "product" of forming the psychologist into the image of Christ in the very doing of psychology, which is the goal of this activity. Of course, this will only be an approximation of the ideal as we develop.

The spirituality-ethics of epistemology and science thesis. Finally, it is clear from the Christian reality of freedom and sin that knowing in general, and doing science/psychology in particular, are both possible and problematic, depending on the goodness or virtues (e.g., the openness and honesty) of the observer. The science of psychology is particularly problematic, for the object of investigation is the human self, the same kind of self or person doing the investigating. Psychologists are free to do their observations, reflections and theorizing well or poorly, honestly or dishonestly. Thus, one's ability to do psychology and understand the person well is partly determined by what kind of person the observer is. One's character health, or lack of health, and one's ability to participate in and actualize one's personhood affects what the person can see or is willing to acknowledge about true personhood (Wood, 1998).

The epistemic role of virtue and holiness in doing psychology. One's journey in union with God and conformity to Christ's character is not only the telos of doing psychology but the determining factor for doing psychology well. The business of our own experiential growth is the foundation for developing a deep, unified, conceptual psychology as well as for doing psychotherapy and helping others. The reason is clear within the logic of the Christian faith but has escaped modern attention, namely, that holiness and spiritual health preserve the person in honesty to be open to the reality of human nature, sin and health rather than to miss or distort what is real and true of human beings. Of course, this is understood as a process throughout life.

As hinted at earlier, psychological health does not guarantee that one's product (research, reflections or praxis) will be excellent psychology, but it does help protect the scientist from distortions *due to unhealthy passions*. Personal psychopathology may limit the horizon of human experience of the self, resulting in potentially truncated observations, reflections and theorizing. This is especially a danger in psychology, since the psychologist is an invested or "interested" party in understanding (or misrepresenting) his or her self. For example, if God really exists, then the atheistic psychologists are necessarily skewing dimensions of human experience (e.g., unbelief, shame and guilt in relation to God) by ignoring or explaining away the supernatural or by construing belief in God as pathological. At best they will reduce God-talk to merely representations of early, internalized relational experiences with others. Of course, the same could be said of a believer who is closed to the reality of what is taking place within the self and in relation to God and others. In the area of research, it may be that dishonesty coupled with ego aggrandizement moves theorists and researchers to an unwarranted dogmatism or adherence to a theory despite evidence to the contrary, potentially blinding them to certain realities altogether.

The epistemic need for expanded horizons of experience in doing psychology. In general, one's experience or lack of experience of various realities often becomes the limiting horizon of theorizing, which is just as true for the Christian as the non-Christian. The reason for this is not only one's tendency to distort reality and fit it to oneself, but because in psychology, one's own self is a major datum for one's observation and reflection, and there seems to be a human penchant toward self-deception and universalizing one's experiences onto the world as the possible horizon or limit of what is true and real. For example, if a Christian doing psychology has little or no conscious experience of the Spirit or of the possibility of union with the Spirit, then her lack of experience may become the limiting horizon in her theory-making about the human spirit and its experience of God. Moreover, a Christian psychologist who has difficulties with vulnerability and maintaining deep relationships with others may downplay the role of human relationality in understanding the person or may, in reaction, overplay the role. Furthermore, a Christian who has been trained in a certain *naturalistic* approach to psychology, change and therapy (whether it be cognitive, relational, family systems, etc.) may or may not be open to the role of the Spirit, the role of demons, or appropriate uses of prayer, discernment with the Spirit and the spiritual disciplines in theory or therapy.

On the other hand, psychologists who have experienced the presence of the Holy Spirit in prayer will be more sensitive to understand and explore this experience in their theory and research, as well as with their believing clients when appropriate. In general, psychologists who are open to understanding themselves in relationship to the self, Christ and others will be well situated to understand human intrapsychic and interpsychic realities. They can look at these phenomena for what they are, more or less, without having the need to distort or reduce them to some other kind of phenomena. They still might misunderstand reality due to error or lack of effort, but at least it will not be due to the blinding effects of psychopathology. In all of these cases, not only the health and dysfunction of the psychologist but also the experience or lack thereof (the personal-existential component) is all-important for the right manner of doing psychology in the Spirit (the methodological-process component), as well as for good theorizing (the theoretical-product component).

The life of the psychologist as central to doing psychology. If one's psychological health and honesty determine the doing of psychology, then it may not be far from the truth to say that a true psychologist is one who knows oneself truly—and one who truly knows oneself is a true psychologist. Perhaps the maxim could be expanded to the following: *a true psychologist is one who is becoming truly healthy,* and *one who is becoming truly healthy is a true psychologist.* Only one who has experienced a good range of psychological health knows the boundary conditions of what can be experienced, what in fact is pathological, what makes up and contributes to true health, and what results if certain elements of experience are missing from life and theory. If one has not dealt with personal fears, anger, guilt, shame, and the need of the Spirit and one another, then these will perhaps be distorted, eliminated or reduced to something else in one's psychology.

We believe the above maxim holds as a general principle for both

Christian and non-Christian psychologists alike. That is, non-Christians' ability to discover truth will be limited by their own pathology, and it will be aided to the degree that they are emotionally and psychologically healthy. The difference here is that one's relationship with Christ has the power to assist the Christian psychologist in this growth process, which in turn can facilitate her ability to (1) pursue psychology as a means to loving God and neighbor; and (2) discover truth about the nature of the human self that the unbeliever may be unable or unwilling to see. Of course, just being a believer does not ensure doing excellent psychology. In fact, the believing psychologist may be just as limited by an unwillingness or inability due to psychopathology, laziness, ill-training or an inadequate methodology/theory.

The role of the spiritual disciplines in doing psychology. If the process and product of honest and insightful science are enhanced and preserved by good character, which results from union with God and the resulting conformity into Christ's character and the love of neighbor, then a startling implication emerges: *spiritual disciplines that foster union with God and good character in Christ are essential to doing good psychology.* The character of the psychologist lays the foundation for his or her openness to reality and the study of it. Spiritual disciplines develop this kind of character and, thus, are linked to the *transformation of the person* doing psychology, the *process* of doing good psychology and to the end theoretical *product* of psychology.

There will be a kind of learning-spiral between the doing of psychology and therapy and the spiritual disciplines. While the doing of spiritual disciplines protects the doing of psychology, we also gain insight from psychology about the nature and manner of doing spiritual disciplines well or poorly, openly or defensively. That is, practice in open and honest confession of one's sin and the development of humility can help guard one from distorting one's evidence or research due to arrogance or some need for significance. On the other hand, psychological insight into one's childhood relationship with a domineering and overly critical parent can reveal how this may transfer into a prayer life of performance and dishonesty in order to please a demanding God, which preempts open and loving self-disclosure in prayer. We can only imagine what it would be like to study at a school of psychology that is consciously committed to growth in psychological insight, as well as to growth in the life of prayer and in the spiritual disciplines—to personal growth as well as growth in greater union with God by the Spirit. The modern ethos of science precluded this from happening, blithely insisting that rationality and critique alone would protect science from error.

Other psychologists on the importance of the person and the spiritual-ethical element. Interestingly, a number of theorists have echoed the centrality or at least the importance of the person and the spiritual-ethical element in doing psychology in faith. As early as 1979, Carter and Narramore (1979) had already hinted at the relationship of knowing and the product of doing psychology with the kind of *person* doing the integration. They pointed out that virtues such as humility, awareness of limitations, tolerance for ambiguity, openness to the scientist's own fears and anxieties—human character—are essential to relating psychology to faith (p. 117). Tan (1987, 2001) likewise pointed out that "personal integration" and the "spirituality" of the psychologist are most fundamental to relating psychology and faith (2001, pp. 18-28; 1987, pp. 34-39).

In fact, there is evidence of change on the horizon for how a new generation of Christians, standing on the shoulders of their predecessors, are looking into more holistic, relational and experiential models for relating psychology to faith. Some are finding insights for new models in neuroscience, emotion research and attachment theory; others are exploring older spiritual traditions of soul care and spiritual formation for models of science to help understand, experience, and assist others in transformation (Benner, 1998; Evans, 2007; Johnson, 2007; McMinn, 1996; Moon and Benner, 2004; Sorenson, 1996a, 1996b). This change, in turn, is opening new doors of exploration for students in training. All of this is to be applauded. We believe this movement toward a more holistic, embodied, existential model is a *predictor* for the next stage in developing a distinct transformational model for doing psychology in the Spirit that specifically addresses how the personal-spiritual informs the conceptual and the very process of doing psychology.

CONSTRUCTING THE CONTOURS OF A TRANSFORMATIONAL PSYCHOLOGY

Given these foundational thoughts about the nature of transformational psychology, there is a need to reforge some of the contours of the whole enterprise of doing psychology in the Spirit. Much of the insight of prior theories and their categories will be retained, but within a slightly different orientation and structure. Our proposal for the contours of a transformational approach to psychology is sketchily outlined in the diagram below (for a further discussion, see Coe & Hall, chaps. 10-17, 2010). No doubt this transformational psychology could be construed differently, while retaining the same fundamental commitments and principles.

Levels 1-5 of the transformational psychology depicted in figure 3 are foundationally related to one another and are interdependent—though in real experience they ebb and flow together. The logical flow between levels is as follows: (1) becoming the kind of person-scientist characterologically by the spiritual disciplines, which encourages and protects (2) the methodology of doing science in God in order to (3) produce a body of knowledge of the person, leading to (4) the fruit of praxis of soul care and (5) the transformation and training of the scientist/therapist/psychologist in the love of God and neighbor.

Level 1: The transformation of the psychologist by spiritual-epistemological disciplines and virtues. Level 1 is the foundation of transformational psychology that focuses on the *transformation of the psychologist* by the spiritual-epistemological disciplines and virtues. These disciplines help protect and maintain the *process* and *product* of doing psychology in the Spirit at all the other levels. Spiritual disciplines assist the psychologist in being open to the reality of what one is studying and to a healthy process of study and research. They also guard the learner from pathological influences like being unwilling to see the truth of what a self is (deceit) or being driven by vices, false agendas, fantasies, grandiosity, overconfidence, timidity, which would hinder one from being open to reality. Central to the spiritual-epistemological disciplines are those of presenting oneself to God, the prayer of recollecting the self in one's true identity in Christ, exercising honesty-truthfulness and contemplation.

Level 2: Methodology, research and doing psychology in God. The process and method of doing psychology in level 2 are based on a realist methodology: that there is an external world containing dynamic, law-like structures that can be known for the sake of wisdom (psychological health versus dysfunction by means of introspection, observation and reflection), and there are realities that can be known by faith (from Scripture and religious

Level 5: Spiritual-Transformational Goal for the Psychologist and the Training in the University

Union with God   Conformity to Christ   Love   Glorifying God

(Contemplating the object of science in God)

Level 4: Praxis of Psychology in the Spirit as Soul Care

Twentieth-century therapeutic interventions (psychoanalytic, depth relational, existential, humanistic, cognitive behavioral, etc.)   Spiritual direction   New paradigm?

Level 3: Theorizing and Development of the Body of Knowledge for the Sake of Serving the Spiritual Formation Needs of the Church

Nature of the Self	Sin and Psychopathology	Psychological Health
1. The self as a spirit (personal identity and freedom)	1. Original sin	1. Health without Christ
2. The self as having a nature	2. Sins of the heart	2. Parental love as model for God's transformative love
3. The self as relational	3. Being sinned against	3. Health in Christ by the Holy Spirit
4. The self as beyond relationality to union with God	4. The demonic	4. The cross redeeming us to love God and neighbor in the Spirit a. Developmental spirituality b. Spiritual disciplines and discernment

Level 2: Methodology, Research and the Process of Doing Psychology in God (Old Testament Sage as Model for Social Science)

Observation on creation and the Word in the love of God   *Reflection* on creation and the Word in the love of God   *Interaction* with reflection of others in the love of God

Level 1: Transformation of Psychologist by Spiritual-Epistemological Disciplines and Virtues for Doing Psychology and Science in the Spirit

Presentation   Recollection   Honesty-confession   Discernment   Contemplative prayer

Figure 3. Contours of a transformational model of psychology

experience), both of which are united in a single vision of love in understanding the person. Scripture, of course, provides a unique datum insofar as it is an authoritative, God-authored interpretation of certain dimensions of reality that ground, transform, and need to be in continual dialogue with our observations and reflections on creation.

Level 3: Theorizing and development of a body of knowledge. One of the central goals for the transformative psychologist is to produce a body of knowledge and theory in the Spirit, which approximate reality in order to serve the faith of loving God and neighbor. Volumes could be written on each dimension—and perhaps better categories could be developed that are still consistent with the vision of the model than the ones given below.

A. The Nature of the Self

    1. The self as a spirit (understanding the uniqueness of personal identity and freedom)

    2. The self as having a nature (a developmental understanding of human capacities and relationality)

    3. The self as understood for relationship and union with God

B. Sin and Psychopathology

    1. Original sin and resulting impaired psychological and relational dynamics

    2. Sins of the will, vice habits of the heart and other impaired defenses

    3. Being sinned against and the negative psychological effect of unhealthy relationships

    4. The potential impact of the demonic on human experience and impairment

C. Psychological Health

    1. The potential of human psychological health apart from Christ

    2. Parental love as a model for God's transformative love in the matrix of healthy development

    3. Psychological health based on Christ's redemptive work by means of the indwelling Holy Spirit

    4. The developmental growth-dynamics of loving God and neigh-

bor (includes a developmental approach to spirituality, the role of the spiritual disciplines, and the dynamics of healthy relationships with the Spirit and one another)

Level 4: Praxis of psychology in the spirit as soul care. There is a logical move in this spiritual formation model of psychology from theory *to* praxis, from understanding *to* treatment, from reflection *to* loving others. That is, if the goal of developing a theory of the person is the love of God and neighbor, there must be a way to help others in this understanding and transformation process. Both the secular world and Christianity have historically developed various forms of mentoring, education and teaching. Psychology in its nineteenth- and twentieth-century manifestations has provided unique forms of mentoring—or ways of *being with* another person in the form of depth therapy, and in various types of relational, cognitive and behavioral interventions for the sake of addressing psychopathology and human functioning.

We believe there to be a compelling and promising vision of psychotherapy, a broad relational paradigm that draws out the implications of our view of the self as relational-knower. This relational paradigm represents a convergence of multiple fields and disciplines including affective neuroscience, attachment theory, relational psychoanalysis, intersubjectivity theory, emotion-focused therapy (EFT) and family systems theories, and this paradigm provides a contemporary, scientific view of change that has been missed in the more classical cognitive and behavioral traditions. This relational paradigm of doing therapy and soul care also converges with recent developments in helping people grow within a more classical Christian form of spiritual direction and discipleship. In the name of peering behind the veil at these traditions of soul care, we are also open to the development of possible *new paradigms* for ways to encourage psychological and spiritual growth, as well as encouraging the love of God and neighbor, which brings together elements of relational therapy and spiritual direction.

Level 5: Spiritual-transformational goal for the psychologist and training. The very acts of doing science, making theories and practically applying them for neighbor-love all serve the final end of transforming the scientist in the love of God. None of us do these things well, but it is the aim of a robust transformational psychology. One can only imagine the dramatic implications that this transformational approach to psychology (and science) could have for research, education and clinical training in the academy and church in caring for the university, seminary, church and world.

CONCLUSION

The focus on the person and process (the ethical-spiritual-methodological) are at the heart of a transformational psychology, and we believe the implications, as we have tried to articulate, are compelling. Science and faith do not involve two separate acts, for doing psychology *truly* is to do it in faith, in the love of God—to contemplate God in the object and the object in God. This helps us—theoretically and pragmatically—to avoid truncation, to keep our work focused on the end goal and to do our work in the manner for which God created us.

Furthermore, psychology (and science in general) and faith are not about relating two separate domains or realities, studied by two different methodologies, that need to be brought together by some subsequent non-scientific method. A transformational psychology is committed to developing a science or methodology for psychology as a single vision of study that is open to all relevant reality as legitimate data for psychological theory, research and therapy.

Finally, because the personal growth of the psychologist is central to doing psychology, there needs to be dramatic rethinking about the training of psychologists with respect to the transformation of the person, the process and the products of psychology in university and clinical training programs. Christian graduate schools of psychology and undergraduate departments need to rethink their course goals regarding how the subject matter, classroom experience and assignments could aid in the transformation of the professor and student doing psychology (Coe, 2000). What a dramatic difference it would make were this training fundamentally about spiritual and relational growth, which we have argued, is the ground for healthy and true observation-reflection in the doing of psychology and therapy.

REFERENCES

Adams, J. (1972). *Competent to counsel*. Grand Rapids, MI: Baker, 1972.

Aitken, K. T. (1986). *Proverbs*. Philadelphia: Westminster Press.

Aquinas, T. (1892). *A translation of the principal portions of the second part of the summa theologica*. (Joseph Rickaby, Trans.). London: Burns and Oates.

Benner, D. (1998). *Care of souls: Revisioning Christian nurture and counsel.* Grand Rapids, MI: Baker.

Carter, J. D., & Narramore, B. (1979). *The integration of psychology and theology: An introduction.* Grand Rapids, MI: Zondervan.

Coe, J. H. (2000). Intentional spiritual formation in the classroom: Making space for the Spirit in the university. *Christian Education Journal, 4,* 85-110.

Coe, J. H. (2007, November). The spiritual-epistemological disciplines for studying/doing theology in obedience. Paper presented at the annual meeting of the Evangelical Theological Society, San Diego, CA.

Coe, J. H., & Hall, T. (2010). *Psychology in the Spirit: Contours of a transformational psychology.* Downers Grove, IL: IVP Academic.

Evans, C. S. (2007). The concept of the self as the key to integration. In D. H. Stevenson, B. E. Eck & P. C. Hill (Eds.), *Psychology and Christianity integration: Seminal works that shaped the movement* (pp. 170-75). Batavia, IL: Christian Association for Psychological Studies.

Foster, J. D., Horn, D. A., & Watson, S. (1988). The popularity of integration models, 1980-1985. *Journal of Psychology and Theology, 16,* 3-14.

Johnson, E. L. (1997). Christ, the Lord of Psychology. *Journal of Psychology and Theology, 25,* 11-27.

Johnson, E. L. (2007). *Foundations for soul care: A Christian psychology proposal.* Downers Grove, IL: IVP Academic.

MacIntyre, A. (1984). *After virtue* (2nd ed.). South Bend, IN: University of Notre Dame Press.

McMinn, M. R. (1996). *Psychology, theology and spirituality in Christian counseling.* Wheaton, IL: Tyndale House.

Moon, G. W., & Benner, D. G. (Eds.) (2004). *Spiritual direction and the care of souls: A guide to Christian approaches and practices.* Downers Grove, IL: InterVarsity Press.

Rad, G. V. (1972). *Wisdom in Israel.* Nashville: Abingdon Press.

Rawls, J. (1971). *A theory of justice.* Cambridge, MA: Belknap Press of Harvard University Press.

Sorenson, R. L. (1996a). The tenth leper. *Journal of Psychology & Theology, 24,* 197-211.

———. (1996b). Where are the nine? *Journal of Psychology & Theology, 24,* 179-96.

Tan, S. Y. (1987). Interpersonal integration: The servant's spirituality. *Journal of Psychology and Christianity, 6,* 34-39.

———. (2001). Integration and beyond: Principled, professional, and personal. *Journal of Psychology and Christianity, 20,* 18-28.

Willard, D. (1984). *Logic and the objectivity of knowledge.* Athens: Ohio University Press.

Wood, W. J. (1998). *Epistemology: Becoming intellectually virtuous.* Downers Grove, IL: InterVarsity Press.

A Levels-of-Explanation Response to Transformational Psychology

David G. Myers

JOHN H. COE AND TODD W. HALL HAVE AN ambitious agenda: to "redesign our traditional way of thinking of psychology in relation to Christianity, as well as rethinking the very nature of science itself" (p. 199). Their bold wish is to transform psychology and science into "something that is intrinsically a single act of faith and love" (p. 200). To accomplish this, they have *"set off on our own course to reexperience and redesign the process of doing psychology and its end product"* (p. 202).

Although it's unclear to me what this new "science" would look like, reading their chapter triggers three thoughts.

First, go for it. And then show psychological scientists what new knowledge and insight transformational psychologists have been able to produce. If "you will know them by their fruits" (Mt 7:16 NASB), then what will transformational psychology teach us? What insights from it might be the basis for future AP and GRE psychology exams?

Second, the Christian origins of modern science can prepare us to appreciate and respect the revelations of science. For those at institutions with a Reformed heritage, John Calvin offers a model with his "great admiration" for the secular scholars of his day, whose praiseworthy work ultimately comes "from God" (Calvin, *Institutes*, Vol. 1., p. 247).

Third, although they are right that psychological science merits critique, perhaps a more modest agenda would be appropriate. Both history and the Bible's own witness show that people—including people of faith—are fallible creatures. The rains of truth and illusion fall on us all. The "realities of the faith redeem the possibility of doing psychology according to reality and not merely the dictates of our fantasies and perceived needs," note Coe and Hall (p. 204). But are Coe and Hall and fellow Christian psychologists immune to their own fantasies and needs? Aren't we all fallen creatures, whose worldviews and values shape our understandings? And isn't science, by putting our cherished ideas to the test, a potential corrective for unrestrained bias?

When Coe and Hall go on to give more definition to their transformational psychology, some devout Christians will likely question their assumptions. Is "an immaterial human spirit" (p. 203) an essential faith-rooted part of their new psychology? I would infer yes when they say that "'Christian realities' (e.g., the existence of immaterial objects)" are ones that "secular, modern science has excluded" (p. 206). However, a growing number of Christian scholars offer a biblically based understanding of humans as *embodied creatures* whose eternal existence is rooted not in an essential immaterial nature (possessing an undying immortal soul, as Plato supposed) but rather in God's promise of some form of bodily resurrection. (See recent books by Fuller Theological Seminary faculty such as Nancey Murphy, Warren Brown and Joel Green for an explanation of biblical faith that is much closer to today's cognitive neuroscience than to Coe and Hall's Platonic idea of an immaterial soul.) So who is privileged to say what is reality: the evangelical Christians Coe and Hall? Or the evangelical Christians at Fuller who have quite a different understanding?

Thus when Coe and Hall ask "is the transformational psychologist doing something other than 'psychology'" (p. 206), I answer, indeed yes: he or she is doing *religion*. A "nonnaturalistic methodology in science" is nonscience in science; it's a contradiction in terms. Better to respect religion as religion and science as science, and then to build bridges between them. For example, Coe and Hall could offer us a bridge between today's social psychology—with its explorations of the human "need to belong"—and the Christian assumption that, in their words, "life is relational" (p. 213).

And would Coe and Hall really want to explain to secular psychological scientists why "the nonbeliever is unable *fully* to do psychology" (p. 214)? How would they explain transformational psychology's superiority at studying memory formation, cognitive changes with aging, color vision, the genetic foundations of personality and intelligence, hemispheric information processing, the biochemistry of disorder, and myriad other topics that form the stuff of psychological science's investigation of human nature?

So while I appreciate Cole and Hall's effort to weave scientific and spiritual understandings into one harmonious fabric (that much we agree on), I respectfully dissent from their effort to transform "psychology" into religion. If someone were to seek to "transform" Christianity into a New Age spirituality, Coe and Hall would surely object: "You can't just make up what the word *Christian* means without regard to its agreed-on historic meaning." Likewise, *psychology* has an agreed-on meaning, as reflected in textbook definitions ("the science of behavior and mental processes," as in my own texts) and in standard dictionaries:

- "the science of the mind or of mental states and processes" *(Random House Unabridged Dictionary)*

- "the science that deals with mental processes and behavior" *(American Heritage Dictionary of the English Language)*

- "the science that deals with mental processes and behavior" *(Miriam Webster)*

- "scientific discipline that studies mental processes and behaviour in humans and other animals" *(Britannica Concise Encyclopedia)*

Christian students reading this book are offered two distinct paths to doing psychology Christianly. Both are well-intentioned. Both have advocates. One path, represented by Coe and Hall (and by Powlison, as well as Roberts and Watson) is to come apart from the "biased" world of secular psychology and to create, off in a corner, a focused Christian psychology where conservative Christians talk among themselves. The other path takes us into the playing fields of mainstream psychological science. There, as part of worshiping God with our minds, we can enthusiastically use the tools of science to explore the human creature, while also seeking to be part of God's leaven in the loaf.

As for me, the chosen path is not the separatist enclave. Although Christian scholars will want to be true to observed reality *and* to their own values, many of us feel called to seek to follow the tradition of the apostle Paul, who was not apart from the world but rather was Greek to the Greeks and Jew to the Jews (1 Cor 9:20-23)—seeking to understand the world, engage it, learn from it, talk its language and leaven its discourse.

An Integration Response
to Transformational Psychology

Stanton L. Jones

THERE IS MUCH TO COMMEND AND AFFIRM in this description of the transformational psychology view of the relationship between Christianity and psychology. Some of the most important features are that

- the approach evidences a clear commitment to biblical authority and a fundamental grounding in a biblical view of persons (which is articulated well, though briefly, in this chapter) and indeed of all reality.

- this chapter articulates a clear commitment to critical realism (Jones, 1994), the affirmation that objective reality exists independent of our perceptions (realism), but that, nevertheless, we engage and come to know that objective reality through the traditions or worldviews to which we are heirs (making it *critical* realism). In John Coe and Todd Hall's words, "we do science open to the truth" but always "within a tradition" (p. 201).

- Transformational psychologists seek "*a single, unified—though complex—science/psychology of reality*" (p. 207), a goal shared by the integration approach.

- There is a clear willingness by Coe and Hall to engage, learn from and contribute to all of psychology.

- They embrace the Old Testament "sage" as an appropriate model to emulate.

- They encourage the use of classic spiritual disciplines, and the pursuit of spiritual transformation more broadly, as foundational for the Christian psychologist.

- They edifyingly identify love as the final and appropriate end for all of our efforts.

Since Coe and Hall's goal is to "provide the general outlines or contours of this transformational model, as well as distinguish it from previous models" (p. 200), I will now focus on what distinguishes this model and some concerns with those distinguishing points, despite the commendable qualities listed above.

First, Coe and Hall, in seeking to differentiate their model from previous models, label only one view with which they are sharply distinct: the integration view. They present a distorted characterization, however, of the integration view and hence of its limitations. They describe the integration view as "a relating of two separate kinds of studies involving two different kinds of methodologies that are mutually exclusive, which the believer then brings together in some fashion with its own peculiar methodology" (p. 206). They argue that their transformational psychology, in implicit contrast to the integration view, does not "relegate a piece of theology as something to be *integrated with* science" (p. 203, emphasis in original). Perhaps most pointedly, in clear reference to the integration view, they say "psychology (and science in general) and faith are not about relating two separate domains of realities, studied by two different methodologies, that need to be brought together by some subsequent nonscientific method" (p. 225).

This, however, is not the integration view but rather an unflattering caricature of it. None of the founding authors cited in my chapter—neither Gary Collins, nor Carter and Narramore, Evans, Van Leeuwen or any of the other stalwarts of the integration movement—suggested that the psychological/scientific and the spiritual/theological domains were distinct realities to be studied by sharply distinct methods, culminating in some sort of alchemistic and forced amalgamation. Instead, integrationists have called for precisely the sort of holistic reconstruction of psychology (per Collins's early title *The Rebuilding of Psychology*) that Coe and Hall themselves call for based on a biblical view of persons and reality, of science and of knowing. Indeed, when I finished reading their description of the transformational view, I was uncertain of what distinguishes this approach from the family of integration views properly understood. While their view manifests some unique emphases and perhaps idiosyncrasies, they embody the core commitments I have always associated with an integration view.

Second, and perhaps most importantly, I am intrigued but concerned by the seeming spiritualized individualism of the transformational view. This concern was triggered early in the chapter by the following exhortation:

"we want to become aware of overdependence on a tradition(s). *The goal here is to set off on our own course to reexperience and redesign the process of doing psychology and its end byproduct.* . . . The goal, then, is for each generation in the Spirit to allow *reality* and *faith* to shape this endeavor" (p. 202, emphasis in original). While I have argued for radical rethinking of the very nature of psychology in contexts that are both religious (Jones & Butman, 1991) and nonreligious (Jones, 1994) and have urged a courageous distancing from prevailing paradigms, this exhortation for the individual Christian psychologist to set aside the wisdom of all prior work was breathtaking in its scope. Should every new generation of Christian psychologists, indeed every individual psychologist in training, scrap all that has come before to start again from scratch? What happens to the progressive accumulation of wisdom and of knowledge if we are to "set off on our own course to reexperience and redesign the process of doing psychology and its end product"?

As the authors went on to develop their views, however, it became clear that this was no mere tangent in their argument. They argued that their approach is "driven less by any one theory and tradition and more by the person and the process of doing psychology" (p. 203). In fact, "this transformational model affirms that *the transformation of the psychologist is the determinative and foundational element for the process and product of doing psychology*" (p. 206, emphasis added). This emphasis is reiterated over and over, including their identification of the first "transformational psychology thesis" as "the transformed person as most fundamental" (p. 213), a thesis reinforced by their depiction of the "Transformation of Psychologist" as level 1 of their whole model in figure 3.

At one level, I must and do agree with aspects of this emphasis and have previously made a version of this argument myself: arguing that psychology in particular and science more generally can never be understood as impersonal processes implemented by automatons, but rather are intrinsically human processes. If it is human individuals who do science and who do psychotherapy, then our humanness will shape every facet of what we do. In addressing students of psychology, I concluded a long meditation on the integration of psychotherapy theories (Jones & Butman, 1991) with a chapter that focused on the personal transformation of the Christian psychologist. This included an extended discussion of the virtues that should characterize us, and of our calling to "imaging" or embodying or incarnating, in our persons and in our work as godly counselors, God's roles or offices, God's character, and God's concerns. Such embodiment of the likeness of God must be understood as intertwined with true spiritual transformation, with God's work of sanctification.

Individualism is a great strength and a great weakness of evangelicalism. Our individual focus ensures that we take the call to follow Christ personally, that we take individual piety seriously, that we each understand the call to pick up our cross and follow Christ as a call that demands a personal decision from each of us. But the dark side of this emphasis on the individual is manifested in the continued splintering and fragmentation of the Protestant movement—and of evangelical churches and ministries in particular. The freedom and responsibility to respond personally sometimes becomes license to ignore the communal integrity of the entire body of Christ, to ignore our obligation to seek unity (John 17). This engenders a type of hubris that imagines we can ignore the wisdom and labors of past generations of believers whose theological and life understandings are a great gift from God.

The call of Coe and Hall to considerable freedom from past ways of thinking about Christian psychology jarringly contrasts with the call of Roberts and Watson to master the great resources of Christian psychology from the past. In focusing on the spiritual transformation of the individual psychologist as their foundational principle, Coe and Hall risk disagreements among psychologists (over, for example, ways to formulate psychological understandings) degenerating into which psychologist is more spiritually mature or transformed. Coe and Hall are gracious individuals, but if spiritual transformation is foundational and if I disagree with aspects of their views, is that disagreement rooted in my failure to be spiritually transformed? Might, it be argued, the reason that I disagree with them be that I am simply not spiritually mature enough to see that they are right?

Make no mistake: There are times when it is right to invoke just such an argument. Romans 1 speaks of a kind of willful moral blindness that can prevent those in bondage to sin from seeing the world rightly. It is God who can free us from such bondage and give us eyes to see rightly. The New Testament epistles contain arguments that boil down to some variant of an apostle asserting that "those of you who are spiritually mature can see that I am right." But should those of us who are not apostles invoke such reasoning as we seek to construct a Christian psychology? As I would expect from esteemed colleagues, Coe and Hall make no such allegations, but if spiritual transformation is foundational and if bringing together psychology and Christian faith is fundamentally a product of the individual spirituality of the inquirer, how do we understand and work out our disagreements?

My third concern is their indirect criticism of other (unidentified) approaches as understanding their Christian foundations as mere assumptions instead of actual knowledge: "Further, our transformational psychology does not merely *assume* certain Christian beliefs to be true. . . . Rather, the Christian apprehends or knows these specifically Christian realities" (pp. 203-4, emphasis in original), and "We are *not* saying that these tenets or beliefs are presuppositions, if one means by 'presupposition' something that I know by assuming or supposing it to be true. Rather, they are true because they correspond to or are born out in the experience of reality" (p. 205, emphasis in original).

Once again, I cannot be sure who they are criticizing on this point, but it could even be my own work. In Jones and Butman (1991), we outlined our approach to integration by saying in chapter one:

> Ideas about human character and personality do not arise in a philosophical vacuum. As Browning (1987, p. 95) has said, 'the modern psychologies function within larger contexts of meaning about the way the world is.' . . . These assumptions and presuppositions are of crucial importance for the Christian academician, clinician or researcher, especially those that pertain to our notions of personhood and philosophy of science. (pp. 30-31)

And then in chapter two, we elaborated:

> But if we are not searching [the Bible] for a personality theory, what in the Scriptures is it reasonable to expect to find? In brief, we believe that our foray into theological and biblical anthropology will give us the essential foundation for a more true and more complete understanding of persons by giving us 'control beliefs' (Wolterstorff, 1984) or presuppositions. These control beliefs are the 'givens,' the assumptions that control or shape all other thought. (p. 40)

Are we then guilty of "merely assuming" certain Christian beliefs to be true because we used the words *assumptions* and *presuppositions?* Absolutely not. The philosophical waters are deep here, but we were writing in the tradition of Reformed epistemology (Plantinga, 1984; Wolterstorff, 1984). This is a tradition that recognizes that things we take as utterly and foundationally true (such as God's existence) may nevertheless not be demonstrable as true to the standards demanded by others (such as determined atheists). Nevertheless, we are still within our "epistemic rights" (in the words of Plantinga) to take such beliefs as fundamental to our approach to knowing. Writers may use such words as *assumptions* and *presuppositions* without giving up on truth.

Finally, Coe and Hall are not innovators in proposing that we as Christian psychologists see ourselves as following in the footsteps of the Old Testament sage; in Jones and Butman (1991, chap. 16), we drew on the same proposal from Tidball (1986) who himself documented a long heritage for such an understanding.

REFERENCES

Browning, D. (1987). *Religious thought and the modern psychologies.* Philadelphia: Fortress.

Jones, S. (1994). A constructive relationship for religion with the science and profession of psychology: Perhaps the boldest model yet. *American Psychologist, 49*(3), 184-99.

———. (1996). Reflections on the nature and future of the Christian psychologies. *Journal of Psychology and Christianity, 15*(2), 133-42.

Jones, S., & Butman, R. (1991). *Modern psychotherapies: A comprehensive Christian appraisal.* Downers Grove, IL: InterVarsity Press.

Plantinga, A. (1984). Advice to Christian philosophers. *Faith and Philosophy, 1,* 253-71.

Tidball, D. (1986). *Skillful shepherds: An introduction to pastoral theology.* Grand Rapids, MI: Zondervan.

Wolterstorff, N. (1984). *Reason within the bounds of religion* (2nd ed.). Grand Rapids, MI: Eerdmans.

A Christian Psychology Response
to Transformational Psychology

Robert C. Roberts

My AIM IN THIS COMMENT is to support and clarify some of the main claims in the essay by John Coe and Todd Hall.

Their essay stresses the epistemology of a Christian psychology. In fact, one could think of their paper as an essay in epistemology. Epistemology is the study of knowledge—what it is, how we acquire and communicate it, and how it is related to our practices. Coe and Hall contend that the character of the psychologist himself (that is, his virtues and vices) makes an enormous difference in what he comes to know as a psychologist. But they say little about the nature of the knowledge in question. Here I may be able to help out a bit.

In a book titled *Intellectual Virtues: An Essay in Regulative Epistemology*, Jay Wood and I distinguish three kinds of knowledge, each of which depends on the virtues of the knower (Wood & Roberts, 2007). But the three kinds of knowledge depend on virtues in somewhat different ways, so if we don't have a clear idea of what knowledge is, we may not be very precise about how it depends on the virtues. The three kinds of knowledge are propositional knowledge, understanding and acquaintance. Following are some simple illustrations.

Let's say that Harry knows that *light travels from the moon to Earth in about 1.255 seconds at the moon's mean orbital distance from Earth*. This is an instance of propositional knowledge because what Harry knows is a proposition (indicated by the part of the sentence in italics). For Harry to have this kind of knowledge, three conditions have to be met: (1) Harry has to *believe* the proposition, (2) Harry's believing the proposition has to *result from some respectable belief-producing process* (for example, getting the belief from an authoritative scientific source), and (3) the proposition has to be *true*.

To have knowledge of the above proposition, Harry doesn't need to understand very much, but there's plenty to understand in the neighborhood of this proposition. Let's say that Harry's friend Trevor understands the moon's movements relative to Earth. For example, Trevor can explain why, though the moon orbits the Earth every 27.5 days, it shows the same phase to the earth only every 29.5 days. Understanding is a grasp, mastery or "seeing" of the regular connections among things, the principles that govern them, and thus often yields an ability to explain. Generally, understanding is much more sophisticated and demanding than propositional knowledge, and it constitutes a great portion of what scientists and other intellectuals (including psychologists) seek under the title of "knowledge."

Yet a third kind of knowledge results from firsthand experience. You can well imagine somebody who is not satisfied with mere propositional knowledge about the moon, or even profound theoretical knowledge, but who wants to become acquainted with the moon itself. Giles would like to look at the moon through a powerful telescope and even go walking around on it to feel what the moon dust is like under his feet, to experience the great reduction in gravity as compared with Earth and to climb down into a crater or up the crater's ridge. Wood and I call this kind of knowledge "acquaintance" because it is firsthand in a way that neither propositional knowledge nor understanding needs to be.

All three kinds of knowledge are found in psychology and also in Christian life. Empirical research papers often give us a conclusion (proposition) that is true and provide data that support its claim to be true. Clinical theories provide frameworks for explaining how psychological dysfunction originates and why some favored type of intervention is effective against the dysfunction. A person who masters such a framework can use it to understand (at least putatively) particular clients' problems. And in clinical work the therapist often gains firsthand acquaintance with a client's problems and emotions.

These three kinds, or aspects, of knowledge interact. Research papers often propose (sometimes speculatively) an explanation of their results, and thus engage in understanding, which can lead to further beliefs that are well supported partly by the understanding. Understanding often starts with or depends on beliefs that the thinker takes to be true and well grounded. Acquaintance often provides support for our beliefs and is also notoriously shaped by our understanding: we tend to "see" what we think we ought to see, because we process what presents itself in conformity with our patterns of understanding. The result is that our understanding of something influences the experience we have of it.

We see the same interdependence of knowledge in the Christian life. The creeds contain propositions that Christians believe, and they are well supported by the Bible and church tradition. A person might believe the creed without much theological understanding, but we expect mature, thinking Christians to have a good understanding of what they believe, as well as propositional beliefs. Theology and Bible study are disciplines designed to deepen our understanding of our faith, our ability to connect the various parts of our faith in a way that makes sense to us and allows us to see its application to the world we live in and to our actions.

But for the Christian life, it is not enough to know the truths presented in the creeds and to have a profound understanding of theology and knowledge of how to apply it to our lives. It is also crucial to know, by personal experience or acquaintance, what it is to be a sinner in need of redemption, what it is to be the object of God's redeeming love, what it is to love one's neighbor as oneself, what it is to be indwelt by the Holy Spirit. No amount of mere justified believing of Christian truths, or profound theological understanding, can substitute for personal experience of the things of Christian faith. In fact, our justified believing and theological understanding are themselves shallow or incomplete if we have no personal acquaintance with the things of the gospel.

One of the important theses of transformational psychology is that there is no clear or strict line between spiritual and psychological well-being, or between spiritual and psychological knowledge. Acquaintance with oneself as a sinner in need of redemption *is* a kind of psychological acquaintance with oneself. And acquaintance with the Holy Spirit by way of his indwelling presence *is* a kind of acquaintance with psychological well-being.

Another important thesis in the chapter by Coe and Hall is that the kind of knowledge that is distinctive of the Christian psychologist depends on a proper development of the Christian virtues. As I've indicated, I'm sympathetic with both of these theses. I hope to have helped their argument a bit by clarifying the concept of knowledge as it relates to their endeavor, and I hope to help a bit more in the remainder of this response by exploring briefly what it is about the Christian virtues that makes them function as a prerequisite for Christian psychological knowledge.

The chief Christian virtues are faith, hope and love. Other Christian virtues mentioned in Scripture are humility, patience, self-control, forbearance, gratitude, gentleness, compassion, generosity and forgivingness. It would be a useful exercise for some transformational psychologist with a philosophical bent to explore how each of these virtues in the practicing psychologist is a source of psychological knowledge. Here I must limit myself to a brief discussion of just one of these virtues.

Faith is far more than taking the propositions in the Apostles' Creed to be true. The person who has faith in the Father of Jesus Christ lives in worshipful communion with God and his Son, calling on them in moments of decision, trouble and joy—consulting them in decision, trusting them in trouble and praising them in joy. Faith is thus a personal relationship, a kind of intimacy or friendship with God characterized by daily interaction. It involves an attentiveness to what God has done, is doing and will do—an alertness to God in his involvements in the events of the Christian's daily life. It is possible to believe the propositions of the Creed, in the sense of sincerely assenting to their truth whenever the question comes up, but without the question coming up very much. Belief is thus "dispositional," a *readiness* to say yes *if asked*. But faith is active participation in the life of God. This active participation is emotionally qualified—by awe of God's greatness, gratitude for God's provision, sorrow about one's treachery of God, peace concerning one's troubles.

It is just a fact of life that we gain knowledge through participating in rich and challenging activities. From such a rich ongoing interaction as the life of faith, it seems obvious that one will gain understanding and acquaintance (experience) of a psychological kind. One will get to know oneself better. One will come to understand one's strengths and weaknesses, as well as one's needs as a creature made for communion with God. Such a disciple will have an understanding of the inner dynamics of the life of faith, which is a life of healing, and will be profoundly acquainted with the evil and folly that reside in the depths of the human soul. I think we can see from this brief sketch that the Christian virtues are likely to bear their epistemic fruit primarily in the areas of understanding and acquaintance. But it would be wrong to think that they do not contribute at all to knowledge as justified true belief.

It is admirable that Coe and Hall take seriously the importance of thinking carefully about the nature of the knowledge that psychologists seek and prerequisites of that knowledge, and I think they are right that an important prerequisite of Christian knowledge of the human psyche is the spiritual transformation of the psychologist. However, this insight, which seems to be the major emphasis of their contribution to the present volume, does not distinguish transformational psychology from what Watson and I call Christian psychology. I read their paper as a supplement to Christian psychology—as an essay on one aspect of the epistemology of that psychology.

That transformational psychology really treats only one aspect of that epistemology is suggested by Paul Watson's careful, Christianly informed attention to scientific methodology, as illustrated in the second half of our main essay in this volume. At the beginning of their paper Coe and Hall also seem to minimize the importance of studying the various psychologies of the past, as discussed in the first half of our paper—though, in the body of their paper, they show that in fact they value such historical work. I commend them for their concern with epistemology, though as this brief commentary indicates, their insights need to be refined, deepened, broadened and made more precise.

REFERENCES

Wood, J., & Roberts, R. C. (2007). *Intellectual virtues: An essay in regulative epistemology.* Oxford: Oxford University Press.

A Biblical Counseling Response
to Transformational Psychology

David Powlison

THIS CHAPTER GREW ON ME. At first, the fuzzy language and absence of concrete examples obfuscated more than illuminated. Even after careful rereading, phrases such as "doing psychology in God" and "studying all reality in the Spirit" are nonstarters (though I think I eventually caught the drift). But when John Coe and Todd Hall note that the "realities of the faith redeem the possibility of doing psychology according to reality and not merely the dictates of our fantasies and perceived needs" (p. 204), they communicate profoundly what it means to understand and help people with the gaze and intentions of Christ. Their sense that the Christian orientation to reality calls for a comprehensive reorientation of our approach to all things psychological, beginning with the person of the would-be psychologist, is on target. Personal transformation in Christ is the sine qua non for accurate psychological knowing and true helpfulness to others. Knowledge, especially practical knowledge of people, is never abstracted from any knower's core beliefs and intentions.

Coe and Hall deserve high commendation for reckoning with sin's skewing intellectual effects. Their awareness that sin systematically distorts even psychological perception is refreshingly clear-minded. *Reality* has to do with God. Claims to objectivity and neutrality are pretense if the science and therapy systematically defect from reality. This core perception mirrors Coe and Hall's bold appreciation for the reorienting effects of God's mercies.

Coe and Hall's call to engage in fresh firsthand work is on target. Too many discussions treat Christianity as a set of fixed doctrinal-ethical contents, and Psychology as a neutral methodology that generates proven scientific findings. The result is a "patchwork quilt in which some theorist . . . is artificially stitched together with certain fundamental doctrines of the Christian faith" (p. 202). A truly Christian gaze demonstrates unique and comprehensive coherence. When we study people afresh, biblical faith and practice demonstrate a seamless depth and relevance regarding all things psychological.

Most significantly, Coe and Hall propose a comprehensive vision that intends to produce five very good things (pp. 221-25). I will restate their five goals slightly[1] and then will interact with several of them. They aim for:

1. personal transformation by the Word written and incarnate, so that we come to see and engage people the way God does (as *persons* changed into his image)

2. an intentional search for detailed knowledge of human beings in their total life situation (*processes* of learning from many sources)

3. an articulate, systematic, practical theology that increasingly "approximates reality" (producing a deep, wide-ranging *body of knowledge*)

4. the care and cure of souls, forming others into Christ's image (producing effective *praxis*)

5. transformed institutions engaging in and facilitating the realization of these wisdoms (producing effective *research, education* and *training* programs)

These ambitions are admirably coherent and comprehensive. In terms native to Christian faith, these are the goals of a *practical theology* of counseling ministry. They are the express goals of biblical counseling.[2]

Where then do I differ with Coe and Hall? I think they stumble as they seek to bring their proposal to fruition because of their reliance on the monastic tradition. The form of Christianity that they bring to the table in engaging psychology expresses problematic distinctives of the "spiritual formation" tradition: for example, contemplative prayer's wordless interiority; pursuit of beatific vision in contemplation of God and creation; pursuit of ineffable experience of the divine being; pursuit of mystical union

---

[1] I hope I illustrate Coe and Hall's own conviction: "No doubt this transformational psychology could be construed differently, while *retaining the same fundamental commitments and principles*"; "perhaps better categories could be developed that are *still consistent with the vision of the model* than the ones given" (pp. 221, 223, emphasis mine).

[2] As a label, "biblical counseling" highlights the fourth goal. But this label does not do justice to biblical counseling as a comprehensive practical theology that entails the five goods that Coe and Hall describe: personal transformation, case-wise savvy, an intellectually coherent body of knowledge, a variety of practical applications to counseling (and other) ministries and fruitful institutions. These five goods (what I term Psych-1, 2, 3, 4 and 5, respectively) lead to a sixth good that Coe and Hall don't mention (but no doubt would heartily agree with): cultural transformation (Psych-6).

of the self with God ("beyond relationality"); transmuting the spiritual disciplines to serve contemplative purposes.

Interest in ancient and medieval church mysticism has grown among evangelical psychologists in the 2000s, including not only Coe and Hall but also Larry Crabb, Gary Moon, David Bennerand and others. This interest does express three very good impulses. First, these authors are hungry for greater spiritual reality and personal integrity. Second, they have grown weary of the dreary secularity of the psychologies. Third, they have been repelled by routine shallowness in various evangelical traditions: moralism, doctrinalism and experientialism. I share their impulses, but do not think the contemplative tradition provides adequate direction and a framework to bring such impulses to a fruition that honors Jesus Christ.

For starters, contemplative spirituality does not track with the troubles and struggles of everyday people. It does not track with Scripture. It does not track with Jesus. It is an "upper-story" spirituality, not a feet-on-the-ground way of life. I will illustrate my concerns by briefly discussing Coe and Hall's last three goals.

What shape will the intellectual product take, the *systematic body of knowledge?* Will it concretely express the way that Scripture manages to be simultaneously God-centered and earthy? In contrast, the hazy spirituality of mystical encounter with the divine in a noumenal realm of privatized experience drifts away from earthed humanness. The Bible everywhere treats everyday human experience, and it never gestures toward monastic super-spirituality. The contemplative tradition tends toward an elite, strenuous, privatized spirituality that is impossible for garden-variety people. I think that Coe and Hall's chapter evidences this tendency.

But histories and prophets, psalms and proverbs, the actions and teachings of Jesus, and the epistles of his apostles speak to the garden-variety troubles of strugglers. Jesus has a wonderfully deft way of touching people who are sweating out life: peasants, fishermen, illiterate mothers, impoverished widows, disabled people, street people. Jesus speaks to the powerless, the weak, the addicted, the outsider, the remorseful. He brings elites—powerful, rich, educated, spiritually refined—down to earth. When Coe and Hall allude to a self that is "beyond relationality" in its "union with God" (figure 3, p. 222), they express the quintessence of contemplative spirituality's defection from reality. There is nothing deeper or higher than relationality: within the triune Godhead; in our corporate and individual relationships to Father, Son and Spirit; in our relationships with each other.

What actual *system of ministry praxis* will be produced? Will it be a hybrid of "spiritual formation" and psychotherapy? In themselves, the terms "soul care," "spiritual direction," "spiritual formation" and "spiritual disciplines" are good terms awaiting particular meaning. But when operating under the influence of the mystical tradition, they become vectors for upper-story spiritualizing. Such a turn leads away from the church's long tradition of hard-won pastoral counseling wisdom. God's self-revelation walks the earth in Jesus's practical mercies to us. He gradually forms us into the same shape of practical mercies toward others. This vision for human, humane, well-reasoned, psalmic and proverbial insight and practice has shaped the church's tradition of earthed wisdom. Thomas Oden's four-volume *Classical Pastoral Care* largely traces how the broad stream of pastoral wisdom has wrestled with how to understand people truly and love people well, not with how mystics interpret their private agonies and ecstasies. The privatized spirituality of desert monks and medieval monastics moves in a different direction from the community-oriented pastoral care and cure of souls, as expressed, for example, in Gregory, Luther, Baxter, Bonhoeffer and in the intentions of the contemporary biblical counseling movement. I suggest that mature biblical counseling is the answer to Coe and Hall's query about whether a "new paradigm" of counseling might emerge to supplant both the modern psychotherapies and spiritual direction!

What *institutional systems* do Coe and Hall envision? Are the university and the therapy office the primary loci for developing a body of knowledge and for delivering care? If "one who truly knows oneself is a true psychologist" (p. 218), why would professional psychologist-mystics play lead in the wisdom business? Where is the church as a community of care, a community of wise counsel, a community of change? Where is the place for true pastoral care, pastoral wisdom, pastoral counseling, pastoral theology? Or is there a monastic drift to Coe and Hall's proposal that separates insight and expertise from the daily lives we live with one another?

6

A Biblical Counseling View

David Powlison

Christian faith *is* a psychology.

A coherent, comprehensive understanding of how people work is intrinsic to thinking Christianly. The revelation of Jesus Christ offers a distinctive interpretation of the "thoughts and intentions of the heart," those schemata and motivations that structure and animate human behavior. Scripture offers a distinctive interpretation of "nature" (i.e., constraints and potentials of the body) and of "nurture" (i.e., enculturating voices and interpersonal experiences). God reveals a distinct image of human flourishing toward which counseling aspires, and a distinctive change process by which we move toward that ideal. A Christian understanding systematically differs from how other psychologies explain the same phenomena.

Christian ministry *is* a psychotherapy.

Intentional, constructive conversation is indispensable to practicing Christianly. The revelation of Jesus Christ creates a distinctive conception of the relationship between counselor and counselee, a distinctive understanding of methodology, a distinctive social location for counseling practice to flourish. This care and cure for the soul systematically differs from how other psychotherapies deal with the same problems in living.

This is not to say that a Christian psychology and psychotherapy come ready-made in the pages of the Bible. Nothing comes ready-made. Biblical-counseling wisdom is an ongoing construction project, like all practical theological work. It is one outworking of biblical faith into the particulars of our time, place, problems and persons.

Our call to do this work raises the question of how Christian faith and practice relate to other psychologies and psychotherapies that inhabit our sociocultural surround. What are the similarities and differences between other psychologies and Christian faith between other psychotherapies and Christian practice? How do other psychologies and psychotherapies challenge us? What helpful things can we learn from them? (Christians ask these questions, hence a book such as this one.) What should they learn from us? How do we challenge them? (To their detriment, non-Christian psychologists don't ask these questions.) We share all things in common regarding subject matter. We share a desire to help make right what goes so wrong in personal and interpersonal life. Yet we see with different eyes and proceed with different intentions. The similarities, analogies and commonalities create reasons for extensive interaction, expecting to learn from each other. The differences, disparities and antinomies create reasons for thoughtful disagreement, seeking to persuade each other.

This article will do three things. First, I will mention several underlying assumptions of a Christian point of view, and will indicate orienting implications for how we understand and help people. Second, I will deconstruct the word *psychology,* teasing apart a half-dozen distinct meanings that must be borne in mind as we consider the various ways Christian faith relates to this entity known as Psychology. Third, I will present a case study, sketching how a biblically construed understanding and practice engages the realities of people and their problems.

CREDE UT INTELLIGAS

"Believe so that you may understand," as Augustine put it. Disbelieve, and you discard the key to true knowledge. Misbelieve, and you systematically deviate from reality. Unbelieve, and you forfeit even "the beginning of wisdom." Believe so that you may understand, or Jesus' words will bite: "Can a blind man lead a blind man? Will they not both fall into a pit?" (Lk 6:39[1]). Wisdom keeps the true God consciously in view when considering humankind. You may accumulate an infinitude of psychological facts, encyclopedic information about people, but without keeping God in view, T. S. Eliot's (1963) words will bite: "Where is the wisdom we have lost in knowledge? Where is the knowledge we have lost in information?" (p.

---

[1]All Scripture quotations used in this chapter are taken from The Holy Bible, English Standard Version.

147). Wisdom is the crown jewel: "nothing you desire can compare" (Prov 3:15).

Believe so that you may understand. This is obviously the case when it comes to knowing God. But it equally applies to understanding persons who intrinsically *are* image of God, accountable to God, deviant from God and renewable by God. The psyche's dynamics operate Godwardly—whether we know it or not, whether a theory reckons with it or not, whether a therapy addresses it or not.

Let's briefly orient to underlying assumptions of this Christian point of view, noting a few psychological implications. We'll start by considering three strands of the Nicene Creed.

First, we believe that God is the *maker of all that is*. By implication, we have been handmade by a Person, down to the idiosyncrasies of personal history and social location; of genetic code, hormone levels, disease process and dying; of individual quirk, character and bent of heart. Every person exists as a dependent, and operates vis-à-vis this Person of persons to whom we owe our lives. To be fully human is to know and love this Maker by name. Such knowing is the pervasive psychological reality in a sane human being: heart, soul, mind and might. Such sanity fully takes to heart the interests and welfare of other persons besides ourselves. Christian faith understands psychology and psychotherapy as implications and outworkings of this God-centered point of view. We are told about God . . . and we realize the God-referential psychodynamic running through every human heart. We are told about God . . . and we learn what it means to be human. When other psychologies abstract people out of this true context, they theorize about an abstraction, never quite seeing the person. They will manufacture, research and counsel a humanoid, while the essential humanity slips through their fingers.

Second, we believe that the Lord is *judge of the living and the dead*. By implication, we are thoroughly known and evaluated: the innermost thoughts and intentions; the cries of anguish, confusion, outrage, fear or joy; every casual word or habitual choice; always amid the threats, pains and constraints, the hopes, felicities, and opportunities of physical and social circumstance. The one who searches all hearts and understands every plan and thought, the one to whom we must give account, misses nothing and considers everything (1 Chron 28:9; Heb 4:13). Actual psyches love either God or something else. A fierce Christlessness is the universal, obsessional neurosis. God is jealous for our loyalty, and he notices whenever other choices condition current psychological reality. He finds us wanting, fatally flawed by self-serving bias as the pervading psychological reality. Life and death hang on what happens next.

Third, most wonderfully, we believe that Christ *came down for us and for our salvation*. By implication, we've not been left to ourselves and our fate. God pursues us in person. All that goes wrong—our sins and miseries, a body breaking down, a social world breaking down, the madness in our hearts (Eccles 9:3)—can and will be made right by Christ. "He restores my soul" (Ps 23:3). The restoration of our humanity involves restoring our primary relationship. The restoration of our humanity is a psychological reality, among other things, engaging every aspect of psychological functioning: sense of identity, operations of conscience, thought, feeling, choice, memory, anticipation, attitudes, relationships. Psychotherapy ought to restore your soul. It ought to cure you of your variant on the universal, obsessional neurosis and make you sane.

Maker, Judge and Savior orient us as we seek to make sense of the psychological functioning of creatures who are made, judged and redeemable. The implications hold true down to the microscopic individual details of human psychology. Of course, this credo supplies none of the myriad psychological facts and details—far from it. There's work to do and much to learn from many sources. But the credo orients, teaching us to see facts in their true context.

How does Christian faith relate to the incalculable quantities of information, the diverse theories and therapies, the powerful institutions and professions, and the broadly influential social force that we know as psychology?

PSYCHOLOGY?

The word *psychology* serves us well in the same way that the words *religion, philosophy* and *politics* serve us. Each is a general term, and it may mean many different things, depending on how it's used. Furthermore, each is inescapably plural when it refers to specific content. There are many religions, many political views, many psychologies. Many different phenomena, activities, theories and interventions nestle under the broad heading

Psychology. In order to clarify how Christian faith and practice relate, it is of first importance to tease apart the different meanings of the word.

The word *psychology* is a good word. How can we use it accurately, helpfully and Christianly? How can we sift through the semantic ambiguity in how it's commonly used? The word is protean, the semantic field huge. In this section I will discriminate the major uses by slicing the semantic pie into six pieces.

PSYCH-1: HOW YOU WORK

Human beings operate psychologically. The torrent of experiences, thoughts, feelings, motives, attitudes, memories, volitions, beliefs, assumptions, schemata, perceptions and so on is what I mean by "Psych-1." Your psychology includes all these phenomena begging for description, explanation and intervention. Psych-1 is *you* in interaction with your entire life situation. A dynamic interplay takes place between

- what comes out of you: behavior (actions, words, emotions, cognitions, etc.)
- what surrounds and infuses you: innumerable situational and biological influences of nature and nurture
- what rules you: internal motives and schemata

Putting the same thing in biblical terminology, a dynamic interplay takes place between

- what comes out of you: manner of life (works, fruit, hands, feet, tongue, etc.)
- what surrounds and infuses you: complex life situation, both bodily and situational, sufferings and blessings, temptations/trials and opportunities, gifts and disabilities, voices and images that are both true and false
- what rules you: heart, soul/*psyche*, mind, conscience, desires, will, eyes, ears
- the living God, the one with whom you have to do

The first set of descriptions tends to be heard as crammed with feet-on-the-ground secularity, the second set as crammed with head-in-heaven piety. But they refer to the same actualities.

Psych-1 is the stuff of life. It simply describes how we operate in the world we inhabit. Imagine yourself stuck in a traffic jam on the way to an important appointment. You become tense, irritated, anxious, competitive. Here's a descriptive psychology (what is going on inside of you, what comes out of you and what impacts you) of this lowest-grade road rage.

What happened? You left the house ten minutes late because a talkative neighbor dropped by. You're meeting an old friend for lunch, hoping to reconcile after an estrangement. An accident ahead has seriously clogged traffic. You will arrive very late. You left your cell phone on the kitchen counter. . . .

What goes on in your body? Adrenaline surges through your bloodstream; blood vessels dilate; you squirm with muscular tension. Your temperament from birth has created your family reputation: impetuous, vocal frustration! To top it off, you're hungry. Why did you book lunch for 1:00 p.m.? You won't eat until after 2:00, and hunger puts a sharper edge on your discontent.

What is the impact of other people? Other drivers edge in. Your father provided a lifelong role model of volatility in such circumstances—you learned aggression from a master teacher. A culture of edgy entitlement reinforces the expectation of getting your own way. It's legitimate—even admirably self-assertive—to blow off anyone who shows you disrespect or gets in your way.

How do you show frustration? You press up to the bumper of the car ahead, eyes fixed straight forward, tracking neighboring vehicles in your peripheral vision. You successfully cut someone off. The grimaces, sighs of disgust and muttering under your breath could be videotaped. You surf the radio impatiently. After ten tense minutes, you remember you've got comfort food on hand. You grab the Snickers bar out of your briefcase or purse and inhale it in two bites.

What are you feeling? You're "tense." That's a complex feeling state. Irritation plays melody in the treble clef, while undercurrents of anxiety, misery and regret dominate the bass clef. You feel a simmer of loathing and generalized hostility. Impulses of guilt dart through the turmoil when you remember the ICHTHUS sticker displayed on your rear bumper.

What's running through your mind? Remember to scrape off that sticker. Rehearse the train of events leading up to this wreck of your day. Second-guessing and if-onlys. Self-recrimination for forgetting the cell phone. Mental scenarios of slinking into the restaurant. Rehearse the excuses you'll offer, mentally play-acting tone and posture. Imagine hostile intentions of the driver to your right who's trying to cut in. Why does this always happen to me? Why does God do this to me? I can't stand idiots who drive aggressively and cause accidents.

What expectations, fears, desires and underlying beliefs operate, whether you're semiaware or wholly unaware? You naturally want—and fully expect—in fact, you direly NEED to get to this appointment on time. You fear being thought ill of by your former friend. Your current life purpose? Get ahead of cars to either side. Your functional, implicit belief system? It's a dog-eat-dog world. My will be done. No God is on scene. No Judge is taking notes. No one cares if I cuss and complain. No Savior needed or wanted. No one is looking out for me. No need to consider the interests of other drivers.

The consequences of irritation and aggression? Stony looks and an obscene gesture from the driver to your right. A minor fender scrape that's not worth stopping for. Successfully cutting ahead of two cars, so you'll get where you're going a full seven seconds earlier than otherwise, richly demonstrating that aggression works. Overall tension affects the rest of the day. You're jumpy and defensive when you finally meet your former friend.

Other factors in play? A minor tiff with your spouse or roommate this morning over a stack of dirty dishes. Overtired because you stayed up too late last night playing *Grand Theft Auto*. It rained every day this week. You've been under a lot of pressure with deadlines.

All this (and more) simply runs the video. This torrent of significant internal and external phenomena is your psychology in the pretheoretical, presystematic, human subject, Psych-1 sense.

Notice two things about the description I've given. First, I sought to be relatively atheoretical in narrating a few significant psychological factors playing out in the traffic jam. Any reader should be able to identify with the story.

Second, like any psychologist, I couldn't even describe what happened without revealing some of my core assumptions (Psych-3). For example, I didn't mention that your birthday is in early spring, and that an Aries is supposedly quick-tempered. I think those facts are irrelevant to the situation at hand. I also didn't mention the supposed fact that anger reactions became hard-wired in your genes because primitive people who got angry in threatening situations had a higher survival rate than primitives who remained placid. In my opinion, that's a convenient fiction, adding nothing to what we know or need to know. Both astrology and evolutionary psychology offer mythical explanations for the significant things going on when you're stuck in traffic. Neither theory orients us toward meaningful self-knowledge or animates a constructive change process. But some people disagree and would tell the story a different way. Core assumptions always come into play.

Furthermore, I mention several things that tip my hand to what I do believe. First, in describing schemata and expectations, I not only use religious metaphors, but I allude to explicitly "religious" motives: fear of man, pride and implicit unbelief. I hint that petty irritability, aggression and anxiety intrinsically operate vis-à-vis God rather than in a moral vacuum. In other words, feeling "tense" expresses failures of faith and love. God vanishes from sight and other human beings morph into enemies. In other words, what's happening registers as "sin," both as a motivational set and as a lifestyle.

Second, I described such motives as more or less conscious, sometimes wholly unconscious. That's significant. I distance myself from the old heresy that limits sin to conscious volition. Most sins are complexly motivated and structured: "unintentional intentions." For example, in unbelief—erasure of God as a significant actor in the cosmos—we usually "just do it," never realizing what we are doing. Becoming more conscious of one's choices is actually a step of growth.

Third, the way I told the story shows that I think it is important to locate our moral reactions in context, amid an array of significant situational variables. I don't give final cause status to these variables. To cite Jesus: it is out of the heart that evils come (Mk 7:20-23). But the situation does matter. If you hadn't been stuck in traffic, you wouldn't have gotten angry. Volatile fathers actively misdisciple their children into their image. By temperament some of us are more prone than others to anger. By validating the significance of such factors, I distance myself from the old heresies of pietism and moralism, which isolate the soul with God, *mano a mano* on the mountaintop. Our physical embodiment and social embedment form the significant stage on which the human moral drama plays out.

Psych-1 is most like a *good novel* or *film,* a story that brings significant complexities to light. So what is the bottom line regarding Christianity and Psych-1? Like good art, like the modern Western psychologies, and like the world and local religions that take the place of Psychology in non-Westernized places, Christian faith is *about* Psych-1. That's why Jesus, Luke, Paul, David and the writer of Job are so often recognized as master psychologists. They *know* people. It's why the Bible speaks with such vigorous immediacy to modern readers.

PSYCH-2: DETAILED KNOWLEDGE OF HUMAN FUNCTIONING

The *field* of psychology, with its innumerable subdisciplines, isn't simply the telling of psychologically revealing stories. That's the stuff of Scripture, literature, history and talking with your friends. Psych-2 refers to organized knowledge, to close observations and systematic descriptions of human functioning. Psych-2 is the thing about psychology books and psychologists in person that makes them so interesting. They know a great deal about people. The ability to supply descriptive riches and a feel for how people work—whether case experience or research findings—is attractive. Psych-2 is why a piece of psychological literature can ring bells of human experience.

Three factors contribute to the depth and breadth of knowledge one often finds in psychologists, whether theoreticians, researchers or clinicians. First, they intentionally go about acquiring knowledge. Researchers acquire "nomothetic" knowledge, broad principles arising from systematic investigation of populations (e.g., social science) or of physiology (e.g., cognitive neuroscience). Clinicians acquire "idiographic" knowledge, a feel for individual differences and dynamics, arising from case experience.

Second, psychologists spend time with people who willingly open their lives to inspection. Research subjects sign up to be studied. Counsel-seekers bring their woes and confusions to the table. If you probe patiently and pay attention to what others say and do, you learn many things worth knowing.

Third, psychologists are often willing to open their own lives to self-examination or outside scrutiny. Include yourself in the human predicament, and you build bridges of sympathetic understanding.

The Psych-2 aspect of psychology intuitively seems the most objective, the most "neutral," the most "scientific." This observational-descriptive aspect of psychology helps us get to know the myriad, significant psychological facts. Psych-2 is useful to Christianity for its descriptive acuity and the questions it asks. But it is not uniquely useful. A wealth of information and feel for people is common property with many others besides psychologists. We must place Psych-2 in the context of many other sources of significant knowledge.

First, read the Bible for the humanity portrayed, as well as for the divinity revealed, and above all, for the interaction between the two. Though myriads of significant details about individuals and social groups are not contained within the Bible, learning to think the way Jesus thinks will rightly align all that you learn from all other sources.

Second, know yourself. Deal honestly with your sins and sufferings. You can gain insider knowledge of only one human being (and this knowledge, too, needs corrective realignment). When you learn truly about yourself, you gain sympathetic understanding for others.

Third, get to know other people. Talk about things that matter. Anton Boisen (1936/1962) rightly stressed the need to study "living human documents." You'll find every person to be wildly different from you—and that there are even deeper continuities and commonalities (1 Cor 10:13; 2 Cor 1:4).

Fourth, drink deeply of good novels, poetry, drama, film, music, visual arts. They capture experience. The better the art, the closer it will be to the realities that the Bible illuminates, explicates and addresses.

Fifth, read history, biography, culture studies, cultural anthropology. You want to know people, and astute observers give you descriptive riches. No person or discipline is value-neutral. But, at their best, practitioners of these disciplines tend to openly acknowledge their assumptions and work hard to make those assumptions relatively nonintrusive.

Sixth, read thoughtful writers in psychology and psychiatry. They notice things you've never noticed, and are both informative and provocative. I particularly appreciate the humanistic tradition within psychology and psychiatry—Peter Kramer, Robert Coles, Anna Freud, Harry Stack Sullivan, Armand Nicholi, Irving Yalom and others. They demonstrate an admirable curiosity and a tenderness that humanizes strugglers. They wear theoretical commitments relatively lightly. In their thoughtful humanity, you can discern the rough shape of realities—truth and love—that biblical wisdom brings into bright daylight. However, always read with your radar on. Compared to practitioners of the disciplines mentioned in the previous paragraph, psychologists tend to be unaware of the problematic nature of their underlying assumptions (e.g., implicit or explicit nature-nurture determinism is prevalent). Their insights often overtly suffer from the effects of defective theories (see Psych-3 below), either missing or misinterpreting the most important factors.

A persistent misunderstanding of the biblical counseling view asserts, "You don't believe Christians can learn anything from secular psychology." On the contrary, we can learn, should learn, and do learn from anyone and everyone. But we do seek to be aware of the blinkering and distorting effects of faulty assumptions and explanations (including our own failures to apprehend the Christian gaze and to express wise love). John Calvin's interaction with the Greek philosophers provides a good historical parallel to how biblical counseling interacts with the modern psychologies. On a superficial reading, he seems almost contradictory. He applauds the Greeks for brilliant insights, and in the next breath dismisses them as blind and wrong-headed. But this is exactly the way that a God-centered gaze interprets other gazes, simultaneously appreciative and contrary. To use a mid-twentieth-century metaphor, secular psychologists have "neurotic insights," simultaneously brilliant and distorted.

How then should we view psychological information, whether tumbling out in story (Psych-1) or organized by research or case wisdom (Psych-2), or communicated through many other sources whose epistemological status is the same as the psychologies? Bring it on. It is this stuff of life that Christian faith can frame and weigh properly. With a careful caveat about the theory-ladenness of data and with a well-trained ability to think from your own point of view (Heb 5:14), you can learn from anyone and interact with everything.

Psych-2 is most like what we think of as *science,* the intentional pursuit of organized knowledge. The bottom line regarding Christianity and Psych-2? We can learn a great deal. But bear in mind how faulty assumptions variously overemphasize, exclude, distort or falsify information (see Powlison, 2004).

PSYCH-3: COMPETING THEORIES OF
HUMAN PERSONALITY

When I said that there are many psychologies and that Christian faith is a psychology, I was using the word in its Psych-3 sense: an interpretive and explanatory model that organizes and weighs the torrent of Psych-1 experience and Psych-2 information. Christian faith is a psychology in exactly the same way that it is a theology. True knowledge of people and true knowledge of God correlate. This is a fundamental assumption of Scripture. It undergirds the psychological insight in Augustine's *Confessions*, Aquinas's *Summa Theologica*, Calvin's *Institutes* and Edward's *Treatise Concerning Religious Affections*. The revelatory sourcebook puts Christians to work trying to understand God and man, and to put that understanding into words.

We can know myriads of facts, but what do they mean? Theory and worldview provide the interpretive center of the psychological enterprise, the "doctrinal core." I hinted at this doctrinal core in discussing Psych-1 and Psych-2. I couldn't help but tip my hand about my own personality theory, even in describing an incident of minor road rage. We will see later that a core of doctrinal assumptions will inescapably pervade psychology as therapy (Psych-4), as social institution (Psych-5) and as cultural ethos (Psych-6). Neither knowledge nor application is theory-neutral.

There are many psychologies, many explanations for human behavior. Every personality theory offers an interpretive system, a set of categories, labels and explanations. Each posits some theory of the dynamics of the psyche's desires, hopes, beliefs and expectations. Most theories attempt to weigh the relative contributions of biology and/or social experience. Norms and ideals set standards of human flourishing, against which diagnoses are made, and toward which therapies aspire. The schema guides counseling conversations toward whatever is the desired "image" of a well-functioning human being. In Robert Roberts's (1993) words, the personality theories are "alternative spiritualities" offering "rival 'words' about human nature." They "mean their 'words' to be taken to heart, to shape our souls, and their therapies are potent methods for planting their ideas in us so that we may grow in the shapes that they ordain" (pp. 4, 10). Just as there are many philosophies and many religions, there will always be conflicting personality theories until the kingdom of God is established and everyone faces up to the final truth about our souls.

Psych-3 is most like what we think of as worldview or *theology*. The bottom line regarding Christianity and Psych-3? The personality theories systematically differ from the Christian gaze. Secular Psych-3s diverge from the Christian Psych-3. We will be stimulated and challenged by the questions they ask and by the realities they seek to account for. But they offer false and shallow views of humanness, and we must better account for human experience and offer better answers (see Welch, 1997, 1998, 2001, 2004, 2007; and Powlison, 2003, chaps. 7-15; 2004; 2005, chap. 1). We have work to do.

PSYCH-4: PRACTICAL APPLICATIONS TO PSYCHOTHERAPY

Psych-4 refers to various psychotherapeutic models and skills aiming to redress problems in living.[2] Christian faith informs a "psychotherapy"— cure and care of souls—in exactly the same way that it informs preaching or worship. Counseling is a fundamental task of Christian wisdom. This conviction undergirds, for example, Gregory's *Pastoral Care*, Baxter's *Christian Directory*, Bonhoeffer's *Life Together* and the contemporary biblical counseling movement that this chapter seeks to describe. The redemptive sourcebook puts Christians to work doing constructive conversations.

Psychotherapy is not a neutral, technical expertise. Counseling practices and strategies are designed to facilitate change in beliefs, behaviors, feelings, attitudes, values and relationships. Just as Psych-3 worldviews shape the observations and descriptions of Psych-2, so they guide Psych-4 conversational interventions. One cannot intend to help another change without some ideal for human functioning, usually explicit, and easy to tease out when implicit. Ideals assert criteria of good and evil, true and false, significance and irrelevance, however much practitioners may recoil from acknowledging both the moral nature of their conversations and the omnipresent influence of "suggestion" expressed in their questions, comments and silences. The more thoughtful practitioners know that they are doing "pastoral" work, and recognize that moral values and worldview assumptions come into play in *every* human interaction.

What is this exotic thing termed psychotherapy? I like Sigmund Freud's

---

[2]Applied psychology includes noncounseling attempts to shape and change behavior; e.g., advertising, management, education, propaganda, etc.

(1926) description of the interaction between counselor and counseled:

> Nothing takes place between them except that they talk to each other. [The therapist gets the patient] to talk, listens to him, talks to him in his turn, and gets him to listen. "So it is a kind of magic, you talk, and blow away his ailments." Quite true. It would be magic if it worked rather quicker. Magic that is so slow loses its miraculous character. And incidentally do not let us despise the word. After all it is a powerful instrument; it is the means by which we convey our feelings to one another, our method of influencing other people. (pp. 187-88)

He normalizes the conversation, removing the esoteric mystique. Psychotherapy is simply an intentional conversation in which one person draws another out, listens attentively, and seeks to influence the other in the direction of presumably helpful changes in belief and action. Elsewhere Freud (1916) points out that the therapist "plays the part of this effective outsider; he makes use of the influence which one human being exercises over another." What takes place is an "educative process," a remedial "after-education" under the guidance of an authoritative and caring expert who strategically intervenes in another's life (p. 312). Something similar could be said about any counseling school. Even purportedly "nondirective" counseling simply does these same things covertly.

To put this in biblical language, all counseling attempts pastoral work, shepherding the souls of wandering, suffering sheep. The basic tools of all counseling are the same: "speaking truth in love." Some "truth" about what is wrong, what should be, and how to get there bids to reorient and redirect the soul. Any successful counselee learns to see with new eyes, converts and is discipled. Secular psychotherapy is "pastoral work" done by "secular pastoral workers," as Freud provocatively put it (1926, pp. 255-56).

Biblical counseling fits Freud's generic description in the previous paragraphs (though we have no reason to rule out the occurrence of rapid change along with slow change, and we think that "therapist-patient" language is misleading). The cure and care of souls is the original pastoral work, done by pastoral workers in service to the great Shepherd of the sheep. The church's cure of souls is the prototype, the best, the always renewable, however clumsy or neglected in any particular historical moment.[3]

---

[3]A critique of the competency of the church's counseling theory, training and practice during the

Psych-4 is most like what we think of as *cure of souls*. The bottom line regarding Christianity and Psych-4? We must do better and different than the secular pastorates. We are glad when they accomplish common-grace goods—restraining a suicide, sweetening a marriage, sobering a drunk, walking through a rough patch with a troubled person—just as we are glad when an imam, a self-help guru or mere willpower accomplishes good things. But these other "pastorates" heal lightly the woes and wrongs of the human condition. The competencies of other psychotherapies will stimulate and challenge us, but our calling is to build distinctively Christian counseling ministry that fulfills the mission God has given his people (see Powlison, 2005, chaps. 2-9; 2007). We have work to do.

PSYCH-5: A SYSTEM OF PROFESSIONAL AND INSTITUTIONAL ARRANGEMENTS

Psych-5 refers to institutional and professional arrangements. Knowledge and practice inhabit social roles and institutional structures. The "mental health system" is currently the dominant location for understanding and helping people. But Christian faith has an inherent institutional logic, just as it has conceptual and methodological logics. Ideas and practices do not exist in a vacuum.

The dominant counseling institutions in the West are secular at the moment. Practitioners-to-be are trained in departments claiming disciplinary turf. Psychotherapeutic activity occurs in clinics, hospitals and offices. Boards examine, accredit and supervise, legitimating both education and practice (and implicitly delegitimizing other contexts). Licensing laws and courts reinforce (or destabilize) the social structure of professional practice. Patients link with psychotherapeutic practitioners through a referral system that routinely connects mental health professionals to each other and to various other institutions: educational, medical, judicial, social service, business and, frequently, ecclesiastical. If you need to talk to someone, the pathways are in place that lead you to a mental health professional. Health insurance companies reimburse the conversations of only certain kinds of practitioners. Textbooks, self-help books, newspaper columns, training videos and media gurus propagate views and practices.

---

twentieth century lies beyond the scope of this chapter. See Powlison (1988, 1992, 2010).

Drug companies advertise the salvific effects of medications in major magazines and flood M.D.s with inducements to prescribe. In all these ways and more, psychology as Psych-5 is a mental health *system*.

The social and cultural power that the psychologies wield is not sustained primarily because modern theories are intrinsically more plausible than outmoded religious ideas, or because modern therapies are demonstrably more effective than outmoded religious practices, or because the church is not potentially a far superior institutional setting for curing souls. Power is sustained because theories and therapies are effectively institutionalized in social roles and social locations.

It's beyond the scope of this chapter to discuss the historical reasons for this. But it's worth noting how different psychology is from other social sciences. If a sociologist tried to change society, or a historian tried to change history, we'd call it politics, not good social science. If an anthropologist tried to change a primitive and perceivedly dysfunctional culture, we'd call it cultural imperialism. The attempt to change people is qualitatively different from scientific study and efforts to understand what is. In the nineteenth century the church failed in counseling, though the idea and practice of cure of souls had originated within its ministry. In the twentieth century, that counseling role gradually became attached to various secular professions that had originally served noncounseling purposes. Institutional structures are not givens of the natural order. They are functional, disputable and changeable (see Abbott, 1988).

Christian faith has as much to say about normative institutional structure and professional role as it does about theory of personality or counseling methodology. The classic summary passage is Ephesians 3:14—5:2. God calls his people to mobilize as a countercultural community characterized by transformative mutual counseling.

The mental health system is part church, part social-welfare agency and part research institute. We commend the common-grace good, for example, when a social institution provides a safety net and a sheltered timeout for troubled people. We're glad that a suicidal person can be cocooned out of harm's way. We commend the research intention. But we find the vision of personhood seriously deficient. To the degree that Psych-5 institutions and professions mediate faulty theories and faulty cures for the soul, they compete with the call of the church.

Psych-5 is most like what we think of as *church* (and parachurch). The bottom line regarding Christianity and Psych-5? Build ministry institutions and roles that can mediate the life-rearranging truth and love that is in Christ (see Powlison, 2001, sec. 4; 2005, part 2). We have work to do.

PSYCH-6: A MASS ETHOS

Psych-6 refers to an ethos pervading popular culture, a *zeitgeist*. A psychological way of thinking pervades the popular mindset in the West. When we read about "the triumph of the therapeutic" (Rieff, 1967), or "the culture of narcissism" (Lasch, 1979), or the "empty self" of consumerism and pop psychology (Cushman, 1990), or "psychology as religion" (Vitz, 1977), the word *psychology* is used in its Psych-6 sense.

Christian wisdom intends to be the air we breathe. On the last day, it will become the enduring *zeitgeist,* and every knee will bow to God-defined actuality. But popularized psychological theory and advice shape the very categories of experience and identity. Life experience becomes "psychologized" and, because modern psychologies borrow heavily from medical prestige and metaphors, "medicalized." The Psych-1 and Psych-2 existential and relational realities—pointedly addressed by Christian faith and practice—are reinterpreted as a medical therapeutic drama. Psych-6 is the trickle-down, and the high culture sources may not even be apparent. It isn't necessarily even called psychology. For example, as a piece of pop culture, "He's not meeting my needs" needn't bother to footnote its sources or justify its assumptions. Psych-6 is embedded in film dialogue; it structures conversations between friends; it guides or reproves the way widows grieve; it shapes how parents raise children; it gives language and thought-forms for a diary entry about today's angst; its fingerprints are all over a sermon.

The "spirit of the age" is like climate and weather. It is not a given. It changes. As the church develops into a culture of wise counsel, we will bring about culture change. We will challenge the popular ethos that shapes how people live and converse, because we will live and converse an alternative. Christian faith is demonstrably truer, wiser, more loving, and more effective than the pop psychological ideas and assumptions that sound the keynote in contemporary society.

Psych-6 is most like what we speak of as popular culture or "the world."

The bottom line regarding Christianity and Psych-6? Form a countercul-
ture that breathes the fragrance of biblical wisdom. Our constructive wisdom qualitatively differs from the wisdoms of a psychologized culture.
Our truth qualitatively differs from the therapeutic truisms in the air we
breathe. The ethos of dependency on a Savior and of speaking truth in love
offers a startling contrast to the ethos that dominates the popular mind
and media. The church can do better and must do different (see Powlison,
2003, chaps. 9-15). We have work to do.

Though interrelated, these six meanings of *psychology* highlight different aspects—a person's dynamics, detailed information, explanatory theories, interventive practices, social institutions, and enculturated values and
beliefs. It is important to see how Christian faith and practice relate in
different ways to each aspect of what comes under the monolithic heading
Psychology. But the best way to understand any model, including biblical
counseling, is to get down to cases.

CASE STUDY: "CLYDE"

The case study that follows contains rich descriptive details. Details are
one fruit of caring and of paying careful attention. In part, this case study
reflects the effect of attending to strengths of other psychologies. The
secular psychological endeavor is strongest in Psych-2 descriptions and
feel for people. The psychotherapies are strongest in the caring, probing
and listening aspects of Psych-4. The church has been weakest where secular cures of soul have been strong. The net effect has been that our
strengths in Psych-3 worldview tend to float above the ground, not making contact with the grit of life experience, not connecting in the tenderness of patient, searching relationship. Their strengths rightly reprove us.

But in the long run, Christians will fashion our own richer version of
their strengths. Our work will not have the flavor of the therapeutic but
the fragrance of the Word written and incarnate. In principle, the way of
Christ gives the richest way to describe, to care, to probe, to attend, to
hang in, to engage, to help. As we get our legs under us, distinctively
Christian counseling ministry will grow strong, sweet, insightful and
practical in all necessary wisdoms. Let me seek to illustrate.

What's happening? (Psych-1 and Psych-2). Clyde is thirty-eight years
old, married, with two children. He works as a medical doctor, practicing

internal medicine at a hospital. He is 5'6" tall, weighs 220 pounds, wears thick glasses and seems a bit uncoordinated physically (you're relieved to know he's not a surgeon!). He's evidently intelligent, witty, gregarious and likeable. He's a member of a believing church, is quite generous with his money and knows his Bible fairly well.

But all is not well with Clyde. He has sought help for mounting problems: "My life is out of control. I feel overwhelmed, preoccupied, hopeless. I get so tense and anxious inside that it disrupts my ability to function. Sometimes I feel like ending it all." Marital strife is increasingly frequent, intense and insoluble. Divorce threats hang in the air. Clyde is shamefaced to admit that over the past six or eight months he has been stopping off at a bar on his way home from work for "a few drinks," and that pornography has again become an issue after being quiescent for a number of years.

What more do we need to know? We've learned Clyde's marquee sins and their sequelae: dark discouragement and electric anxiety; heavy drinking and pornography; anger, fear and turmoil in interpersonal conflict; suicidal ideation; confusion, guilt, shame and regrets. But we haven't located his troubles in a comprehensive understanding of the man in his world. What sort of world does Clyde live in? How does he put his world together? Currently we know almost nothing of these things. His marquee struggles appear in a vacuum.

We'll begin with circumstances. What Clyde faces does not explain him, but it locates him: the biblical *peirasmos*, the pressures and influences that shape, try and tempt a person. For starters, he puts in very long hours in a high-stress job. That's important. He's experienced fluttering heart pains in recent months. He knows what that means—either he's developing heart trouble or he's a self-diagnosed mental case. The first option seems plausible: he's obese, sedentary, highly stressed, and his dad died of a heart attack at age forty-six. The second option is equally plausible: he's not dealing well with stress and anxiety. Neither option is a happy thought.

What about family life? His wife, Corinne, is a nominal Christian. She has a markedly shrewish streak, is status- and money-conscious, is highly invested in her own career, and pushes Clyde to be more aggressive in his career and to make more money. Their children are ten and twelve, on the cusp of young adulthood. Clyde has sacrificed a lot of family time for career, and he barely knows them. His mother's health is seriously failing but she won't willingly leave her home. She's increasingly domineering and recalcitrant. His brother and sister are ne'er-do-wells, so it's on Clyde to make and carry out the hard decisions with mom.

Capping off current stressors is something that, at first, was an honor. Eight months ago, his supervisor (a mentor throughout Clyde's career) got him appointed to the hospital ethics committee. The committee proved to be highly politicized. Clyde disagrees in principle with the hospital's abortion policy, but taking an unpopular point of view seems dangerous to his professional health.

What we've said about Clyde's immediate life situation only begins to consider the incalculable variety of influential forces and factors. For example, Clyde lives amid atmospheric cultural values that teach all of us to look down our noses at clumsy, 5'6", 220-pound, middle-aged men. Other atmospheric voices teach us to look up in admiration at medical doctors. Does Clyde have ears for those voices? How does listening affect him? That's only a tiny sampler of what the Bible terms the "world"/*kosmos*. "The Lie" ramifies into a cacophony of voices weighing in to assign relative value and stigma in every single arena.

Those are present tense pressures and voices. But human beings also imagine trajectories reaching into the possible future. Clyde is gripped by intense, barely conscious fears, prophetic voices threatening disaster. Will I drop dead of a heart attack? Will my kids hate me or shrug off our non-relationship with a "Whatever"? Will my marriage collapse into animosity and divorce? If I force my mother into the care facility she needs, will she make my life miserable and cut off my inheritance? Does anxiety prove that I am a weak person? Will I get pushed aside for standing against the power brokers in the hospital administration? What will happen to me?

I've described factors in the present and the anticipated future. But human beings live an unfolding story and always come with a significant past. Clyde points to two particularly significant circumstances. First, his family moved from a town in the South when he was in sixth grade. His dad had been a regional sales manager and was promoted to a vice presidency in New York City. The traumatic move and adjustment were summed up in an event the first week in his new school. His mother visited the classroom and drawled, "Wayull, Clawd honey . . ." The routine viciousness of middle-school bullies took it from there. They'd found a target in this short, clumsy kid with glasses who talked funny: "Clod-honey" became his tagline.

Second, both his mother and father were opinionated, demanding and upwardly mobile. They significantly pressured Clyde regarding major life choices. His dad offered to pay for med school or law school, but if Clyde wanted grad school in English lit, he was on his own. He became a doctor. And his parents pressed him to marry "the right kind of wife," who would enhance the fast track to success. Two artsy and literary college girlfriends didn't fit the ideal, and came in for strong parental disapproval. Corinne fit the ideal.

Case studies tend to major on describing negatives, particularly high-lighting difficult experiences in personal history (a Psych-3 bias toward "nurture-determinism") and "personal problems" (a tendency to reify diag-nostic labels). But Christian faith doesn't share such biases. Just as past, present and future all matter, so positive experiences and strengths count alongside the negatives. Clyde has been greatly blessed. Though mocked by some classmates, his wit and gregariousness made him rather popular on the whole, especially with the girls. He enjoyed many advantages from his family's relative wealth and status: freedom from poverty and danger, opportunity for a good education, entrée into professional circles, great vacations, freedom from debt, nice cars. He's intelligent, successful in his career, and lives far above the norm in financial security and privilege. Despite tensions that thread through his roles as husband and father, he does experience satisfactions and pleasures in relation to his wife and chil-dren. He's not socially isolated (though during his recent troubles, he has kept a lot to himself and feels very alone). Clyde is also a Christian who has known the mercies and goodness of God. He came to Christ during his junior year in college, and rapidly broke away from a lifestyle of drinking and womanizing. He has used his medical skills on a yearly mission team to Haiti, which brings him great satisfaction.

There's a sketch of significant situational factors. What patterns does he bring to the table, his manner of life, the biblical *anastrophe?* We al-ready know what's playing on the marquee: unpleasant emotions, unsavory behaviors, unhappy relationships, ungluing thoughts. What broader pat-terns normally play?

In fifteen years of marriage, Clyde has often enjoyed what's implied in "a pretty good marriage": basic commitment and fidelity, sharing of responsibilities, sexual compatibility, willingness to move on from conflicts. But on the negative side, he tends to move between appeasement, avoidance and arguing, in that order of frequency. Recently that order has been reversed. He finds the increase in mutual hostilities, hair-trigger resentments, parallel lives and secrecy to be quite distressing.

With his children, he can be a genial dad who enjoys play and activities on vacation. On the negative side, he'll move from general neglect (he's busy and preoccupied), to buying their favor (when they happen to show up on his radar), to bullying (when they inconvenience him), again in that order of frequency. With his mother, Clyde mainly tiptoes and tries not to rile her. That's been so since childhood. It's easier to avoid upsetting her than to survive her firestorms.

Then there's the ethics committee. Clyde experiences meetings as poignantly stressful. His actual behavior is polite silence—justified by being the new kid on the block. But, inside that awkward, mute exterior, he plays vivid fantasies of messianic confrontation, where he stands up heroically for truth and right, and is persecuted by the dark forces of powers that be. He trudges out of meetings, extremely dissatisfied with himself, and wanting only to slug down a few cold beers to drown his troubles. As mentioned, he's been feeling overwhelmed, bleak and confused. In darker moments of brooding, he wonders if his whole life has been a big mistake—school, career, marriage. He fantasizes that he should have gone off and become an English teacher or rock star. But he sees no way out, and fleeting thoughts of suicide dangle a promise of relief.

I hope that readers feel a bit overwhelmed—and intrigued. Real life does that.

How do we make sense of all this? (Psych-3). We can't help if we can't organize what we come to know. The secular psychologies offer their labels and explanations. My favorite DSM-IV category is 309.4: "Adjustment Disorder with mixed disturbance of emotions and conduct." That's Clyde, all right. And no temptation overtakes him that is not common to us all! With equal plausibility, Clyde can be squeezed into any of the personality theories. Unmet needs? Conflicting instincts? Poor conditioning of secondary drives? Inauthentic choices? Failure to overcome inferiority complex? Self-defeating thought patterns? Sure, all of the above, and more. And any therapist or researcher prone to favor nature and/or nurture causalities will find overabundant confirmatory data. Every life displays untold riches. There's so much information, and the facts are plastic.

Christian faith offers a distinct perspective on Clyde. We take seriously everything we've noticed and learned—all the situational variables, all the nuances of behavior and emotion. We also know that the springs of life flow from the heart (Prov 4:23). According to Jesus, who gets last say, what's going wrong in Clyde's emotions, behavior and relationships comes "out of the heart" (Mk 7:20-23). Christian faith offers a trajectory of *metanoia*, renewal of mind, a change in the internal "operating system." The goal is love, which comes from a pure heart, a good conscience and a sincere faith (1 Tim 1:5). Clyde has little love right now, and a much-divided heart, a much-distorted conscience and a much-compromised faith. Jesus Christ patiently goes about transforming all that. This language of "heart," "faith," "love" and "Jesus" could be religious platitude (if we ourselves are platitudinous). But it is no platitude in the Bible per se, spoken from the heart of God himself, and backed up with actual mercy at extreme personal cost.

The Bible's description of the "heart" gives God's perspective on the underlying psychodynamic in every human being. Operating inside other potent desires is a prepotent master desire that organizes all others. Anyone can identify life-shaping desires overtly working in people: to gain power or find pleasure, to feel loved or achieve something significant, to find self-esteem or discover meaning, to control events or get rich, to avoid conflict or win the argument, to avoid pain or keep death at bay. The different models of organizing experience and information (Psych-3s) take their pick. But God identifies the master choice that qualifies all lesser choices. All the obvious street-level desires are qualified either by self-serving bias or by faith. Something rules: either the "lusts of the flesh" or the "desires of the Spirit." We love whichever voice we listen to—either the God and Father of Jesus, or any of the pandemonium of other voices. Everyone chooses, however unconscious the experience of choice, and our "instinctive" choice is always wrong. We hear voices rather than listening to sanity.

Christian faith teaches a "psychodynamic theory"—with a major twist. The dynamic does not reduce to intrapsychic, sociopsychological or physio-psychological forces. Clyde, like every human being, is "doing something" with God at each moment. As he engages the multitude of circumstantial variables, what is actually going on in Clyde's individual psychology? For simplicity's sake, I will focus on four particulars that are his version of the ABCDs of human nature as assessed by Scripture.

First, much of his life is organized and controlled by "fear of man." The false love? *I love approval and honor from other people.* This drives deep-seated patterns of avoidance and appeasement, working hard for approval, cowed silence in the ethics committee, caving in to parental pressure, concealment of his vices, much of his depression and anxiety, and some of his anger. It can be subtle. When he absorbs defective value-stigma attributions from his cultural surround, or when he naively takes behavioral cues from other people, he lives in invisible slavery to fear of man.

Second, much of Clyde's life is organized and controlled by "pride." The false love? *I love getting my way. My way is the right way, my agenda and my needs come first.* This drives hostile accusation and self-righteous defensiveness in arguments with Corinne, bullying his children, fantasies of messianic pontification and persecution, recreational choices. It can be subtle. Self-serving bias is nearly omnipresent in all of us.

Third, much of Clyde's life is organized and controlled by "love of pleasure." *I love my comforts and feel-goods.* Food, drink, sex and TV sports provide refuge and escape from stress, pain and discomfort. This drives recreational habits, vices and, when the craving is frustrated, petty anger. It can be subtle. Any of us can fill in the blanks.

Fourth, implicit in all this are various distortions of Clyde's functional belief system. Beliefs provide a complementary perspective to desire/love. Clyde believes he needs each of the things he wants. Each functional misbelief corresponds to the erasure of God from consciousness. "Unbelief" does not mean a vacuum. It means the presence and plenum of other functional beliefs. Clyde's functional unbelief also takes God-referential forms. His stated theology sings of mercy for sinners by the blood of the Lamb. But his functional theology feels miserable, and his functional god is rather like a genie or Paxil, existing to change circumstances or change moods. Unbelief is invariably subtle. It's what simply is, the everyday state of affairs, the madness in our hearts.

Why have I turned up the power of the biblical MRI? It's not because counseling is intrusive and introspective. Biblical counseling is extraspec-tive, tenderhearted and optimistic—faith working through love. But I've focused on the ABCDs of Clyde's inner dynamics because the Christian analytic of the heart collides so directly with culturally dominant Psych-3s. In psychology and Christianity discussions, the Christianity usually comes out looking comparatively obtuse and superficial, the borrower from the superior insights and skills of others. In fact, it is the other Psych-3s that wade in shallow water and stir up sand. Christian faith swims in deep pellucid waters, and brings the bright light of lovingkindness to whatever darknesses come to light.

The counseling process (Psych-4 and Psych-5). A brief article cannot do justice to the counseling or change process. But I will indicate a few basics. First, a constructive conversation begins with conditions of trust. I've told Clyde's story knowing that he chose to trust me and ask for help. That is often the case (but not always) when counseling operates within a healthy church community. Second, apt interpretations and timely interventions are always based on true knowledge and sympathetic knowing of another. I've presupposed the probing and listening aspects of counseling in how I've told his story.

Where did my intervention and reinterpretation choose to focus? Where were the choice points and action steps for Clyde? Process is extremely hard to capture in print. But I will describe one particularly significant moment of change that proved to have far-reaching ripple effects.

Early on, Clyde and I agreed that his response to the ethics committee provides a particularly revealing microcosm. His appointment eight months ago correlates significantly to when his life began to unravel. During and after the monthly meetings, the ABCDs of his heart obvi-ously energized significant works of the flesh: mental chaos, disturbing emotions, destructive actions. Also, the shape of possible faith in God and love for others could be clearly identified, in sharp contrast to all that was currently happening. Such microcontexts are valuable for self-understanding and for actually working out change. They provide a "laboratory" for particular redemption, because cosmic-scale themes play out in microcosmic details.

In the crucible for change, what actually happens? Every psychotherapy traffics in some version of "double-truth." First, it elicits honesty about what's going on: Psych-1 situational and existential realities. A secular psychotherapist and I don't disagree about the facts of the case at hand (though we see them in a different light). Second, the counselor embodies and speaks some interpretive framework that bears on the existential and situational realities. This interpretation claims to make sense of the chaos and misery. It gives an explanation, offers hope, bids to reorganize future beliefs, desires and choices. In any decisive counseling moment, Psych-1 realities sit down and talk with a Psych-3 message. The two persons connect; the two truths overlay and merge. Accurate honesty triangulates with a trusted new interpretation/interpreter. A once disoriented person reorients. Life makes a different sort of sense, and the new truth begins to rewrite the script of life choices. A secular psychotherapist's message will differ essentially from mine.

I chose to map Psalm 40 onto Clyde's experience. It's not a proof text, and the reasons for my choice lie far beyond the scope of this article. But notice how it contains all the relevant pieces, inviting his particulars: honesty in facing oneself, candor about stressful circumstances, clarity about God. The psalm itself triangulates, as the psalmist moves out of himself, as he brings his actual predicament to the true God.

> As for you, O LORD, you will not hold back your mercy from me.
>   Your steadfast love and your faithfulness will ever preserve me!
>   For evils have encompassed me beyond number.
>   My iniquities have overtaken me, and I cannot see.
>   They are more than the hairs of my head. My heart fails me.
> Be pleased, O LORD, to deliver me! O LORD, make haste to help me! . . .
>   As for me, I am poor and needy, but the Lord takes thought for me.
>   You are my help and my deliverer. Do not delay, O my God!
>   (Ps 40:11-13, 17 ESV modified)

Here we witness complex, honest need actually meeting the true God. In sharp contrast, Clyde's complex need had so far found neither voice nor listener.

Clyde and I talked through the pressures and stressors he faced both in the ethics committee and elsewhere: "encompassing evils." We talked through how he lost connection with his God, living the ABCDs instead, failing to serve the committee, inflicting collateral damage on his wife and children: "iniquities more than the hairs on my head." We talked through what this chaos of suffering and sin felt like: "My heart fails me. . . . I am poor and needy." We talked through God's promises of mercy and help, how Jesus Christ comes in person exactly tailored to his immediate need: "You will not hold back your mercy."

Clyde took it to heart, triangulating his need and his Redeemer. He lived Psalm 40 and found God true. (I am nowhere more painfully aware of the limitations of a case study in print for communicating what happens. Perhaps read the psalm again. Feel the force of its inner logic, and the way it gathers up Clyde's experience and carries him.)

The *metanoia* of a radically altered perspective led to new clarity in his thinking and sense of purpose. We talked through how to walk this out in the ethics committee. The way forward appeared so obvious that Clyde felt a bit chagrined he hadn't thought of it before—but such is our confusion in the midst of storm and stress. He arranged to meet with his mentor before the next committee meeting. He voiced honest appreciation for the appointment to the committee, then candidly apologized for being a nonparticipant. He laid out his dilemma: "I disagree with our hospital's abortion policy, for reasons I think are cogent and important. But I haven't known how to disagree constructively. What do you think I should do?" The mentor might have proved a bigot, but not surprisingly in this case, he proved to be reasonable. He was delighted that Clyde had finally spoken up. In fact he had been wondering why Clyde had seemed so reticent and tense during meetings. He reassured him that thoughtful disagreement was *exactly* the purpose of the committee, and thanked him for bringing the matter up so constructively.

Changes begun within that "laboratory" turned on the lights. It was a small change, but it was a sea change. In Clyde's case, the marquee presenting problems—anxiety and confusion, drinking and pornography, messianic and suicidal fantasies—receded quite rapidly. They actually did not need a great deal of discussion. Given the particulars of the case, that's not surprising. (Of course, it doesn't always work that way!) He'd gained his bearings. In subsequent weeks we continued to work through implications in various arenas: marital, parental, filial, relationship with God and so forth. There were some hard, slow roads: loving and reengaging Corinne proved particularly complicated (again, not surprising).

From the morass of everyday human problems—"Adjustment Disorder with mixed disturbance of emotions and conduct"—a man emerged who knew himself more clearly, knew Jesus Christ more pertinently and loved more intelligently.

A brief case study leaves a thousand good questions unanswered. What if Clyde's sufferings and sins had been far more serious, magnified by a power of ten? What if he and I had not begun with reasons for trust between us? What if he were mentally handicapped rather than intelligent? What if he were committedly non-Christian or even anti-Christian? What if he had been abused by church people, and felt deep hostility and suspicion toward the Bible and God? In thirty years of counseling ministry, I've dealt with each of these situations in innumerable permutations. Counseling adapts to any and all differences in the Psych-1 realities. For a short article I had to choose a relatively simple case, not a tortuous one. Aspects of the counseling process change, unfolding more slowly, even much more slowly. But the adaptations are *quantitative,* not *qualitative.* For example, when God-words are a stumbling block, you put things in your own words for a while. Most biblical counseling with any person is in your own words. People lost in a dark wood rarely get the God-words right even when they like using them. As the real God works, the sweet reasonableness of his mercies and truth patiently disassemble the lies that get tangled up in ugly or trite God-talk.

The payoff question for our purposes is whether or not you ever have to switch from the Christian Psych-3 to a different theoretical orientation. The answer is No. God's outlook on the complex evils of the human predicament illuminates any dark wood. We can camp out wherever we need to, continuing to breathe the same fresh air and see in the same bright light. God's mercies enter any suffering, any temptation, any sin, any complexity and confusion. A counselor will always adapt—always—but *never* need jettison what is true.

A culture of change (Psych-6). The change in Clyde provides a thumbnail sketch of something that changes the world. As people learn to change in that way—faith working through love in the midst of hard realities—it creates communities of increasingly wise mutual counsel (always falling short, of course; always partial, but noticeable and noticeably attractive). Transforming the ethos of any culture comes by the accumulation of innumerable slight changes of exactly this sort.

Beloved, we are God's children now, and what we will be has not yet appeared; but we know that when he appears we shall be like him, because we shall see him as he is. And everyone who thus hopes in him purifies himself as he is pure. (1 Jn 3:2-3)

Believe so that you may understand. Understand so that your own soul may be cured. And in this way may God help you to contribute to the curing of many souls.

REFERENCES

Abbott, A. (1988). *The system of professions*. Chicago: University of Chicago Press.

Boisen, A. (1936/1962). *The exploration of the inner world*. New York: Harper.

Cushman, P. (1990). Why is the self empty? *American Psychologist, 45*(5), 599-612.

Eliot, T. S. (1963). Choruses from "The Rock." *Collected Poems 1909-1962*. New York: Harcourt, Brace, & World.

Freud, S. (1976). Some character-types met with in psycho-analytic work. In *The complete psychological works of Sigmund Freud* (Vol. 14). New York: W. W. Norton. (Original work published 1916)

———. (1976). The question of lay analysis. In *The complete psychological works of Sigmund Freud* (Vol. 20). New York: W. W. Norton. (Original work published 1926)

Lasch, C. (1979). *The culture of narcissism*. New York: W. W. Norton.

Powlison, D. (1988). Crucial issues in contemporary biblical counseling. *Journal of Pastoral Practice, 9*(3), 53-78.

———. (1992). Integration or inundation. In M. Horton (Ed.), *Power religion*. Chicago: Moody Press.

———. (2001). Questions at the crossroads: The cure of souls and modern psychotherapies. In M. McMinn and T. Phillips (Eds.), *Care for the soul: Exploring the intersection of psychology and theology* (pp. 23-61). Downers Grove, IL: InterVarsity Press.

———. (2003). *Seeing with new eyes*. Phillipsburg, NJ: Presbyterian & Reformed.

———. (2004). Is the "Adonis Complex" in your Bible? *Journal of Biblical Counseling, 22*(2), 42-58.

———. (2005). *Speaking truth in love*. Greensboro, NC: New Growth Press.

———. (2007). Familial counseling. *Journal of Biblical Counseling, 25*(1), 2-15.

———. (2010). *The biblical counseling movement: History and context*. Greensboro, NC: New Growth Press. (Original work published 1996)

Rieff, P. (1967). *The triumph of the therapeutic*. Chicago: University of Chicago.

Roberts, R. (1993). *Taking the word to heart: self and other in an age of therapies*. Grand Rapids, MI: Eerdmans.

Vitz, P. (1977). *Psychology as religion*. Grand Rapids, MI: Eerdmans.

Welch, E. (1997). *When people are big and God is small*. Phillipsburg, NJ: Presbyterian & Reformed.

———. (1998). *Blame it on the brain*. Phillipsburg, NJ: Presbyterian & Reformed.

———. (2001). *Addictions: A banquet in the grave*. Phillipsburg, NJ: Presbyterian & Reformed.

———. (2004). *Depression: A stubborn darkness*. Greensboro, NC: New Growth Press.

———. (2007). *Running scared*. Greensboro, NC: New Growth Press.

A Levels-of-Explanation Response
to Biblical Counseling

David G. Myers

"CHRISTIAN FAITH *IS* A PSYCHOLOGY" (p. 245). So begins David Powlison's advice to spurn today's psychological science for a faith that, with its own implicit psychology, has little need for science.

"Believe so that you may understand," urges Powlison (p. 246). Let your human understandings flow from your assumed beliefs. As any psychology student should know, belief does guide perception, which is why I titled an earlier book (with Malcolm Jeeves) *Psychology Through the Eyes of Faith.* Indeed, one purpose of any scientific theory is to organize disconnected observations into a coherent system, and to make predictions that allow us to test and apply it. The virtue of science is that (contrary to those who think psychology is nothing but collected biases) one's initial ideas may be overturned, as have many ideas and theories over time. It was, for example, new scientific evidence that challenged and changed my preconceived ideas about sexual orientation.

Powlison (like Robert C. Roberts and P. J. Watson, as well as John H. Coe and Todd W. Hall) takes psychology to "mean many different things" that are quite unlike what psychology means to the people who write textbook and dictionary definitions, who write for the journals of the American Psychological Association and the Association for Psychological Science, who teach in colleges and universities, and who write the exams for the AP psychology course and the Graduate Record Examination. For all of these, and for those of us who write textbooks reporting on psychology, *psychology is the science of behavior and mental processes.*

Not so for Powlison, for whom psychology is without sharp definition. It may be "how you work" (p. 249) or "like a *good novel* or *film*" (p. 253) or a "worldview" (p. 256) or psychotherapy or a "mass ethos" (p. 261) or knowledge that can be assembled from "learning to think the way Jesus thinks" (p. 254). According to Powlison, psychological insight can come from knowing other people, from taking in poetry and film, from reading history and biography, and from absorbing humanistic psychology. There is little place for mainstream psychological science in all this, although he admits that "secular psychologists have 'neurotic insights,' simultaneously brilliant and distorted" (p. 255).

This leaves me with little to say, other than that when he and I use the word *psychology*, we are not talking about the same thing. Our readers may therefore feel rather like Alice in Wonderland as she spoke to Humpty Dumpty: "The question is whether you can make words mean so many different things."

I don't say that to be dismissive. Rather, biblical counseling, and the pastoral mission of applying biblical wisdom to living (as in the case of Clyde), are utterly different activities than doing psychological science as historically understood and practiced on the college and university campuses that I work at, visit and correspond with. Thus, I feel like an economist asked to critique a business manager, or a social researcher asked to comment on a social worker's ideas. We're simply in different fields.

To be sure, there are brief glimpses in Powlison's essay where our worlds could or do overlap. When Powlison finds us "fatally flawed by self-serving bias[es] as the pervading psychological reality" (p. 248), I say "Amen, brother" and have mountains of supportive evidence in mind. When he dismisses as "a convenient fiction" the idea that certain emotions exist because of their survival value (p. 252), at least that invites a debate over the foundational idea beneath modern biology and evolutionary psychology. And when he proclaims that biblical counseling is more effective than secular counseling strategies that "heal lightly" (p. 259), this suggests conducting a clinical experiment (assigning patients to one therapy or the other) to see if he's right.

But these connecting points notwithstanding, our professional worlds differ more than do baseball and cricket or football and soccer. Is biblical counseling effective counseling? It's not for me to judge.

An Integration Response to Biblical Counseling

Stanton L. Jones

THIS BIBLICAL COUNSELING CHAPTER demonstrates that this approach to relating psychology and Christianity, like any worthwhile approach, continues to evolve and develop. There is much of value here.

In my chapter on the integration approach, I recounted my brief personal meeting with the founder of the biblical counseling movement, Jay Adams. In response to my request for guidance in remaining faithful to biblical truth as a clinical psychologist, he urged me to drop out of my training because there was insufficient value in the field and discipline to justify continuing—and there was so much damage being done to the cause of Christ by psychology. I did not take his advice, but neither did I find his reasoning utterly without merit: we often insufficiently mine the riches of the Scriptures and the Christian tradition in our understanding of people and their problems; we can also be insufficiently critical of secular assumptions and values embedded in the psychologies we embrace; the value of certain approaches to psychology is often vastly oversold; and the damage done by the psychologizing of our culture and of the church is real.

David Powlison is now the intellectual leader of the biblical counseling movement. He follows Adams, who in turn followed the intellectual tracks laid down by his professor and mentor, theologian and Christian apologist Cornelius Van Til. As I explained in my chapter, Adams's work drove me to reflect carefully on what it meant to be committed to a Christian worldview, a Christian vision of all of life grounded in the teachings of Scripture. I remain indebted to this tradition for a fundamental insight: to be committed fully to Jesus Christ as Lord means being committed to anchoring one's approach to all of life in the teachings of the Scriptures, God's inspired Word.

But I learned a pivotal lesson in my early study of the biblical counseling movement. I read as much as I could about what it means to be faithful to a Christian worldview, including a volume dedicated to the thinking of Van Til. In that book, philosopher Hendrik Stoker (1971) issued a gentle challenge to Van Til. In essence, Stoker commended Van Til's basic stance of seeing Christ as Lord of all, of seeing all knowledge as a whole and as founded on certain fundamentals that humans must take on faith, and of the need for Christians to challenge non-Christian presuppositions that are raised up in defiance of the foundations of faith in Christ as revealed in the Scriptures. Van Til's strength, argued Stoker, was in his work as an apologist who helped expose the foundations of secular thought and to lead each person to decide who he or she would follow in faith. Would we follow the Lord of the universe or our own human autonomy raised up in rebellion against God?

But Stoker recognized that Christians through the centuries had engaged secular thought not just for the purposes of evangelism and apologetics, but also to *learn from secular thinkers*. So Stoker asked how our engagement with secular thought would change if the purpose of that engagement was not of apologetics but of the constructive task of cooperating with secular thinkers to better understand our world (including ourselves). Shouldn't a complete understanding of Christian engagement with non-Christian thought include a constructive dimension that seeks to learn from and see what is right about secular thought as well as what is wrong? Van Til replied with an equally gentle acknowledgment that such engagement is a possibility.

In many ways, Powlison's chapter is, in this key area, an advance on the thinking of his mentor, Adams, because Powlison articulates a stance of courageous engagement with psychology: "What are the similarities and differences between other psychologies and psychotherapies versus Christian faith and practice? . . . What helpful things can we learn from them? . . . What should they learn from us?" (p. 246), he asks. At this point, though, the reader might pause and ask, If Powlison really does believe in substantive engagement with and learning from psychology, how does his view differ substantively from the integration view?

My engagement with Adams helped me to refine and clarify my commitment to approaching psychology with biblically grounded commitments while exulting in what we could learn from the science and profession of psychology. In one earlier expression of my thinking (Jones, 1994), I argued there should be three aspects or movements in a Christian's engagement with secular psychology: critical-evaluative, constructive and dialogical.

By critical-evaluative, I mean something like what Powlison means when he says that in our engagement with psychology we must keep "the true God consciously in view when considering humankind" (p. 246). We must realize that there is no such thing as ultimate neutrality, that knowledge is always being woven together for the ultimate purpose either of bringing us closer to or further away from the Creator and Sustainer of all knowledge. Truly, there are times when the best response of the Christian is to "demolish arguments and every pretension that sets itself up against the knowledge of God" (2 Cor 10:5 NIV).

Second, by a constructive movement in our engagement with secular psychology, I mean genuine learning from secular psychology. Note that Powlison speaks of "learning" from psychology, but in his chapter, he has little to say about tangible instances of such learning. Contemporary psychology is "deconstructed" but not much more. In fact, early in his essay, he takes a stance that effectively undercuts any attempt at genuine learning from psychology. In his introduction (p. 245), he suggests that Christianity provides a "coherent, comprehensive understanding of how people work," that a "Christian understanding systemically differs from how other psychologies explain the same phenomena," and he uses some version of the word *distinct* no less than seven times in the first four paragraphs to assert how utterly different a Christian view is from a secular view.

Now, if the Christian view is systemically different, is coherent and comprehensive, and is emphatically distinct from a psychological view, what basis is there to learn from psychology? Why bother? If there is a biblical view that is already systemically distinctive such that it differs essentially and pervasively from other views, and is also coherent and comprehensive (covers everything important), then this is a view that *has nothing to learn from other views*. So it makes sense that we find no real instances of learning from psychology offered in Powlison's chapter.

I do not want to take anything away from the lordship of Christ and the sovereignty and glory of the triune God. With Powlison, I affirm the complete truthfulness of God's Word, the Bible; it should be counted as true in everything it teaches. But to claim that *the Bible is true in everything it teaches* is not the same as claiming that *it teaches the truth about everything in every area* (nor that we perfectly grasp the truth that it teaches). Similarly, the lordship of Christ is not diminished by acknowledging humanity's capacity to learn and grow through reflection on the world. The integrationist position is that biblical truth is our foundation, but that we have much to learn from human labors in psychology and other fields to better understand more about the physical substrates of human life, about the varieties and complexities of human personality, about the brokenness and limitations of our experience, and about the possibilities and limitations of our capacities to change.

This leads me to the third movement in our relationship with psychology. By a dialogical relationship I mean simply that, beyond the times of critical engagement when we become sure that psychology is off base and needs to be criticized, and beyond the times of constructive engagement when we genuinely and joyfully recognize that we have something good to learn from psychology, there are times when we mainly are confronted with our ignorance and hardly know how to think. At these times, in humility, we need to be ready to learn through conversation with thinkers of all stripes.

The reader of this volume is faced with having to make a set of quite fundamental decisions in response to the following questions: Do I believe that God has revealed truth about human nature and life that is binding and fundamental to how I should approach understanding human existence? Do I believe that what God has revealed is so distinctive, comprehensive and different from secular views that I have nothing meaningful to learn from sustained engagement with secular psychology? Is there merit to the corpus of findings, perspectives and theories of secular psychology? Do we as Christians have anything to learn from others?

The "levels" view pushes away Christian perspectives from having any formative place in shaping the way we approach the study of psychology. The biblical counseling and Christian psychology views so exalt Christian perspectives that psychology has no real value for our understanding of persons. Only the integration view, in my mind, properly balances fidelity to the Bible's revealed truth about human nature as binding and fundamental, with a proper humility that recognizes the incompleteness of our Christian understandings and the possibility of rich learning from our engagement with secular thought.

Finally, I would draw the reader's attention to the overall structure of the biblical counseling chapter. After an introduction, Powlison provides three substantive sections: (1) an articulation of key Christian assumptions from the Nicene Creed, (2) an extensive reflection on a "deconstruction" of psychology and (3) an engaging case study. Note first that if the hallmark of a biblical counseling view is that it offers a coherent and comprehensive Christian view of people and our problems, why is some summary of that view not articulated here? Why does Powlison focus on certain Nicene fundamentals, worthy and true as they are, but which themselves do not frame a Christian psychology? We find fragments of such a Christian view of persons in his case study and scattered throughout the chapter, but they are only fragments. Second, while many of his critical points in deconstructing psychology are well-reasoned and edifying, they neither build our understanding of what a biblical counseling view is, nor establish what it is and how it is that we can productively learn from secular psychology. Third, I would ask whether Powlison has really taught us much about the relationship between psychology and Christianity through his case study. His case study of Clyde is of a high-functioning Christian individual struggling with significant life issues that make him ideally suited for a biblical counseling approach. This individual is, indeed, the perfect example of a person for whom the resources of the pastoral tradition are ideally suited and whose referral to a secular psychologist would likely be unproductive and unnecessary. Given the case as described, it is actually hard to imagine any secular psychologists objecting that Clyde was poorly served by the counseling delivered by Powlison. This is a person who is, from the beginning, in little need of the resources offered by psychology. As I have previously argued (Jones & Butman, 1991), the resources of the faith and of the church are often wholly adequate to meet many needs that people face, but it is when those resources are exhausted or insufficient that we rightly seek to supplement and complement (*not* replace) Christian perspectives with additional resources from scientific and professional psychology, thoughtfully engaged. That is integration.

For further elaboration of these criticisms and further concerns about the biblical counseling approach, see Jones and Butman (1991, chap. 1) and Jones (2001).

REFERENCES

Jones, S. (1994). A constructive relationship for religion with the science and profession of psychology: Perhaps the boldest model yet. *American Psychologist, 49*(3), 184-99.

———. (2001). An apologetic *apologia* for the integration of psychology and theology. In T. R. Phillips & M. R. McMinn (Eds.), *The care of the soul: Exploring the intersection of psychology and theology* (pp. 62-77). Downers Grove, IL: InterVarsity Press.

Jones, S., & Butman, R. (1991). *Modern psychotherapies: A comprehensive Christian appraisal.* Downers Grove, IL: InterVarsity Press.

Stoker, H. (1971). Reconnoitering the theory of knowledge of Professor Dr. Cornelius Van Til. In E. Geehan (Ed.), *Jerusalem and Athens* (pp. 25-70). Phillipsburg, NJ: Presbyterian & Reformed.

A Christian Psychology Response
to Biblical Counseling

P. J. Watson

BIBLICAL COUNSELING DESERVES HIGH PRAISE for its commitment to counseling practices that center on the revelation of Jesus Christ. Biblical counseling, as described in this chapter, is nevertheless difficult to embrace as a model for Christian participation in psychology. From the perspective of Christian psychology, the unacknowledged difficulties appear in the frequent statements that "we have work to do." Both *work* and *we* require deeper examination.

First, Christian psychology would challenge any notion that this chapter has exhaustively defined the "work" that Christians in psychology must do. The biblical counseling chapter implies that Christian psychologists should only do counseling. But surely this cannot be true. Even this chapter admits that psychology as a science serves as a useful, albeit limited, source of knowledge for the biblical counselor. The "nomothetic" findings of science, for example, are one of many factors that "contribute to the depth and breadth of knowledge one often finds in psychologists, whether theoreticians, researchers or clinicians" (p. 253). And from psychology as science, "we can learn a great deal" (p. 255). But why assume that Christians do not have a more extensive role to play in a discipline that includes counseling as only one part of its work? Is it not possible and indeed essential for biblical counselors (and other Christian psychologists) to test, expand and defend their perspectives by using scientific methods that have a proven and widely respected ability to yield reliable and valid knowledge? Would it not be useful, for example, to scientifically understand the health-promoting dynamics of Christian beliefs about sin? Would not compelling scientific evidence about this issue have a potential to defend Christian perspectives against critics and to help counselors better understand how sin-related beliefs actually operate within those they counsel (Watson, Morris, Loy, Hamrick & Grizzle, 2007)?

Biblical counseling downplays the work of science by suggesting that other forms of human endeavor have an "epistemological status [that] is the same as the psychologies" (p. 255). Biblical counselors, for example, should "drink deeply of good novels, poetry, drama, film, music, visual arts" (p. 254). Biblical counselors and presumably everyone else should indeed "drink deeply" from all sources of insight. The question, however, is this: In what ways, if any, is biblical counseling different from the well-educated and sympathetic conversations of Christians who live next door? Would it not be important in the work of biblical counselors to articulate formal, professional methods of discernment for evaluating *all* sources of insight? And why even call this work "biblical counseling"? Why not promote instead a "biblical-life hermeneutics" that has little to offer as a model for Christians working in psychology? Why not simply encourage the education of "biblical interpreters" and leave completely behind any even implied connection with the professions of counseling and psychology?

From a different angle, however, the problem with interpretive methods is that they are of course (in)famous for the diversity in perspectives that they support (e.g., Nietzsche, 1887/2000). How can biblical counseling assume that it has the epistemological status to produce interpretations with uncontested reliability and validity? How can the insights of history be read to suggest that Christianity has ever operated as a harmoniously unified biblical-life hermeneutic? Would not at least some formal commitment to science be useful in disciplining the interpretive processes of biblical counselors (as well as all other Christians working in psychology)?

At one point David Powlison argues, "If a sociologist tried to change society, or a historian tried to change history, we'd call it politics, not good social science" (p. 260). This view presumes that the work of the social sciences can and should be objective. Social scientists apparently should "acknowledge their assumptions and work hard to make those assumptions relatively nonintrusive" (p. 254). This kind of thinking is increasingly untenable (e.g., Rosenau, 1992).

Within the postmodern cultural context, Christian psychology, like other forms of Christian thought and praxis, can and should maintain explicit commitments to its worldview. Value neutrality cannot and should not exist. The work of Christians in the social sciences, therefore, is to use scientific methods to intrusively and explicitly promote biblical perspectives on what persons and cultures should be. Scientific methods include qualitative and quantitative forms of analysis that Christians can use to transform the world in ways that are compatible with a biblical worldview. In making those transformations, scientific methods are often invaluable in empirically describing how fallen persons and cultures operate in the present, and then in evaluating the effectiveness of efforts to transform them. A Christian psychologist should explicitly and intrusively use scientific methods to promote biblical perspectives on forgiveness and peace in interpersonal relationships. A Christian sociologist should explicitly and intrusively use these methods to change a racist society. A Christian historian should explicitly and intrusively "work" hard with all the available evidence to challenge any triumphalist narrative of authoritarianism. And Christian psychologists, historians, sociologists and economists can and should explicitly and intrusively work together, united by a biblical worldview, to overcome the grinding poverty that afflicts so many people on this planet.

Again, Christian psychology would also pay careful attention to the use of "we" by biblical counselors. To some important degree, this chapter seems to assume that biblical counseling can operate within a church in which "we" Christians unite in common understandings of how to meet the needs of persons. But again, how can the insights of history suggest that Christianity operates across time as a harmonious community of interpretation? Today, as in the past, Christians criticize Christians. Constantinianism corrupts the church (see, e.g., Yoder, 1984). Paganism infects the worship "we" practice (Viola & Barna, 2008). Dominant forms of Christianity operate under a Western cultural captivity to individualism, consumerism and racism (Rah, 2009). Within the church, no "we" can speak with an uncontested voice of interpretation, and the conflicting voices of the Christian "we" all make appeals to the same authority of the Bible. Resources outside the Bible can help the church better understand where "we" stand. Christian beliefs, along with Constantinianism, paganism, individualism, consumerism and racism, all have empirical indicators that can be studied.

Christians complain, for example, that excessive individualism in the West leads to narcissistic forms of self-actualization that "we" must and can easily reject. Christian concerns about self-actualization undoubtedly have interpretative validity, but empirical methods suggest that any easy, blanket rejection of self-actualization may be inconsistent with at least some biblical perspectives (e.g., Watson, Milliron, Morris & Hood, 1995).

Scientific analysis of these and many other issues can make important contributions to Christian communities. A scientific Christian psychology has an essential, albeit delimited, role in attempts to better understand what "we" believe.

Biblical counseling also cannot avoid operating within the "we" of a wider culture. To help one person at a time is important and can have an impact on changing the wider society, just as David Powlison suggests. However, the "we" that live outside the church will not be moved by this kind of argument. Biblical counseling will not always be successful, and other forms of counseling sometimes will be. The "we" outside the church will also receive frequent news about problems or "sins" within the church, and that wider, cultural "we" will be skeptical about the church. A biblical counseling that only uses biblical language, or "plain" speech that leads to biblical language, will have limited impact within the context of this wider cultural skepticism. Moreover, a biblical-life hermeneutic has been around for almost two millennia now. The history of that hermeneutic has given critics reasonable grounds for, at least sometimes, doubting what the church says about itself and about others who are not part of the Christian "we." Given its historical difficulties, a biblical-life hermeneutic has found itself in retreat over the past five hundred years in competing with alternative perspectives like secularism, different traditional belief systems and new forms of religion.

If biblical counselors perceive this cultural circumstance to be a problem, they will need to broaden the "work" they do and speak more effectively to the "we" that lives outside the church. To get a fair hearing, they will need to embrace new language structures that help them get heard. The scientific method operates as a powerful "language structure" within contemporary culture. A community of interpretation that uses this language to develop reliable and valid knowledge about its own problems and about the problems of other communities will build a city on a hill that is difficult to ignore in the modern world. If on the other hand, biblical counselors do not perceive this cultural circumstance as a problem, they presumably will need to construct a compelling narrative that can convince the "we" both inside and outside the church that the biblical-life hermeneutic has fulfilled or can successfully fulfill its mission to transform people and culture from what they are to what they should be. The skepticism of many makes the possibility of such a narrative seem remote.

But perhaps the goal of biblical counseling is something else entirely. Perhaps the goal is to serve smaller communal enclaves with shared, uncontested interpretations of Scripture. Perhaps the task is not to worry about the hermeneutics used by other Christian communities of "we" or by the "we" of the wider culture. Perhaps, in other words, each Christian community should embrace a kind of Amish option. Leave the world and calibrate life within the enclave to a language that "we" accept as nonproblematic. The Amish are inspiring and can be admired, and if biblical counseling advocates something like this, then surely the approach deserves respect. At the same time, however, the Amish model is not very useful for understanding how Christians should work in psychology. From the perspective of Christian psychology, "we" have "work" to do across Christian enclaves and within the wider culture.

REFERENCES

Nietzsche, F. (2000). *On the genealogy of morals*. In W. Kaufmann (Ed.), *Basic Writings of Nietzsche* (pp. 451-599). New York: Random House. (Original work published 1887)

Rah, S.-C. (2009). *The next evangelicalism*. Downers Grove, IL: IVP Books.

Rosenau, P. M. (1992). *Post-modernism and the social sciences*. Princeton, NJ: Princeton University Press.

Viola, F., & Barna, G. (2008). *Pagan Christianity?* Carol Stream, IL: BarnaBooks.

Watson, P. J., Milliron, J. T., Morris, R. J., & Hood, R. W., Jr. (1995). Religion and the self as text: Toward a Christian translation of self-actualization. *Journal of Psychology and Theology, 23*, 180-89.

Watson, P. J., Morris, R. J., Loy, T., Hamrick, M. B., & Grizzle, S. (2007). Beliefs about sin: Adaptive implications in relationships with religious orientation, self-esteem, and measures of the narcissistic, depressed and anxious self. *Edification: Journal of the Society for Christian Psychology, 1*, 57-67.

Yoder, J. H. (1984). *The priestly kingdom*. Notre Dame, IN: University of Notre Dame Press.

A Transformational Psychology Response to Biblical Counseling

John H. Coe and Todd W. Hall

DAVID POWLISON'S REPRESENTATION of biblical counseling is a genuine, biblical attempt to understand the relationship of psychology and Christianity. Powlison provides a nuanced account of the ways we use the word *psychology* and how biblical counseling relates to each of these. In fact, Powlison offers such a good attempt at providing a biblical view that we wondered whether there is serious disagreement between us. However, after a closer reading, three overlapping contentions emerge:

1. Biblical counseling, unfortunately, fails to adequately critique the modernist approach to science and psychology, so it fails to break away from this truncated methodological approach of studying the person. Therefore, it fails to produce its own unique, thoroughly Christian version of science.

2. Additionally, biblical counseling accepts as science the modernist approach that is purely quantitative and descriptive, which excludes mental objects/phenomena and the prescriptive (values, character and morality) from the purview of science.

3. Biblical counseling fails to take sufficiently seriously the biblical account of doing the firsthand work of psychology as observation-reflection on persons. This observation-reflection method is reflected in the Old Testament wisdom literature, which provides biblical material for discerning values and wisdom for living from a study of human persons.

It is not clear whether Powlison represents the majority of those affirming a biblical counseling view, since others seem to be much less amenable to elements that he permits. While Powlison affirms that the church has been strongest in understanding "psychology" at the worldview level and in the development of a robust theory of the person in God (what he terms Psych-3), it has been weakest in those places that secular psychology has been strongest—in its detailed understanding of the dynamics of human functioning (Psych-2) and its caring for and listening to people (Psych-4). The net effect, according to Powlison, is that the church has tended toward a theoretical approach to the person but has failed to have its feet on the ground to connect and deal with people's real issues. While this seems quite honest and unfortunate, we suggest this same problem is also evident in Powlison's own case study, and we further assert that the biblical counseling view is partially to blame for this. Our goal is to build psychology on a pre-modern view of science that will provide Powlison with the rigorous methodology for doing what he already affirms informally.

Our first contention is that, while Powlison has a commonsense view of how the Christian can understand and interact with the various ways the term *psychology* is employed, he fails to do a thoroughgoing criticism of psychology and scientific methodology in light of a Christian worldview. For example, when discussing Psych-1 as the needed commonsense understanding of the self, he does not provide a methodological approach for this. When he discusses Psych-2 as the science of the person, he says that we can learn from science and critique this within a Christian perspective, but he talks about psychological science as though it were the fruits of outsiders and pagans, not the potential fruits of believers. That is, he assumes that science is the possession of another, and he assumes that science is the modernist model of studying person in a purely descriptive way that excludes distinctly Christian realities from its purview. This is an injustice to what the church could provide for the healing of its people.

Moreover, failing to do a thorough critique of the nature of science and psychology in order to develop a unique, Christian approach leads to a limited application to the counseling/therapy process. Powlison acknowledges and even encourages us to learn from secular psychological theories (pp. 254-55), yet in the case study of Clyde, no psychological theories regarding the formulation of personality and presenting problems are utilized, nor is the change process articulated. This leads to a lot of implicit psychology and a piecemeal approach to therapeutic intervention. Of course, we are not saying that Clyde did not heal and grow, as it seems clear that an initial shift led him down a better path. However, initial shifts often reveal new layers of psychopathology that require a deep and prolonged relationship with a therapist to change things in the "heart," as Powlison rightly emphasizes. Relational psychotherapies, for example, have proven enormously helpful in bringing about such change.

Recent meta-analyses have demonstrated that relational therapies, in contrast to cognitive-behavioral therapies, tend to produce changes that increase over time after therapy (Shedler, in press). We believe this has to do with the process of internalizing the relational capacities with the therapist that come with a "secure-enough" attachment.

There are a handful of metatheories about how healing and change take place, and our critique centers around one's *theory* of how the change process works and the role of the counselor in this process. Like mentioned above, one group of theories suggests that a warm, secure, relational attachment with a therapist will bring about healing and change. Another group of theories suggests that explicit thought processes and behavioral interventions are the primary agents of change, while another suggests that changing family systems is required. Another group of theories proposes that facing existential issues is the key to change, and another argues that bringing unconscious conflict among biologically based drives into consciousness will lead to healing.

Meanwhile, the Bible does not articulate a full-blown theory of the change process or the role of the counselor. It certainly provides controlling ideas and insights, but it does not provide a detailed theory of how to respond if a client asks, "How do I put off envy and excess anger?" We must then work out such a theory of change and our role in it, but the biblical counseling view appears truncated with its lack of details in how to bring about change. We think that this points, again, to the necessity of a robust pre-modern psychology/science from a fully Christian perspective.

Our second point, related to the first, is that the biblical counseling view fails to adequately critique as science the modernist science model that is committed to a universal method of quantification or measurement of bodies and their (efficient) causal relations to one another and, thus, precludes addressing prescriptive human values. The successes of astronomy in *measuring* observables, their movements and relationships to one another was so successful that the modern scientists of the seventeenth and eighteenth centuries wanted to make this the chief language of knowledge of creation, if not all knowledge. However, particular difficulties for science and psychology arose, including how to explain (1) spiritual and nonphysical phenomena and (2) ethics. The modernist scientific methodology of quantification is purely descriptive, not prescriptive, and is capable only of addressing physical realities. So it becomes difficult to intelligibly talk about values (good and bad), moral prescriptions for living (moral "oughts" and prohibitions) and character traits (virtues and vices)—concepts of psychological health and unhealth as in psychotherapy—as well as about nonphysical objects (souls, angels, God, dreams, personal agency, first-person identity, experiences of feelings and thoughts).

The questions that confronted the Christian psychologist were (1) whether and to what degree a legitimate scientific psychology can be developed to address nonphysical and/or Christian realities, and (2) whether the Christian psychologist is doing something other than "psychology" or science when relating psychology and Christianity. The tension is clear: it is not legitimate for modernist science to include Scripture as legitimate data for psychology, nor is it legitimate to address immaterial objects, sin, life in Christ or values. However, Christians include Scripture as a legitimate source of knowledge and are compelled by Scripture, as well as reflection on human nature, to address realities that are inherently unquantifiable. The biblical counseling tradition tends to maintain the modern view of science, keeping distinct the two domains of science and religion-values. We suggest that this has led to a truncated understanding of change and the counseling/ therapy process in this biblical counseling tradition, which is due to not developing and applying a "science" of therapeutic change. We believe that an intrinsically holistic transformational psychology is possible by returning to an ancient classical-realist view of science.

Finally, biblical counseling, given its genuine adherence to Scripture, could greatly benefit from affirming a pre-modern approach to science, where Christian realities and perspectives come to bear on all reflections about reality, particularly human phenomena, while embracing a robust methodology for doing a science of the person. As it turns out, there is an alternate approach to science, affirmed by the ancients, that is capable of grounding a holistic vision for understanding the person in light of *all* reality. The classical and medieval thinkers—those represented in ancient Near Eastern wise men (sages), the Old Testament sage, the Greeks in Plato and Aristotle, the Stoics and numerous medieval thinkers—had an entirely different approach to scientific method than that of modernity. According to the modernist "new science," you begin scientific investigation with a universal method of measuring objects in motion, which predetermines the kinds of objects that are possible to discover and investigate. The classical-realist approach *reverses* this process: *the object of investigation determines the methodology,* which involves the following elements:

1. Science begins with a casual *acquaintance* of the object

2. for the purpose of learning more about the *nature* of the object,

3. which allows the *object of investigation to determine* the best way to further investigate it,

4. resulting in the development of *a method of study* best suited to the object.

Rather than allowing a predetermined way of knowing to determine what is real and what counts as knowledge, this view of scientific method allows *reality* to determine *methodology.* To put it differently, ontology determines epistemology, and a presupposed epistemology does not determine ontology. According to the ancients, one cannot know what is the best way to study what exists until one is adequately acquainted with what exists. On this view of science, the psychological health of the scientist to remain honest and open to reality is central to doing science well, which is foundational to our transformational psychology model.

Consequently a transformational psychology critiques modernist science and attempts to realize science as a single, unified vision of reality in faith and the Spirit. This provides a comprehensive and coherent scientific methodology that is capable of relating psychology to faith, of doing a psychology of Christian realities. This psychology will include Scripture as a legitimate datum of "science" and will include immaterial objects, values, sin and our capacity to be indwelt by God as within the boundaries of psychology. In turn, this process of doing transformational psychology is ultimately grounded in the psychologist who preserves the integrity of this process by being as open as possible to what is real and true about understanding the person. This is precisely what the Old Testament wise man was about, and the biblical counseling tradition, with its fierce adherence to biblical integrity, would be well positioned to champion and build on such a methodology for the sake and good of the church.

REFERENCES

Shedler, J. (In press). The efficacy of psychodynamic psychotherapies. *American Psychologist.*

7

Gaining Understanding Through Five Views

Eric L. Johnson

Mᴜʟᴛɪᴘᴇʀsᴘᴇᴄᴛɪᴠᴇ ʙᴏᴏᴋs ʟɪᴋᴇ ᴛʜɪs ᴏɴᴇ abound in our day: Five Views on the Gifts of the Spirit, Three Views on Postmodernism, Four Views on Septuagint Translation (not yet!). Such books are popular and valuable—not least because they demonstrate that Christians, while agreeing in their core beliefs, hold various beliefs on many secondary topics. In some cases, the positions presented in these books are mutually exclusive, so the readers' task presumably is to determine which presentation has made the best case, or if already convinced that they know what the best view is, to identify problems in the other views and to understand better the weaknesses of their own.

There are undoubtedly aspects of the five positions in this book that are contradictory to each other, and many will inevitably read this book with their minds already made up. But in the case of *this* book, it would be a serious mistake to assume that there is only one correct position among the five such that the others are wholly in error. On the contrary, I want to suggest that this book's vigorous debate points to a larger reality that lies behind all of the views, and this reality requires listening to all of them and appropriating the valid insights of each one, in order to get the "biggest picture" we can. Let's see why and how.

HUMILITY: A VIRTUE PREREQUISITE FOR GAINING UNDERSTANDING

Going back at least as far as the book of Proverbs, believers have recognized that wisdom entails a paradox: the wiser we become, the more aware we become of our lack of wisdom and our need for the help of others. "The way of a fool seems right to him, / but a wise man listens to advice" (Prov 12:15). In stark contrast to humanistic wisdom, the biblical authors repeatedly point out that wisdom comes from without, not from within. It is transcendently from God, and second, it is mediated by other humans who know more than we do. According to Christian wisdom theory (Ford, 2007; Johnson, 1996b; Rad, 1972), the creative insight of the individual is absolutely dependent on God and relatively dependent on the wisdom of others. This is why true wisdom begins with the fear of God (Prov 1:7), and Christians seek their wisdom from above (Jas 3:17) in Christ (Col 2:3).

As a result, Christian understanding seeks first God's understanding. God knows all things; he "knows every truth" (Mavrodes, 1997, p. 236), so his knowledge is absolutely, unsurpassably comprehensive, corresponding perfectly to all reality. Plantinga (1993a) argues from God's omniscience that "the proposition that *p* is true . . . will be equivalent in the broadly logical sense to the proposition that God *knows p,* and also the proposition that God *believes p*" (p. 40). Likewise believing in God's omniscience, Jonathan Edwards (1944) wrote nearly three centuries ago that, "Truth, in general may be defined after the most strict and metaphysical manner: 'the consistency and agreement of our ideas with the ideas of God'" (p. 341). Consequently, for the Christian, the goal of any science is the increasingly comprehensive conformity of our understanding to God's absolutely comprehensive understanding or, as some have said, "to think God's thoughts after him."

In contrast to his perfect understanding, ours is necessarily limited at best. We must confess with the apostle Paul that "we see but a poor reflection as in a mirror" (1 Cor 13:12). In spite of all the technological progress in the careful (scientific) study of God's creation over the past few hundred years, humans cannot know things *perfectly.* We can grow closer to God's perfect understanding, but we can never attain absolute comprehensiveness. There are a number of reasons for this. To begin with, finite creatures can stand in only one place and see things from only one standpoint; as a result, under the best of circumstances, we can never hope to obtain God's "omniscient observer" view of things. Our finitude also means that acquiring knowledge is developmental, so it starts from zero (at conception!) and increases over time through the course of our experiences and study. Even more problematic, we can make mistakes in our investigations, as our understanding is obscured by the limitations of our motives, methods and sources. Finally, our greatest hindrance is due to the fact that our minds and hearts are religiously distorted by the noetic and carditive effects of sin. So while Christians ought to seek God's understanding, we must acknowledge that his alone is perfect, or absolutely comprehensive, and that ours is only a partial reflection or reproduction of the whole.

As a result of these limitations, no human can know everything. God's truth is too big and our minds are too small and corrupted by sin. One simplistic response to this state of affairs is a kind of intellectual apathy called *relativism*: "With all these different approaches, it doesn't matter what a person believes." But as people have reflected more deeply on the nature of knowing, they inevitably recognize that some beliefs are a more accurate reflection of reality, that some persons have a better grasp of things than others, and that it is possible for us to better understand the way things are than we used to. These realizations are assumed by the father in Proverbs:

[Turn] your ear to wisdom
    and [apply] your heart to understanding,
and if you call out for insight
    and cry aloud for understanding,
and if you look for it as for silver
    and search for it as for hidden treasure,
then you will understand the fear of the LORD
    and find the knowledge of God.
For the LORD gives wisdom,
    and from his mouth come knowledge and understanding. (Prov 2:2-6)

Developing a more comprehensive, fuller, richer understanding is not easy; it requires great effort. It also requires virtues like humility (this theme is at the heart of transformational psychology). Wise people "begin" their search for wisdom with the awareness that they lack it. They need the help of God and others. "Give your servant a discerning heart" (1 Kings 3:9). This quest for wisdom glorifies God for at least two reasons: (1) because he is the source of human wisdom; and (2) as we obtain more wisdom, we become a little more like him, and this is a good in the Christian scheme of things.

The philosophical position that humans can actually know reality as it really is, in some measure, is called *realism*. Most Christian philosophers over the centuries have been *realists* (e.g., Augustine, Aquinas, Pascal, Thomas Reid), because they believed that God created our minds and the universe in such a way that our understanding can accurately reflect reality to some degree (in our day, see Alston, 1996; Moreland & Craig, 2003; Plantinga, 1983, 1993a, 1993b, 2000). God's understanding can be likened to the entire landscape that we, in our science, try to paint on the canvas of our discipline. For Christians, the goal of a science is to represent in our understandings God's single, perfect, comprehensive understanding, as best we can. Our goal in a book like this is ultimately to discern *God's* view of psychology and Christianity.

MULTIPLE PERSPECTIVES: THE MORE SITES THE BETTER FOR GAINING UNDERSTANDING

So how can our understanding become more comprehensive, more like God's? There are many ways, of course, but one of them is to avail ourselves of an increasing number of valid perspectives on reality. God's all-encompassing vista can only be approximated by humans collaborating and standing in different locations in order to see something from different standpoints. The "landscape" we are interested in is so big that we finite and sinful beings need different perspectives to get the fullest "picture" possible by combining our various human "paintings" (Frame, 1987).

We see this diversity of perspective in modern psychology. In its early days there were structuralists, functionalists, behaviorists, psychoanalysts and Gestalt psychologists (Heidbreder, 1933). Today there are many more: social cognitive, ecological, behavior genetic, evolutionary, object relations, narrative and positive psychologists, to name just a few. These "schools" tend to arise because of sociohistorical changes in the development of a discipline, the individual differences of psychologists (thinking styles, interests and passions), and the variety of approaches taken to understand different key "problems" or phenomena (and different approaches work better on some problems than others). Doubtless, one of the main reasons that there are so many schools in psychology is the sheer complexity of human nature that may require multiple perspectives in order to get the "biggest picture." Then the different "schools" are maintained through the training students receive by their mentors in college, graduate school or seminary (when these perspectives are most likely to be embraced).

At the same time, Abraham Kuyper (1898) pointed out that "schools of thought" are also a consequence of sin, because to the extent that God does not provide the central unifying motive of human life, we seek to find it in the creation: in ourselves and our conceptual and religious systems and communities. This would help to explain the belligerence that can characterize advocates of different schools. Unfortunately, there is abundant evidence that being a Christian does not necessarily protect one from this kind of party spirit.

All this suggests that we should be wary of an exclusive commitment to one perspective that would reject entirely the contributions of other models. The project of relating the Christian faith to psychology and counseling in contemporary culture is extremely complex. Understanding such complexity will likely require the bigger picture afforded by multiple perspectives, and I would suggest that each of the five views we have considered has something essential to contribute to our understanding. Each provides a different but valid viewpoint on the relation of faith and psychology, and each can help us make some progress toward the goal of greater conformity to God's absolutely comprehensive understanding of these matters. At the same time, this openness does not imply that all five perspectives are *equally* valid. Some may correspond better to God's understanding than the others, some may deal with more important aspects of the relation of faith and psychology than others, some may address specific disciplinary, cultural or spiritual problems better than others, and some, frankly, may be more distorted or truncated than others. As a result, a multiperspective framework entails careful examination and evaluation, and it will usually lead to the favoring of one or more models over other ones.

Location, location, location. Let's be more specific. Perspectives develop somewhere. Each of the five views lies in a hypothetical "location" within the fields of psychology and counseling; each occupies a certain social space vis-à-vis other people, cultural institutions, church priorities, and human and Christian values; and these locations can have many aspects.

For example, the representatives in this book differ considerably in terms of the extent to which they (1) value empirical research, philosophy, historical research, spirituality and Scripture in their psychology and counseling; (2) consider conformity to Christ and a relationship with him to be a topic proper to psychology and counseling; (3) focus their professional energies on the concerns of the church, the academy of our day or public mental health; (4) are concerned more with either the blessings of common grace (or creation grace) in science and therapy or with the agenda of the church as a countercultural community within the broader culture; (5) practice more of a hermeneutic of suspicion regarding modern psychology texts or a hermeneutic of trust; (6) are more interested in either science or in counseling and the care of souls; (7) emphasize facts or values, description or evaluation, the head or the heart; (8) promote either cultural engagement by the church or the purity of the church; (9) are more concerned about either secularism or self-righteous hyperspirituality; (10) are more interested in one's relationship with God or one's relationships with other humans; and (11) consider psychological problems to be more related to biology and socialization or to sin.

These differences together reveal each perspective's "location" in the culture at large and the church. From their various vantage points, the representatives see the world differently; they notice things that one cannot see somewhere else. If each view has *any* amount of validity, the Christian community of psychologists and counselors ought not be ignorant of them, for each location offers a certain ad-vantage[1]; that is, together they increase the comprehensiveness of our overall vision.

Consider the "locations" of just two of the approaches in this book. It is no accident that many of those who advocate the levels-of-explanation approach are academic psychologists who study tightly defined and closely specified aspects of human behavior. Myers, our "levels" author, is a social psychologist whose earlier empirical work focused on studying the behavior of individuals in small groups. His frequent coauthor and equally distinguished advocate of the "levels" approach, Malcolm Jeeves, is one of the world's foremost neuroscientists. These are areas (group dynamics and brain function) about which the Bible has little specific to say. In contrast,

---

[1]*Vantage* means "a place or position affording a good view" (*Concise Oxford English Dictionary,* 11th ed., s.v. vantage).

many of the advocates of biblical counseling are pastors and those who counsel almost exclusively within the Christian community, who deal with concrete problems that are the "bread and butter" of practical ministry. Powlison is theologically trained, and his writings suggest that he is most concerned about the strategies and tactics that should be used in the church to deal with sin and the problems of living as God's people. These are precisely the types of concerns (problems) to which Scripture speaks with the most clarity. What different views on the human soul these two "locations" provide!

Regions of activity. Perhaps then, each view makes the most sense and is the most compelling when applied to "regions" of activity for and within which they were developed. If this is true, we should not simply ask "Is this the correct view," but rather turn that question into a more flexible, conditional one: "Is this a good view for understanding how my Christian faith relates *given this specific aspect of human life or this setting?*" Take two fundamental questions from different ends of the psychological spectrum: How do animals remember and learn? and What are the most basic motivations of the human being? Specific Christian teachings will have much more to say in response to the latter question than to the former. When evaluating each view, it is necessary to interpret it within its context.

Legitimate preferences and divine callings. The issue of individual differences must also be discussed here. Some people are more interested in science and the study of God's creation, while others are more person-oriented and want to help people with their problems; some are more analytical in their approach to complex problems, others are more synthetic. Such variation is a part of God's design, and it ought to be a source of celebration in the kingdom of God and not pit Christians against each other.

Moreover, God may call his people into very different kinds of vocations; for example, some are called to work within the church and others are called to work in the broader culture. Out of charity and a trust in God's sovereignty, Christians have to accept that God may have guided their brothers and sisters into very different vocations than they might expect. Daniel, for example, served with distinction at the highest administrative levels of the Babylonian kingdom, even though it had virtually destroyed the kingdom of Judah, and he was a great witness for Yahweh among that pagan culture's intellectual elite. It seems likely that God would call some Christians to influence the psychological and counseling culture of our day. However, in light of God's soul-healing agenda for the church, many will likely be called to primarily minister to her.

DIALOGUE: THE SOCIODISCURSIVE MEANS FOR GAINING UNDERSTANDING

The format of this book approximates a limited dialogue. To better appreciate the value of such dialogue, we will consider briefly the thinking of the great twentieth-century Russian Orthodox social and literary theorist, Mikhail Bakhtin, whose overall framework has been called *dialogism* (Holquist, 2002), because he considered dialogue to be so foundational to human life. According to Bakhtin, humans are characterized by "addressivity"—the capability of being spoken to—and our lives most fundamentally consist of ongoing conversation: continual cycles of utterance, reply and response, interrupted by periods of silence, which eventually issue into another conversation. In fact, Bakhtin (1986) thought all utterances are in some sense a response to all the previous conversations of one's life: "Any utterance is a link in the chain of speech communication" (p. 84).

Bakhtin believed that dialogue with others is essential in the development of our own understanding. In the best dialogues, we deeply accept the other as our peer, so we listen, expecting to learn about something we cannot know without his or her help. Because others see the world from different perspectives, they invariably expand our horizons. Even when they are dead wrong, we can learn something about how to think better by listening discerningly. But most of the time, we find that others positively enrich our understanding by sharing what they can see that we cannot. Indeed, my dialogue partner sees me in a way I cannot possibly see myself. As a result, if I listen carefully, I will invariably learn something of value in conversation. The other has, compared to me, what Bakhtin called a "surplus of seeing." Others can see things I cannot, and likely will not, without their help.

At the same time, Bakhtin's conceptual evenhandedness is displayed in his recognition that respect for the other ought not compromise one's own being, nor the relative value of one's own position and perspective. I too have a "surplus of seeing" with respect to my dialogue partners, and I too can help them. Each of us has a "location" in the world, a stance in the dialogical flow of human history, that legitimates our perspective and our sharing it as well. However, having lived in the Soviet Union, Bakhtin was well aware that speech can be distorted and oppressive, so others' and our speaking requires continual discernment, a discernment that balances listening with questioning and criticism. In genuine dialogue, then, the conversation partners speak up, listen carefully to one another and evaluate themselves again and again, and as they do, they forge another link in the ongoing conversation of humanity that constitutes human history.

Now let's reflect on the privilege we have had of listening in on the conversations in this book (admittedly constrained by the format). Representatives of five views have shared with each other (and us) their views of psychology and counseling, and building on the previous section of this chapter, we can observe that each viewpoint has a location and sees things that the others (and perhaps we) are leaving out. By listening to each one, our own understanding is challenged and enriched, and in time, ideally, that which is worthwhile in each will be preserved and that which is inconsequential and distorted will be defeated through the dialogue—as we continue to listen and speak and listen again to those who respond to us. Genuine dialogue necessarily makes our understanding more comprehensive.

What makes our dialogue distinctly Christian? As we noted above, Christians begin with prayer (a kind of dialogue), listening to God and asking him to give them wisdom from above (Jas 3:17). We continue the dialogue by listening to wise members of the Christian tradition—first and foremost, by listening to the inspired authors of the Christian canon (the Hebrew and Christian Scriptures) and second, by listening to other Christians who have thought deeply about psychological and counseling matters. Through such dialogue our own voice becomes increasingly, distinctly Christian. Hence the value of a book such as this.

Perhaps we could boil down a dialogical stance to the five views with the following two questions:

1. Given the distinct perspective of the proponents of each of the five views, what does each view address that I don't yet see or fully understand?

2. What valid insights and emphases about psychology and counseling does each view have that I'm leaving out or underemphasizing?

COMMUNAL TRADITIONS: THE SOCIOHISTORICAL CONTEXT OF UNDERSTANDING

So far I have encouraged us to consider how to expand our understanding of psychology and counseling by participating in the book's dialogue between those who come from different perspectives; in doing this, we have been engaging in a hermeneutic of trust regarding the five views. Next we will develop its opposite—a hermeneutics of suspicion—for there are also great challenges in dialogue from multiple locations. To aid us, we will return to Alasdair MacIntyre's (1984, 1988, 1989, 1990) discussions of the role of the community in understanding.

As we noted in chapter one, MacIntyre (1984, 1988, 1990) has written that humans can only make progress in understanding by means of their intellectual tradition, and a living tradition is constituted by conflicts between the rival interpretations of members of its intellectual community. Moreover, "it is not merely that different participants in a tradition disagree; they also disagree as to how to characterize their disagreements and as to how to resolve them. They disagree as to what constitutes appropriate reasoning, decisive evidence, conclusive proof" (1989, p. 146). The present book demonstrates that in the areas of psychology and counseling, Christianity is a living tradition, composed of at least five subtraditions, whose representatives disagree regarding a host of foundational issues, some of them spelled out explicitly in the foregoing chapters and others operating implicitly in their basic assumptions.

MacIntyre (1989, 1990) has argued that a community's intellectual crisis is created by the compelling intellectual resources of a rival tradition—in our case, that of modern psychology. He also suggested that those best able to contribute constructively to resolving the crisis are those who are the most conversant with *both* traditions. Though Christians in the field will react differently to that claim—some likely rejecting it—MacIntyre here offers additional criteria for assessing divergent views. Accordingly, one could evaluate each view by the extent to which it is (1) grounded in and reflective of the Christian tradition in its thought and practice and (2) familiar with and informed by the positive accomplishments of modern psychology.

Falling short on criterion 1 would seem to limit a view's capacity to advance a recognizably Christian agenda. Adjusting this criterion slightly, one could evaluate each view by the extent to which the modern tradition is *more dominant* than the Christian tradition. In this latter case, a view would be in danger of compromising its own Christian identity and, in the extreme, of undermining its claim to be an authentic expression of the Christian tradition. So, perhaps, the most important conclusion to draw from MacIntyre's work is that an intellectual tradition must be most faithful to its own resources or it risks its own self-destruction through absorption into a rival tradition.

On the other hand, falling short on criterion 2 would seem to insulate and isolate a view from benefiting from the scientific accomplishments of those outside the church, and furthermore, it would limit a view's capacity to impact contemporary psychology. This issue may not concern those who are called primarily to the church, but those called to broader cultural engagement may have to look to other views for help in communicating and participating in legitimate and relevant ways with those outside Christianity.

MacIntyre's analysis also drives us to question the extent to which the proponents of the five views properly interpret and utilize the Christian tradition they claim to reflect. Fidelity to one's tradition is a claim that must be constantly assessed. Simply because one desires to be especially committed to Christianity or the Bible does not mean that one is, in fact, doing justice to the Christian tradition or using the Bible appropriately (according to its God-intended revelational purposes). On the other hand, we must also beware of claiming the Christian tradition has developed conceptual or scientific resources equal to those of modern psychology, if in fact they are, in certain respects, inferior. Such defensiveness does not glorify the God of truth (the source of all truth), and it risks discrediting Christianity in the eyes of those who know better. Faithfulness to one's tradition has its own liabilities, as fundamentalism has made all too clear.

Explorations of the communal traditions that have shaped people help us to make sense of and evaluate their arguments more accurately than if we only read what they write. Understanding necessarily develops within communities, and scholars, scientists and counselors are trained (and socialized) to approach their tasks in certain ways. They, in turn, join particular professional groups; read and contribute to certain books and journals; and attend some conferences and not others. These social-institutional realities affect what counts as knowledge and good practice, as well as influence the way individuals approach the object of their study (Danziger, 1979, 1990, 1997) and their people-helping (Cushman, 1995). If the physical sciences are affected by these influences (Kuhn, 1962), it seems even more likely that the human sciences (like psychology) would as well, a suspicion that has received a good deal of documentation (in addition to Danziger, see for example, Ash & Woodward, 1987; Buss, 1979; Campbell, 1979; Foucault, 1965; Rose, 1990). As a result, when trying to understand each view, it is helpful to keep in mind the training of its proponents and the community of scholars or counselors with whom they most identify. This enables us to interpret more accurately what they are saying, because we are better able to read their statements in the full light of their foundational communal context.

CRITICAL ABILITY: ANOTHER VIRTUE PREREQUISITE FOR GAINING UNDERSTANDING

In our desire to avoid the vices of arrogance and obstinance, we must also avoid their opposite: a bland, unedifying "agreeableness." There is a false kind of harmony that actually obscures the value of our different perspectives from one another in the interest of seeming to be friendly. This sentimental view of dialogue resists taking positions and avoids statements that might cause conflict in order to maintain the illusion that we're all getting along, when we are really refusing to be fully human. At its root, this relational passivity is slothful cowardice masquerading as love. True love involves respect, and respect in dialogue involves taking seriously what another says and identifying significant errors, or places of disagreement, when they are found. Education can only occur when we take positions, recognize differences and decisively criticize one another's perspectives (as well as our own!).

Truth itself is not ill-defined and amorphous—though our understanding always is, compared to God's. Truth is beautiful and good. Understanding the truth is a delightful fulfillment of human nature. Understanding is a well-sung song, a faithful portrait, a fitting correspondence in which our minds, hearts and lives veritably match reality, more or less. The joy of truth has made men enemies, but this real danger ought not to keep us from vigorously holding beliefs that seem to us to be true and from humbly identifying problems in the thought of others. So long as we are in these bodies (and maybe forever) misunderstanding is everyone's portion, but we owe others, God and ourselves the gift of kind criticism of human discourse.

As we carefully examine the five views we have read, we will need to sift them and inspect the thoughts, attitudes, values and assumptions of their representatives in order to do our best to detect illogic, overstatements, blind spots and faulty renderings. Depending on our motives, this search for truth can be loving or self-seeking. If we strive to love our dialogue partners, keeping our affection for them in mind and the unity of the church as our goal, then our quest for understanding will involve the dialectics of listening and speaking, questioning and answering, truth and falsehood, trust and suspicion. It will entail a conflict of ideas, traditions, perspectives and practices. But if conformity to the mind, heart and life of Christ is our goal—and the greater that conformity, the greater Christ's glory is manifested on earth—then the quest for truth is a virtuous and very spiritual task, worthy of our energies.

CHRISTIAN POSTFORMAL RECONSTRUCTION: THE GOAL OF ADVANCED UNDERSTANDING

Engaging with others in dialogue and subjecting their positions to gracious critique are important parts of the challenge we face when reading a book like this. Another part is formulating or constructing a new understanding based on the new things we have learned through the foregoing processes, and we must personally, actively engage in this if this construction is ever to occur. We must *search* for wisdom (Prov 2:4). This is not a passive endeavor, but it takes a great deal of effort on our part. So the kind of learning that this book requires involves both critical dialogue with others and our own active involvement, as we go about continually reconstructing our understanding-in-community. Researchers on the kind of reconstruction needed have termed it "postformal thought," which we will consider from a Christian perspective.

Evaluating each model. The first task to be done in the development of a postformal understanding of these views is the articulation, in *our* own words, of each of the approaches on *its* own terms. We put it in our own words, because that is what best guarantees that we understand it, but we strive to understand it on its own terms, so that we are true to its actual emphases and avoid misrepresenting it. Each of the five views is a system of thought—a rational, coherent set of beliefs, attitudes and practices regarding psychology and counseling—and it can therefore be evaluated individually for its coherence and validity, resulting in an assessment of its strengths and weaknesses.

However, we must admit that conducting an objective analysis of each model is an *ideal.* The reality is that we can never analyze models apart from our own preferences, prejudgments and prior learning. Whenever we read or think about anything, we have no choice but to make use of our own "preunderstanding"—formed through previous experiences, dialogue, training and study—which guides our present reflections and predisposes us to see things in certain ways. So a purely objective analysis of each model "on its own terms" is actually beyond our abilities, but it remains an important goal nonetheless. We all have to start somewhere (that is, beginning with our preunderstanding), but we should nevertheless strive to be as fair an evaluator as we can. Truth seems to be disclosed best when we prayerfully assume a kind of critical fairmindedness.

Constructing a metasystem. After articulating each model as best as we can, given our preunderstanding, our next step is to develop a way of appropriating as much as possible of what is valid from each view. This requires developing a "metasystem." Researchers in the field of early-adult cognitive development have documented that some adults develop the capacity to form such a metasystem (Basseches, 1984; Kegan, 1982; King & Kitchener, 1994; Kramer, 1990; Richards & Commons, 1984, 1990; Rybash, Hoyer & Roodin, 1986; Sinnott, 1998).[2]

Presystemic thinking. These studies have found three broad stages of human thought. Piaget, the great cognitive-developmental psychologist, studied the first two. Although Piaget actually identified three stages of

---

[2]This quality of thought has been called *postformal* in adult-cognitive-development literature. For Christian discussions of postformal theory, see Johnson (1996a, 1996b, 1998, 2002) and Reich (1994, 2002). Certain philosophers have also recognized and used this type of thinking (e.g., Hegel, Kierkegaard and Ricoeur) and so have some evangelical theologians like D. A. Carson (1981), Frame (1987) and Poythress (1987). (The latter two were influenced by C. Van Til's notion of "limiting concepts" [1972].)

childhood cognition (sensorimotor, preoperational and concrete operational), we'll just call the childhood stage "prelogical," because typical children can only grasp surface features of the physical world (they are "preoperational," PO) or derive simple generalizations (concrete operations, CO) from it. Children cannot deduce more complex rules or principles because they lack formal operational (or logical) abilities. They are mentally embedded in their *perceptions* (in PO) or *thoughts* (in CO) and are incapable of reflecting *on* their thoughts (Kegan, 1982). As a result, they cannot subject their thoughts to logical scrutiny and organize their beliefs into a coherent, linear system, so their understanding is likely to have logical inconsistencies, in which some beliefs they hold contradict some of their other beliefs.

Systemic thinking. Piaget found that in adolescence some children begin to develop the ability to think logically or systemically (in the stage of formal operations).[3] Persons at this stage can think about their thoughts, which are abstracted from the concrete world, so they can organize, compare and evaluate them in a linear fashion (e.g., from cause to effect). Only with formal logic can people develop a logically consistent system of thought.

Such thinking is profoundly important in modern life. Without such logical abilities, experimental research would not have developed, because in order to devise a meaningful experiment, the scientist must be able to abstract a number of variables that are relevant to the research question and hypothesize how they might be related, so devising a "system" of causal relations between the variables. But it's not just scientists who use formal logic. It is needed to understand any abstract "system" of thought—for example, complex mathematics (like calculus), government systems (like democracy and fascism), economic systems (like capitalism and communism) and theological systems (like Islam and Eastern Orthodoxy). That's why students typically don't study such topics until late high school or college; before then, they usually do not have the requisite reasoning ability to understand such purely mental organizations of propositions or beliefs. We use formal reasoning to analyze each of the five views as a discrete system of thought.

---

[3]Though it is probably in college that students really develop this way of thinking—and then only in some areas. In fact, only about 50 percent of college seniors appear to use formal operations consistently on tasks devised to assess such thinking (Pascarella & Terenzini, 1991).

However, in spite of its tremendous power, single-system, linear reasoning has limitations. It has a hard time grasping what happens when systems change and when variables (and systems) interact with each other (as in the weather or in complex social interactions that are bidirectional or reciprocal). Simple formal reasoning struggles in real-life problem-solving contexts where all the information necessary to solve the problem in a clear-cut way isn't available (e.g., should I talk to someone in the company about difficulties I'm having with my immediate supervisor?). And most important for the task facing us in this book, a linear use of logic has difficulty synthesizing a number of single systems into a bigger picture—a metasystem if you will—of multiple systems, contexts, purposes and values (Richards & Commons, 1984, 1990; see also Basseches, 1984; Kegan, 1982; King & Kitchener, 1994), like we find characterize the five views herein.

The fact is that the world we live in has features that are not capable of being grasped within a single, linear reasoning system. For example, how can light be both a wave and a particle? How can an adult child best show love to a verbally abusive mother? How can God be both three and one? Do we best help the poor by giving them assistance or by encouraging them to help themselves? The nature of much of reality seems to require metasystemic thinking. Really complex topics defy simple formal-reasoning abilities. Hearty debates in college dorms often result when two inflexibly consistent thinkers get together (imagine a debate between Rush Limbaugh and Bill Maher). Both can be logically consistent given their particular assumptions or frames of reference, while holding opposite positions on an issue. So long as they view the topic only from that one standpoint, they appear to be logically incapable of grasping the insights found in the other position(s). Linear-reasoning thinkers, embedded in their own framework, seem unable to grasp the truth in another system, insofar as its truth appears to contradict their own. Debates between those inflexibly committed to their own frameworks are sometimes productive, but they often end in frustration. And of course, while the goal of a good debater is to expose the logical inconsistencies of the *other* person's thinking, dialoging with these folks can be quite helpful, since their vigorous consistency often reveals inconsistencies and defensiveness in *our own* thinking.

But what happens when a linear thinker starts to realize there is truth in a system that seems to contradict his or her own? That often creates anxiety, and that anxiety can have many responses that generally lead in three possible directions. One response is to revert back to prelogical thinking and just ignore the problems. A more advanced approach recognizes the logic problem this poses to one's current understanding, but tragically concludes that it must not be possible to know the truth for sure. This is the "solution" of relativism. Both of these resolutions can lead a person to become "eclectic," that is, to choose whatever beliefs (or practices) he or she wishes, without attempting to fit them together into a more comprehensive metasystem. As a result, they can lead to contradictions in one's thinking and practice, and ultimately they inhibit the search for more comprehensive solutions, so they keep the individual from moving to more advanced, complex levels of understanding that can embrace more of the big picture of God's perfect understanding.

A third response to complexity is to cling rigidly to one's present formal understanding and deny the insights and benefits of other approaches. Many intelligent Christians get stuck here and draw sharp lines between their ("entirely correct") system and the ("entirely false") opposing system(s) and defend their own view at all costs. They have no need to take seriously other positions, since they already have all the truth. Since they are not open to admitting they could have limitations in their understanding, a deeper grasp of the whole truth is beyond their reach. But there is a fourth possible approach to take.

Metasystemic thinking. Early-adult cognitive-developmental researchers (like those cited above) have found that some adults move beyond prelogical, relativistic and systemic thinking. The very structure of their thinking processes are changed and they learn how to apply logic in a "metasystemic" way that transcends the limits of simple linear reasoning. This "postformal" way of understanding synthesizes the truths of multiple systems that are *apparently* contradictory (at the level of linear reasoning). It requires listening carefully and respectfully to others, extending logic into higher-order and more inclusive domains, and the intuitive understanding that allows the genuine insights of different systems to be grasped *in their respective contexts* (or locations). This kind of thinking results in the construction of a new, more comprehensive "metasystem," which avoids the unexamined, haphazard and, ultimately, irrational understanding of prelogical and relativist thinkers and transcends the rigid, formal exclusiveness of systematic thinkers.

Christian teaching requires postformal understanding (the Trinity, God's providence and human agency), and it frees Christians from a "party" spirit (e.g., "I follow Paul, . . . I follow Apollos." [1 Cor 1:12]), thus enabling them to embrace all the truth they can get, to describe as much of the big picture as they can and to get a little closer to God's absolutely comprehensive, meta-metasystemic understanding.

But back to this book. The contributors have presented five coherent systems for viewing psychology in light of the Christian faith. Yet it must be pointed out that each of the views is likely to be a metasystem itself, the result of years of searching, sifting and reflecting on such matters by the contributors. Even so, there remain striking differences between these views. As just noted, one approach to these differences is the single-system model: pick one, defend it against the others, and resist recognizing the strengths and insights of the others. Or we can begin the task of developing our own postformal synthesis, forging the best metasystem we can at this point in time, a system that incorporates as much of the value of all five views as possible, without reverting to relativism or unreflective, logical inconsistency.[4]

Christian postformal thought entails, on the one hand, plenty of curious and respectful dialogue with others within the Christian tradition, and on the other hand, a good deal of private contemplation, where we set about reflecting on what we've heard or read, putting it together into as valid and coherent a metasystem as we can manage—a task that finite persons will never complete! At the same time, this active reconstruction process requires firmness of conviction and perseverance in what one knows to be true. Postformal dialogists use their present understanding as a guide, while they listen respectfully to the perspectives of others, hoping to discover some new understandings that they hadn't seen before.

Genuine versus apparent contradictions. In a postmodern day like ours, when relativism is so common, an important clarification is probably in order. Postformal dialogism does not lead to the affirmation of

---

[4]Perhaps this is the place for me to admit that I am personally committed to working within the model of Christian psychology. Nonetheless, I am simultaneously committed to the project of this book, because my own journey has convinced me that each model has value that I need to factor into my own account.

beliefs that are truly (and not just apparently) contradictory to each other. Openness to postformal thinking is not license to believe mutually incompatible things. Early in the semester, a student hears Professor Jones declare, "Molecules are actual entities!" Later in another class the same semester, Professor Anderson is heard exclaiming "Molecules are theoretical fictions!" Metasystemic thought does not entail figuring out how to synthesize two antithetical assertions. No, some propositions truly contradict other propositions.

Learning to distinguish when ideas are *actually* incompatible from when they are only *apparently* incompatible (but are actually harmonious at a deeper level) is a difficult but essential reasoning skill for the postformal thinker. The laws of logic (like the law of noncontradiction) still hold in metasystemic thinking. A statement cannot be true and its opposite (its contradictory) also be true. However, postformal thinking allows us to affirm truths that appear to be contradictions—but for both of which there is good evidence (e.g., biblical texts that teach that Christ is human and that he is God)—while we perhaps formulate new ways of understanding such complex topics (e.g., the doctrine of Christ's incarnation).[5] If some of the beliefs of the authors of this book are truly incompatible with some of the beliefs of the others, we cannot use postformal magic to put together what logic genuinely renders asunder. However, if the evidence demands it, the metasystemic thinker is willing to hold beliefs that may appear to be contradictory now, with the hope that further understanding may lead to greater clarity and the ultimate confidence that God's understanding contains no genuine contradictions.

Logic is essential for all human thought (Moreland & Craig, 2003). Postformal thinking provides no license to think sloppily, that is, *il*-logically. It is not illogical; it is supralogical. It integrates two or more simple logics into a higher logical order, without abandoning logic's laws. Furthermore, many things in life are best understood with linear thinking. But when the available evidence compels us (as in the present book), we are bidden to develop a more comprehensive understanding than a single viewpoint alone could accomplish.

---

[5]Apparent contradictions are called *paradoxes* by logicians today, and they can be fruitful sources of insight into the nature of things (Erickson & Fossa, 1998; Quine, 1976). Such apparent contradictions in theology have been called *mysteries* in the Christian tradition (Johnson, 2002).

GAINING UNDERSTANDING THROUGH PEACEMAKING

There are many good reasons for a book like this, but one of the most important is peacemaking (Mt 5:9). The Christian counseling community has been experiencing something like a "Forty Years' War," in which various factions have alternately criticized, denounced and ignored one another, each firmly convinced that its approach is the only valid one. I hope that the readers of this book will have sufficient reasons to be conscientious objectors in this conflict, will challenge a warfare mentality when they encounter it, and will themselves work hard to respect, listen to, learn from and share with, as they have opportunity, their Christian brothers and sisters in psychology and counseling who hold different positions than they do. I am grateful to the contributors of this book for modeling so well peacemaking dialogue.

All Christians want to realize God's will within the spheres of their callings. In the sciences, that will always entail drawing near to Christ, in whom are hidden all the treasures of wisdom and knowledge (Col 2:3). As Jonathan Edwards (1980) suggested, "All the arts and sciences, the more they are perfected, the more they issue in divinity, and coincide with it, and appear to be as parts of it" (p. 397). For the Christian, the science of psychology and the art of counseling are fundamentally religious enterprises, as is all of life. May God be pleased with our dialogue, conduct and journey together toward him in the field of psychology and the practice of counseling.

REFERENCES

Alston, W. (1996). *A realist conception of truth.* Ithaca, NY: Cornell University Press.

Ash, M. G., & Woodward, W. R. (Eds.). (1987). *Psychology in twentieth-century thought and society.* Cambridge: Cambridge University Press.

Bakhtin, M. M. (1986). *Speech genres & other late essays.* Austin: University of Texas Press.

Basseches, M. (1984). *Dialectical thinking and adult development.* Norwood, NJ: Ablex.

Buss, A. R. (Ed.). (1979). *Psychology in social context.* New York: Irvington.

Campbell, D. T. (1979). A tribal model of the social system vehicle carrying scientific knowledge. *Knowledge: Creation, Diffusion, Utilization, 1,* 181-201.

Carson, D. A. (1981). *Divine sovereignty and human responsibility: Biblical perspectives in tension.* Atlanta: John Knox Press.

Cushman, P. (1995). *Constructing the self, constructing America: A cultural history of psychotherapy.* Reading, MA: Addison-Wesley.

Danziger, K. (1979). The social origins of modern psychology. In A.R. Buss (Ed.), *Psychology in social context* (pp. 27-45). New York: Irvington.

————. (1990). *Constructing the subject: Historical origins of psychological research.* Cambridge: Cambridge University Press.

————. (1997). *Naming the mind: How psychology found its language.* Thousand Oaks, CA: Sage.

Edwards, J. (1980). *The works of Jonathan Edwards: Scientific and philosophical writings,* Vol. 6. (W. E. Anderson, Ed.). New Haven: Yale University Press.

Erickson, G. W., & Fossa, G. A. (Eds.). (1998). *Dictionary of paradox.* Lanham, MD: University Press of America.

Ford, D. F. (2007). *Christian wisdom: Desiring God and learning in love.* Cambridge: Cambridge University Press.

Foucault, M. (1965). *Madness and civilization* (R. Howard, Trans.). New York: Random House.

Frame, J. (1987). *The doctrine of the knowledge of God.* Phillipsburg, NJ: Presbyterian & Reformed.

Heidbreder, E. (1933). *Seven psychologies.* New York: Appleton-Century.

Holquist, M. (2002). *Dialogism: Bakhtin and his world* (2nd ed.). New York: Routledge.

Johnson, E. L. (1996a). The call of wisdom: Adult development within Christian community, Part I: The crisis of modern theories of post-formal development. *Journal of Psychology and Theology, 24,* 85-92.

————. (1996b). The call of wisdom: Adult development within Christian community, Part II: Towards a covenantal constructivist model of post-formal development. *Journal of Psychology and Theology, 24,* 93-103.

————. (1998). Growing in wisdom in Christian community: Toward measures of Christian postformal development. *Journal of Psychology and Theology, 26,* 365-81.

————. (2002). Can God be grasped by our reason? In D. S. Huffman & E. L. Johnson (Eds.). *God under fire: Modern scholarship reinvents God* (pp. 72-103). Grand Rapids, MI: Zondervan.

Kegan, R. (1982). *The evolving self: Problem and process in human development.* Cambridge, MA: Harvard University Press.

King, P. M., & Kitchener, K. S. (1994). *Developing reflective judgment: Understanding and promoting intellectual growth and critical thinking in adolescents and adults.* San Francisco: Jossey-Bass.

Kramer, D. A. (1990). Conceptualizing wisdom: The primacy of affect-cognitive relations. In R. J. Sternberg (Ed.), *Wisdom: Its nature, origins, and development* (pp. 279-313). New York: Cambridge University Press.

Kuhn, T. (1962). *The structure of scientific revolutions.* Chicago: University of Chicago Press.

Kuyper, A. (1898). *Encyclopedia of sacred theology.* New York: Charles Scribner's Sons.

MacIntyre, A. (1984). *After virtue* (2nd ed.). South Bend, IN: University of Notre Dame Press.

————. (1988). *Whose justice? Which rationality?* South Bend, IN: University of Notre Dame Press.

————. (1989). Epistemological crises, narrative, and philosophy of science. In S. Hauerwas & L. G. Jones (Eds). *Why narrative? Readings in narrative theology* (pp. 138-57). Grand Rapids, MI: Eerdmans. (Original work published 1977)

————. (1990). *Three rival versions of moral enquiry: Encyclopaedia, genealogy, and tradition.* South Bend, IN: University of Notre Dame Press.

Mavrodes, G. (1997). Omniscience. In P. L. Quinn & C. Taliaferro (Eds.), *A companion to philosophy of religion* (pp. 236-42). London: Blackwell.

Moreland, J. P., & Craig, W. L. (2003). *Philosophical foundations for a Christian worldview.* Downers Grove, IL: InterVarsity Press.

Pascarella, E. T., & Terenzini, P. T. (1991). *How college affects students.* San Francisco: Jossey-Bass.

Plantinga, A. (1983). Reason and belief in God. In A. Plantinga & N. Wolterstorff (Eds.), *Faith and rationality: Reason and belief in God* (pp. 16-92). South Bend, IN: University of Notre Dame Press.

————. (1993a). Divine knowledge. In C. S. Evans & M. Westphal (Eds.), *Christian perspectives on religious knowledge* (pp. 40-65). Grand Rapids, MI: Eerdmans.

————. (1993b). *Warrant and proper function.* Oxford: Oxford University Press.

————. (2000). *Warranted Christian belief.* Oxford: Oxford University Press.

Polanyi, M. (1958). *Personal knowledge: Toward a post-critical philosophy.* Chicago: University of Chicago Press.

Poythress, V. (1987). *Symphonic theology.* Grand Rapids, MI: Zondervan.

Quine, W. V. (1976). *The ways of paradox and other essays.* Cambridge: Harvard University Press.

Rad, G. V. (1972). *Wisdom in Israel.* Nashville: Abingdon.

Reich, K. H. (1994). Can one understand rationally Christian doctrines? An empirical study. *British Journal of Religious Education, 16*(2), 114-26.

————. (2002). *Developing the horizons of the mind: Relational and contextual reasoning and the resolution of cognitive conflict.* New York: Cambridge University Press.

Richards, F. A., & Commons, M. L. (1984). Systematic, metasystematic, and cross-paradigmatic reasoning: A case for stages of reasoning beyond formal operations. In M. L. Commons, F. A. Richards & C. Armon (Eds.), *Beyond formal operations: Late adolescent and adult cognitive development* (pp. 92-119). New York: Praeger.

————. (1990). Postformal cognitive-developmental theory and research: A review of its current status. In C. N. Alexander & E. J. Langer (Eds.), *Higher stages of human development: Perspectives on adult growth* (pp. 139-61). New York: Oxford University Press.

Rose, N. (1990). Psychology as a 'social' science. In J. Shotter & I. Parker (Eds.), *Deconstructing social psychology* (pp. 103-16). London: Routledge.

Rybash, J. M., Hoyer, W. J., & Roodin, P. A. (1986). *Adult cognition and aging: Developmental changes in processing, knowing and thinking.* New York: Pergamon.

Sinnott, J. D. (1998). *The development of logic in adulthood: Postformal thought and its applications.* New York: Springer.

Van Til, C. (1972). *Common grace and the gospel.* Phillipsburg, NJ: Presbyterian & Reformed.

Westphal, M. (1993). *Suspicion & faith: The religious uses of modern atheism.* Grand Rapids, MI: Eerdmans.

Name Index

Subject Index

Spectrum Multiview Books

From IVP Academic